Readings from the Edges

STUDIES IN LATINO/A CATHOLICISM

A series sponsored by the Center for the Study of Latino/a Catholicism
University of San Diego

Previously published

Orlando O. Espín and Miguel H. Díaz, editors, *From the Heart of Our People: Latino/a Explorations in Catholic Systematic Theology*

Raúl Gómez-Ruíz, *Mozarabs, Hispanics, and the Cross*

Orlando O. Espín and Gary Macy, editors, *Futuring Our Past: Explorations in the Theology of Tradition*

María Pilar Aquino and Maria José Rosado-Nunes, editors, *Feminist Intercultural Theology: Latina Explorations for a Just World*

Néstor Medina, *Mestizaje (Re)Mapping Race, Culture, and Faith in Latina/o Catholicism*

Carmen Nanko-Fernández, *Theologizing en Espanglish: Context, Community, and Ministry*

Readings from the Edges

The Bible and People on the Move

Jean-Pierre Ruiz

ORBIS BOOKS

Maryknoll, New York 10545

Founded in 1970, Orbis Books endeavors to publish works that enlighten the mind, nourish the spirit, and challenge the conscience. The publishing arm of the Maryknoll Fathers and Brothers, Orbis seeks to explore the global dimensions of the Christian faith and mission, to invite dialogue with diverse cultures and religious traditions, and to serve the cause of reconciliation and peace. The books published reflect the views of their authors and do not represent the official position of the Maryknoll Society. To learn more about Maryknoll and Orbis Books, please visit our website at www.maryknollsociety.org.

Library of Congress Cataloging-in-Publication Data

Ruiz, Jean-Pierre, 1958-
   Readings from the edges : the Bible and people on the move / Jean-Pierre Ruiz.
      p. cm.
   Includes index.
   ISBN 978-1-57075-944-4 (pbk.)
   1. Bible—Criticism, interpretation, etc. 2. Emigration and immigration—Religious aspects—Catholic Church. 3. Theology—Latin America. 4. Catholic Church—Doctrines. I. Title.
   BS511.3.R85 2011
   230'.041—dc22

2011010929

Contents

PART II: LOOKING TO THE TEXTS

Acknowledgments

Friends and colleagues have claimed that I coined the phrase "the anthological imagination" to frame the ways in which Latino/a theologians and biblical scholars have worked to shape theologies that find expression less as the solo *oeuvre* of an individual thinker but in the shared energy of intense discussion and of the sort of in-depth analysis that is only possible in an atmosphere of deep trust and shared commitment. That approach is grounded in a theological anthropology according to which being human is always a matter of being in community with others, where the first person *singular* always implicates the first person *plural* so that who I am has much to do with who *we* are. The pages of this book bear witness to the best of that give-and-take when I have been attentive to the insights of my friends, colleagues, and conversation partners in many venues. These opening pages provide me with the opportunity both to acknowledge their direct and indirect contributions with gratitude and to admit that the work's shortcomings are the likely result of those occasions when I have been inattentive or resistant to their promptings.

In that spirit, I begin with words of deep appreciation to the Center for the Study of Latino/a Catholicism at the University of San Diego and to its director, Orlando O. Espín, for accepting this book into its series Studies in Latino/a Catholicism. As director of the Center, it was Orlando who actively nurtured the sort of intensely collaborative process that brought together scholars from a variety of theological disciplines to work on projects that bore fruit in two earlier volumes in this series, *From the Heart of Our People: Latino/a Explorations in Systematic Theology* and *Futuring Our Past: Explorations in the Theology of Tradition*. It was my privilege to contribute to both of these books, and in so doing I became convinced both of how important it is for biblical scholars, systematic theologians, moral theologians, and church historians to work with and to learn from one another, and of the remarkable synergies that such interdisciplinary endeavors can yield.

As I explain in chapter 2, it is to an Orbis book—Gustavo Gutiérrez's *A Theology of Liberation*—that I trace the beginnings of my conviction that theology can make a difference when it is deeply engaged in the lived daily reality of ordinary people, including those on the margins of society. For

Orbis, "a world of books that matter" is so much more than a marketing slogan, for it expresses their long-standing commitment to make room for many voices to enter into the classroom, the church, and the community. I offer my thanks to Robert Ellsberg and to Susan Perry for the patience and the gentle persistence with which they have brought this book into print. If this book matters, it will be thanks in no small measure to them and their colleagues at Orbis.

I am convinced that the work of biblical studies and of theological scholarship is an ecclesial vocation, one that takes place at the heart of the church for the sake of its mission to witness to the goodness and the justice of God in the world. I arrive at that conviction thanks to the faith communities that have nurtured and challenged me, that sometimes nagged me into paying attention to texts and contexts I might otherwise have ignored. These too find their place in the pages of this book, and I have sought to be faithful to their spirit and their voices. I am indebted to the people of Our Lady of Loreto parish in Brooklyn, New York, and to the leadership of East Brooklyn Congregations, to the people and pastoral ministers at St. John Vianney parish in Flushing, St. Patrick's parish in Long Island City, and Sts. Joachim and Anne parish in Queens Village. Special thanks go to Robert M. Robinson, pastor, mentor, and longtime friend, in whose company the kitchen table has often been a place for nourishment of mind and soul.

It is my privilege to serve on the faculty of the Department of Theology and Religious Studies at St. John's University in New York, and this book owes much to the integrity with which St. John's embraces its mission as a Catholic, Vincentian, and metropolitan university. Founded in 1870 to educate immigrants and the children of immigrants, St. John's has remained both faithful and forward-looking. From the St. John's community, I single out for special thanks Margaret John Kelly, DC, executive director of the Vincentian Center for Church and Society, and Mary Ann Dantuono, its associate director. Their invitation to serve as a research fellow of the Center has provided me with many opportunities to explore the range of concerns that affect people on the move. Thanks to them I have begun to articulate a theology of migration in conversation with scholars from disciplines ranging from economics to education, as well as with service providers and community leaders who share a vision inspired by the Vincentian charism of service to the marginalized.

This book would not have been possible without the dedicated efforts of my secretary, Mrs. Lois Horan, or of my graduate research assistants at St. John's University, among them Evelyn Cruz, Louis Maione, and Richard Omolade. The "Mighty Women of Theology" at St. John's, Jane Gutloff, Kathy Schlossmacher, and Mary Ann Spanjers, OSF, deserve a special shout-out of their own for knowing how to keep me from sidestepping hard and important questions.

There is not a page of this book that fails to reflect the influence of my *compañera* and *colega* Carmen Nanko-Fernández, whose candor and keen editorial eye contributed much-welcome clarity to my prose, and whose insights have helped me to find grace mysteriously at work in the most unexpected places—from Yankee Stadium in the Bronx to the Fullerton underpass in Chicago.

Together with many others, Carmen and I both have drawn strength and sustenance *en la lucha* from the scholars who form the Academy of Catholic Hispanic Theologians of the United States (ACHTUS). I owe much to the members of ACHTUS, who recognize the ongoing need for a space where Latino/a theologians and biblical scholars can accompany each other as we wrestle with the lived daily experiences of our communities. Among them, I extend special thanks to Gilberto Cavazos-González, Miguel H. Díaz, Raúl Gómez Ruiz, and Gary Riebe-Estrella.

I am likewise indebted to those with whom I have been honored to work as a part of the Hispanic Summer Program and the Hispanic Theological Initiative, among them doctoral fellows Armando Rodríguez, Gregory Lee Cuellar, Jacqueline Hidalgo, Neomi Rosenau De Anda, David Sánchez, and Gilberto Ruiz, together with José Irizarry, Efraín Agosto, Daisy Machado, Joanne Rodríguez, and Sharon Ringe.

The Latino/a Theology Consultation of the Catholic Theological Society of America and the Latina/o Religion, Culture, and Society Group of the American Academy of Religion have provided opportunities for fruitful consideration of migration as a theological issue *en conjunto* with Jonathan Tan, and I am grateful to him for the insights that have come from those discussions.

Earlier versions of several chapters of this book have appeared elsewhere, and I am grateful to the original publishers for their permission to include revised versions of these publications here. These include "Good Fences and Good Neighbors? Biblical Scholars and Theologians," originally published in *Journal of Hispanic / Latino Theology* (May 29 2007) (http://latinotheology. org/2007/fences_neighbors); "Abram and Sarai Cross the Border: Reading Genesis 12:10-20 with People on the Move," originally published in *Border Crossings: Cross-Cultural Hermeneutics*, ed. D. N. Premnath (Maryknoll, NY: Orbis Books, 2007), 15-34; "An Exile's Baggage: Toward a Postcolonial Reading of Ezekiel," originally published in *Approaching Yehud: New Approaches to the Study of the Persian Period*, ed. Jon Berquist (Semeia Studies 50; Atlanta: Society of Biblical Literature, 2007), 117-36; "'They Could Not Speak the Language of Judah': Rereading Nehemiah 13 between Brooklyn and Jerusalem," originally published in *They Were All Together in One Place? Toward Minority Biblical Criticism*, ed. Randall C. Bailey, Tat-Siong Benny Liew, and Fernando F. Segovia (Semeia Studies 57; Atlanta: Society of Biblical Literature, 2009), 79-95; "The Bible and People on the Move: Another Look at Matthew's Parable of the Day Laborers," originally published in *New Theology Review* 20, no. 3 (August 2007): 15-23.

Introduction

Latino/a Itineraries

Even though I did not realize it then, this book began in the heart of Rome, during a conversation over lunch between two doctoral students at the Gregorian University, one a Mexican American from El Paso, Texas, the other a Nuyorican, *this* New York Puerto Rican. Listening to Arturo Bañuelas speak about his dissertation and about the people of his borderlands diocese with equal passion was a *¡Si, se puede!* moment, making it clear to me that engagement in biblical and theological scholarship need not come at the cost of disengagement either from our communities of accountability or from our own Latino/a identities.

We were working on very different projects: Arturo's dissertation was entitled *The Exodus in the Theologies of Liberation of Gustavo Gutiérrez and J. Severino Croatto*, while mine tackled a text from the Apocalypse—a document at the edge of the New Testament canon written by an author who draws attention to his own being out-of-place "on the island of Patmos because of the word of God and the testimony of Jesus" (Rev 1:9).[1] Even so, our concerns converged not only in commiserating about the arcane rites of passage to the doctorate, but also about the payoff question, wondering together whether what we were writing would make any real difference to anyone outside the university library where our work would be catalogued and shelved. The memory of that discussion between a systematic theologian and a biblical scholar far from home and across disciplinary borders is a lasting reminder to me that people on the move have been and remain a crucial focus for the energies of many Latino/a theologians, Arturo Bañuelas and myself among them.[2]

Being on the move is a thread woven through the fabric of so many of our own personal and communal stories. It is at the heart of our story as church, and it even finds a place in the complex encounters that began our (hi)story in the Americas (as I suggest in chapter 9). It is a key piece of the big picture, of the sometimes deliberate and the sometimes unintended consequences of globalization, but it is also a matter of the little stories, of people like five-year-old Marisol, about whom Bañuelas writes so tellingly:

1

Each year between 80,000 and 100,000 children are caught by the border patrol trying to cross illegally into the United States. In our parish we have a ministry with these children, children like 5-year-old Marisol, a beautiful little girl from Guatemala. She was caught trying to cross the border with a coyote, who had been paid to bring her to the United States.

When she was caught, she had a piece of paper in her hand with a phone number in her Guatemalan village. During the whole trip she had kept it in her hand, but when the officers opened it, most of the numbers were missing. This little girl will perhaps forever be separated from her family.

Immigrants like Marisol show us that immigration reform is more than simply a matter of human rights for undocumented immigrants. It is a matter of survival for the poorest. No child of God should ever have to leave her family at 5 years of age to be able to eat and survive in our world. Like the majority of people who cross the border, these are not terrorists or drug smugglers but our brothers and sisters.[3]

Bañuelas argues that immigration "is a defining issue that is about us—all of us Latinos—and about how we will shape the future of our church and our country." After all, as he suggests,

Since the majority of the more than 90 nationalities that daily cross our borders are from the Americas, it is our *Latinidad* itself that is being attacked. We know that the root causes of immigration include extreme poverty, unemployment, political and military corruption, and government instability in the countries of origin. However, we Latinos and Latinas throughout the Americas also know that the United States shares in the responsibility for these conditions that drive immigrants north across our borders.[4]

Latino/a biblical scholars and theologians who have directed our attention to people on the move do so not out of disinterested academic curiosity at the latest demographic trends that are so rapidly and so dramatically reshaping our churches and our society. We do so because their stories are our stories as well, stories of our parents and grandparents, stories of the communities with whom we worship and whose struggles we share. We do so because so many of us stand at the intersection of *pastoral de conjunto* and *teología de conjunto*, as Latinos/as for whom scholarship and ministry are richly interwoven, for whom scholarship is a matter of engagement with and not flight from lived daily experience.

It is this commitment that led the Academy of Catholic Hispanic Theologians of the United States (ACHTUS) to issue a statement on just, comprehensive, and humane immigration reform in 2006. We pledged,

"Through our scholarship and our ministries, we commit ourselves to dispel falsehoods about immigration, to protect civil rights, to promote justice, and to make known the gifts, talents, and contributions of immigrants to our society," because, as we insisted, "Failing to stand for just and comprehensive immigration reform impoverishes us all."[5]

In 2009 ACHTUS issued a statement supporting the passage of the DREAM Act, the Development, Relief and Education of Alien Minors Act, which would provide a path to U.S. citizenship for young people who were brought to the United States as minors. The members of ACHTUS, the statement explained, "stand in solidarity with our alternately documented immigrant youth who, because of their lack of legal status, live in the shadows with limited access to the educational options necessary for a secure future." We insisted, "In keeping with our mission to accompany *nuestras comunidades* in the United States, and faithful to the social teachings of our Church, we are compelled to advocate for just means that provide educational opportunities for our children to participate in our shared destinies as a nation and as a Church."[6]

The aggressive, even vehement negative feedback we often receive when we speak up about immigration is convincing evidence that we have not yet gotten through to some of our own—to fellow Christians and even to fellow Latinos/as. For example, on November 29, 2010, one anonymous reader of the electronic version of Bañuelas's *U.S. Catholic* article entitled "The Lies Are Killing Us: The Need for Immigration Reform," commented,

> Lies are killing us—Yes they are and they happen to be coming from the Msgr. Illegal aliens cost the the (*sic*) US citizens $120 billion annually. That they pay $90 billion in taxes is a figment of his imagination. Many are paid "off the books" and pay no tax and where did he get $90 billion in taxes no where (*sic*) on the 1040 is there a box that says if you are an illegal paying taxes check here. The border should be enforced, illegals should be deported, entitlements to illegals should be ended, employers should be prosecuted. With a 9.6% unemployment rate (with a true rate of 15%) we need jobs for our citizens not for lawbreakers. I am not interested in the new nation the the Msrg. (*sic*) envisions. I agree our nation should care for its poorest citizens and that is key "citizen" the Msrg (*sic*) should stick to "spiritual" concepts and stay out of politics.[7]

On November 28, 2010, Hugo Peña, a reader who identifies himself as a Catholic and as an "American of Mexican descent" argued,

> Msgr. Banuelas (*sic*) misses the point that crossing into the U.S. without a permit is to break the law. His analogy of equating these illegals as the Jews wandering the desert with Moses is ridiculous. The clergy

needs to stay out of these issues because they have no experience in the legalities of law. Yes, it is a tough situation for these people that are taking a chance on entering illegally into this country but the law is the law. As a Catholic, as an American of Mexican descent we need stronger border enforcement. Msgr. Bnuelas (*sic*) needs to study history and find out that those countries that do not enforce their border, language or culture will find themselves in the dust bin of history.[8]

The insistence of such commentators that pastoral ministers should "stay out of these issues" makes it that much more urgent that biblical scholars and theologians continue to insist, together with Archbishop José Gómez, that "We cannot separate our faith in Jesus from the policies we advocate as citizens." Addressing a February 2010 gathering of Catholic CEOs and business leaders in Florida, Gómez urged, "We need you to help remind our neighbors that we are all brothers and sisters, children of God—no matter where we come from, or how we got here, or what kind of documents we possess."[9] The more our resistant audiences tell us to mind our own business and to stay out of public policy debates, the more insistently we need to affirm that the concerns of our brothers and sisters on the move must be our concerns as well.

Being on the move is not *just* about Latin American immigration to the United States. The pervasive reach of globalization means that issues of immigration, of refugees, of internally displaced and stateless persons are issues that affect people on every continent. For instance, as I put the finishing touches on this book, thousands of Tunisian refugees have fled the upheaval in their own homeland and have made their way to the Italian island of Lampedusa. In the western part of Côte d'Ivoire, the Office of the United Nations High Commissioner for Refugees is working to relieve overcrowding at facilities that seek to accommodate some of the more than 38,000 people who are internally displaced because of ongoing civil and political unrest in their country.[10]

Gemma Tulud Cruz eloquently shapes an intercultural theology of migration that draws on the experiences of Filipina domestic workers in Hong Kong, women marginalized in multiple ways who struggle with the challenges of life on the edge.[11] Reflecting on the broad range of perspectives provided by the contributors to *Realizing the America of Our Hearts: Theological Voices of Asian Americans*, a volume edited by Fumitaka Matsuoka and Eleazar Fernandez, Hispanic Catholic theologian Carmen Nanko-Fernández maintains that this breadth challenges "the temptation to create a theology of migration by insisting on the distinctiveness of each migration and its respective context. One size does not fit all, there are no universal experiences of migrations, and this admission has implications not only for our theologies but for our ministries and our social policies as well."[12]

Duly dissuaded by a postmodern distaste for grand narratives from attempting to weave the many threads of human migration into a single, monochromatic tapestry, we are instead challenged to appreciate all that is at stake in the convergences and divergences of many "little stories" of people on the move.[13] That no *single* theology of migration can make sense of the whole range of what people on the move experience need not lead theologians to seek some least common denominator among these experiences, nor should it move us to seek some safe higher ground from which we can claim familiarity with *the* big picture.

While it is undeniable that the transnational forces identified under the convenient rubric of globalization exert their impact on every continent and in every community, theologies of migration that concentrate on the global at the expense of the local run the risk of further marginalizing those who are already pushed to the edges of society, dislocated beyond the borders of human dignity, anonymized and reduced to silence through the sin of academic othercide—erasing them by pretending to speak in their place.[14]

READING AROUND THE EDGES

Appeals to the Bible to stir Christian consciences to action on behalf of people on the move often focus on biblical legislation regarding the treatment of foreigners, frequently citing texts such as Exodus 23:9, "You shall not oppress a resident alien; you know the heart of an alien, for you were aliens in the land of Egypt," as well as Leviticus 19:33-34, "When an alien resides with you in your land, you shall not oppress the alien. The alien who resides with you shall be to you as the citizen among you; you shall love the alien as yourself, for you were aliens in the land of Egypt: I am the Lord your God."[15]

Thus, for example, *Strangers No Longer: Together on the Journey of Hope*, the 2003 pastoral letter of the U.S. and Mexican Catholic bishops' conferences concerning migration appropriately devotes attention to "migration in the light of the Word of God" and makes reference to these texts before turning attention to migration in the light of Catholic social teaching.[16] Side by side with imperatives from the Hebrew Bible that are addressed afresh to twenty-first century Christians, the bishops appeal to the New Testament in ways that call on their readers to see the face of Christ in the face of the migrant and that invite migrants to recognize the Christ who is one with them: "Recalling the migration of the Chosen People from Egypt, Jesus, Mary, and Joseph themselves were refugees in Egypt: 'Out of Egypt I called my son' (Mt 2:15). From this account the Holy Family has become a figure with whom Christian migrants and refugees throughout the ages can identify, giving them hope and courage in hard times."[17]

Appeals like these have a vital place among the resources that can be brought to bear in the challenging work of advocacy on behalf of people on the move. In *Christians at the Border: Immigration, the Church, and the*

Bible, M. Daniel Carroll R. deploys just such an argument very effectively, explaining

> My intention is to try to move Christians to reconsider their starting point in the immigration debate. Too often discussions default to passionate ideological argument, economic wrangling, or racial sentiments that dominate national discourse. Among Christians, my experience has been that there is little awareness of what might be a divine viewpoint on migration. This book is a modest attempt to help remedy that shortcoming.[18]

Carroll's book is a valuable tool for Protestant and Catholic Christian leaders whose "preaching to the choir" on issues of migration still meets with stiff resistance. After all, as Carroll maintains, "All people from the Christian heritage can gather around this sacred Word, which they share, and listen to the voice of God."[19] Calling attention to the title of his book—*Christians at the Border*—as a *double entendre*, he calls readers to make up their minds: "We must determine whether the place we choose to stand in the national debate will be based on the Word of God or whether we will ignore its teaching and defend our opinion on other grounds."[20]

Carroll's book is compelling and convincing, but I have written a very different sort of book, one that very intentionally directs attention to biblical texts that are rarely marshaled in the service of arguments on behalf of people on the move or of public policy reform regarding immigrants and refugees. In some sense, then, this book is about "little stories," read, as it were, around the edges.[21] These readings are very deliberately informed by what Fernando F. Segovia has called "a hermeneutics of otherness and engagement." As a reading strategy,

> it begins with and aims for contextualization—it puts aside and calls into question any claim to be objective and scientific, neutral and impartial, universal. Likewise, it opts for humanization and diversity—it resists both dehumanization, any divestiture of all those identity factors that constitute and characterize the reader as reader, and rehumanization, any attempt to force all readers into one and the same particular and contextualized discussion. Finally, it seeks to acknowledge, respect, and engage the other—it opposes any attempt, implicit or explicit, to overwhelm or override the other, to impose a definition upon it, to turn the other into an "other."[22]

Attending to otherness without falling prey to the temptation to commit what Stavans and Nanko-Fernández refer to as "othercide" involves attention to what Segovia calls the "voice of otherness," which he suggests "begins with contextualization and aims for it." Thus,

In reference to biblical criticism, it argues that contextualization is imperative with regard to the biblical texts as well as with regard to their readers and critics. In effect, it sees a genuine exchange with otherness—the otherness both of the text and of other readers of the text—as impossible without a preliminary renunciation of presumed universality and objectivity and a corresponding admission and acceptance of contextuality.[23]

The ethical payoff of such a hermeneutic? In recognizing others, the others we encounter in texts (biblical and otherwise) and the others who are fellow readers of texts,

> the voice of our otherness becomes a voice of and for liberation: not afraid to expose, critique, and provide an alternative vision and narrative; grounded in mixture as something not to be eschewed and marginalized, but valued and engaged; and committed to the fundamental principles of freedom and justice.[24]

Explicitly engaging in such a reading strategy makes it possible to recognize my own situatedness as a flesh-and-blood reader with a variety of distinctives and complex, overlapping identity markers (for example, as a male, as a Roman Catholic, as a Nuyorican, as an academic), while recognizing that other readers with whom I enter into dialogue about biblical texts may or may not share either my convictions or my context. That does not prevent me from reading *with* another, even if the presuppositions with which we arrive at the task of reading are very different. Nor does it prevent me from seeking common ground with other readers or from seeking solidarity based on a shared commitment to such principles as justice and human dignity. Embracing a hermeneutics of engagement and otherness likewise makes it possible to recognize that the diversity of readers in the world *in front of* the text, to borrow an expression from Paul Ricoeur, reflects analogous diversity in the world *behind* the text.[25] Thus it follows, the Bible does not speak with a *single* voice, and to read as though this were not the case fails to do justice to its complex textures.

In this book I have very deliberately sought to avoid the language of correlation and correspondence, an approach that is too often the default rhetoric of well-intentioned theologians who are concerned with what the Bible may or may not have to "say" to and about people on the move. As Carmen Nanko-Fernández has noted, "Models of correspondence, frequently favored by theologians, even those with pro-immigration stances, inevitably dissolve into proof-texting scripture. Lost are the real struggles, warts and all, of communities interpreting these texts in their own times, and addressing the age-old issue of people on the move."[26]

The concern for the oversimplifications involved in correlational reading strategies makes me cautious about the hermeneutical and ethical side effects of affirmations like, "The parallels of the immigrant narrative to the Exodus story are striking (Ex 13:17-17:7)."[27] Such correlations run the risk of doing disservice both to the world behind the text (by reducing the complexity of its generative matrix) and to the world in front of the text (by imposing *one* reading of the biblical text as normative). Furthermore, when deployed in arguments that seek to counteract the denigration of immigrants, such correlations yield an equally inaccurate romanticized view of migrations and of people on the move. A hermeneutics of otherness and engagement offers a salutary alternative, suggesting instead that mapping relationships between texts and their contexts, between readers and their contexts, and between texts and readers across contexts, is a matter of complex negotiation and not linear correspondence.

MAPPING THIS BOOK

This book is the outcome of several years of reflection, and I am grateful to the biblical scholars, pastoral agents, theologians, students, and others who have patiently listened to me think out loud as it came together in fits and starts, and whose own insightful readings of the biblical texts I consider in these pages often challenged me to rethink and reframe my own understandings. Although each chapter can stand on its own, and while earlier versions of a number of them have appeared elsewhere, this book's trajectory through texts not often considered with people on the move in mind is itself an experience of reading around the edges of the biblical canon, of looking in unexpected places and being surprised at what comes to light in so doing.

The first three chapters in Part I address key questions of method and readings strategies. The first chapter, "Good Fences and Good Neighbors? Biblical Scholars and Theologians," looks beyond the one-time commonplace that limited the charge of the biblical exegete to formulating an understanding of what ancient texts *meant* and then left it to the systematic theologian to consider what it *means*, a division of labor between retrieval and recontextualization, between translation and actualization. If *teología de conjunto* in the service of our constituencies means anything at all in practice, then Latino/a biblical scholars and theologians have good reason to move freely across the artificial disciplinary borders that others have set up. Chapter 2, "The Bible and Liberation: Between the Preferential Option for the Poor and the Hermeneutical Privilege of the Poor," re-examines the interrelationship between a key ethical principle and a key principle of interpretation. Both emerged from the context of the Latin American church, and both converge to help us better frame the question of *who* are the subjects of biblical interpretation. This problematizes the distinction between "academic" and "popular" biblical interpretation by considering whose interests are (or are not) advanced under the rubric of liberationist agendas.

In chapter 3, "Reading *en voz alta*: Latino/a Biblical Studies as Public Theology and the Case of U.S. Immigration Reform," I work to re-imagine biblical studies as something more than a highly specialized academic discipline, considering the role of the sociopolitically engaged biblical scholar as a public intellectual whose responsibility for the production of new knowledge is neither ethically neutral nor inconsequential vis-à-vis the shaping of public opinion. I make a particular case for the responsibility that sociopolitically engaged Latino/a biblical scholars bear with respect to the complex ways in which the Bible portrays people on the move, inasmuch as the Bible is often foundational to faith-based arguments advocating just policies and practices.

In Part II, "Looking to the Texts," subsequent chapters build both directly and indirectly on the platform of biblical scholarship that is reconceived on the basis of the arguments in these first three chapters. Thus, the texts from the Hebrew Bible that I consider in the chapters that follow are presented in canonical order, beginning with Genesis (chapter 4), moving on to Ezekiel (chapters 5 and 6), turning next to a postexilic text from Nehemiah (chapter 7), and then to the New Testament with a parable from Matthew's Gospel (chapter 8), before concluding with a chapter that considers the late medieval apocalyptic exegesis of Christopher Columbus (chapter 9).

There is a mildly transgressive agenda intentionally at work in the range of texts I offer in this book, for it violates the ethos of hyperspecialization that characterizes much of biblical scholarship. I have chosen to consider a range of texts across the canon, selecting these not because they are at the "heart" of the canon but because reading them from the edges invites us to think differently about people on the move both in the texts and among the specialists and nonspecialists who may read these texts in our own time.

In Genesis 12 Abram and Sarai are economic refugees forced by famine to make their way to Egypt. Ezekiel 12 and 20 present the prophet-as-political-exile, wrestling with the multiple traumas of forced displacement. Nehemiah 13 offers a postexilic perspective on language and assimilation, focusing on Nehemiah's consternation that the children of mixed marriages "could not speak the language of Judah."

Taking the oppressive economic and political circumstances of first-century Palestine into consideration informs a very different reading of Matthew's parable of the day laborers. Finally, a consideration of the apocalyptic fervor that motivated Christopher Columbus offers a valuable lesson about the enormous influence of the Bible, particularly its place in shaping the Spanish colonial enterprise in the Americas. In a sense, considering Columbus as an interpreter of the Bible brings us full circle in this discussion of people on the move. Reading around the edges of the biblical canon across the centuries with people on the move affirms Arturo Bañuelas's contention that migration "is a defining issue that is about us—all of us Latinos—and about how we will shape the future of our church and our country."

PART I

Reading Strategies

1

Good Fences and Good Neighbors? Biblical Scholars and Theologians[1]

BUSINESS AS USUAL?

In mainstream Roman Catholic academic circles after the Second Vatican Council, the division of labor between biblical scholars and theologians—systematic and otherwise—came to be inscribed as a methodological commonplace, typically along the lines suggested in the famous 1962 article on biblical theology in the *Interpreter's Dictionary of the Bible*, by the Lutheran biblical scholar Krister Stendahl, whereby the biblical scholar was assigned responsibility for determining what the text *meant*, while it was left up to the theologian to explicate what the text *means* for believers today.[2] Thus, in his highly influential *Method in Theology*, Bernard Lonergan suggested that it is the work of the exegete *qua* exegete to attend to the understanding of texts, an activity "which pertains to the first phase of theology, to theology not as speaking to the present but as listening, as coming to listen to the past."[3] When addressing theological colleagues, says Lonergan, the exegete

> will appear to be happy to proceed slowly, and often he will follow the ways of beginners. His descriptions will convey a feeling for things long past; they will give the reader an impression of the foreign, the strange, the archaic; his care for genuineness will appear in the choice of a vocabulary as biblical as possible; and he will be careful to avoid any premature transposition to later language, even thought that language is approved by a theological tradition.[4]

For Lonergan, the biblical exegete's contribution to the larger theological enterprise is indispensable: "While every theologian has to have some training in exegesis, he cannot become a specialist in all fields." However,

13

the theologian *qua* theologian goes further than exegesis: while the exegete of ancient texts very properly gives an impression of the foreign, the strange, the archaic, his readers cannot be content to leave it at that."[5]

In their handbook *The Bible for Theology: Ten Principles for the Theological Use of Scripture*, Gerald O'Collins and Daniel Kendall begin by noting, "For much of Christian history theologians and biblical interpreters were identical; the same persons faced the task both of exegeting the whole Bible and translating it into their theology. In the last century or two scriptural scholars and systematic theologians have normally belonged to distinct specializations. When using the Bible, theologians need to ask among other things: What are the exegetes saying?"[6] In what follows, they articulate and illustrate ten principles for the use of the Bible in systematic theology that they recommend "as guidelines in moving from the scriptures to theology."[7] These principles are the following:

1. *The Principle of Faithful Hearing.* The Scriptures require theologians to be faithful and regular hearers of the inspired texts.
2. *The Principle of Active Hearing.* Responsible theologians are active interpreters of the Scriptures, appropriating them within the contexts of prayer, study, and action.
3. *The Principle of the Community and Its Creeds.* The Scriptures call for a theological interpretation and appropriation within the living community of faith and in the light of its classic creeds.
4. *The Principle of Biblical Convergence.* Convergent biblical testimony can bear on the theological questions being examined.
5. *The Principle of Exegetical Consensus.* Where available, the consensus of centrist exegetes guides systematic theology.
6. *The Principle of Metathemes and Metanarratives.* Theological appropriation of the Bible takes account of metathemes and metanarratives.
7. *The Principle of Continuity within Discontinuity.* Various discontinuities within continuities affect the theological "taking over" of the Bible.
8. *The Principle of Eschatological Provisionality.* Their eschatological provisionality regulates the theological role of Scriptures.
9. *The Principle of Philosophical Assistance.* The passage from the Bible to theology takes place in dialogue with philosophy.
10. *The Principle of Inculturation.* The task of inculturation helps to shape any theological appropriation of the Scriptures.[8]

Although a detailed consideration of O'Collins and Kendall lies outside the scope of our concerns in this chapter, it is sufficient to note that they, like Lonergan, accept the de facto division of labor between exegetes and systematic theologians. Their ten principles suggest that the differences between exegetical discourses and systematic theological discourses are actually mutually enriching and not irreparably irreconcilable. Their fifth principle, however, does call for some comment. O'Collins and Kendall explain that by the "principle of exegetical consensus" they propose "the willingness of theologians to prefer, all things being equal, the line taken by widely respected, centrist biblical scholars, or at least the majority of them." They further suggest,

> In reflecting on the scriptural texts, theologians ought not plunge forward by themselves and ignore what professional exegetes have to say. However they cannot remain stuck on major questions, waiting for a universal consensus to emerge in biblical studies; experience shows that such a consensus on some questions may never emerge. It is also obviously ill-advised to take over into theology adventurous, even maverick, theses advanced by individual biblical scholars or a small group with its own particularist agenda.[9]

What remains unsettled by O'Collins and Kendall is the important question of the criteria by which any given systematic theologian might discern who the "centrist" biblical scholars and who the "mavericks" might be on any given question. Indeed, the identification of "centrist" biblical scholars and how one might distinguish them from advocates of particularist agendas is a matter that is fraught with difficulty. After all, if, as O'Collins and Kendall suggest, consensus among exegetes is not always (or even often) forthcoming, it follows that consensus over what constitutes centrist exegesis is at least as hard to come by. Furthermore, the determination of where the center lies depends on who is drawing the maps. More bluntly stated, these determinations often have as much to do with the agendas of academic and ecclesiastical gatekeepers as they have to do with the persuasive power of the exegetes' own arguments.

The rocky reception history of the historical critical approach within Roman Catholic circles in the second half of the twentieth century itself serves as a convenient illustration of this dilemma. At one extreme, consider, for instance, the hostility of George Kelly (among others) to Scripture scholars such as Raymond E. Brown.[10] The characterization of Brown's exegetical and theological attitudes by his friends and colleagues as a matter of extraordinary equanimity notwithstanding, elements of the Catholic right wing in the United States spilled no small amount of ink going after Brown and other Catholic exegetes for their embrace of what they (mis)perceive as the insidious historical-critical subversion of the church's received understanding of the Scriptures.[11] A few years earlier, in his January 1988 Erasmus Lecture at St. Peter's Lutheran Church in New York, Cardinal Ratzinger began in the following way:

In Wladimir Solowjew's *History of the Antichrist*, the eschatological enemy of the Redeemer recommended himself to believers, among other things, by the fact that he had earned his doctorate in theology at Tübingen and had written an exegetical work which was recognized as pioneering in the field! With this paradox Solowjew sought to shed light on the ambivalence inherent in biblical exegetical methodology for almost a hundred years now. To speak of the crisis of the historical-critical method today is practically a truism.[12]

In *The Interpretation of the Bible in the Church*, the Pontifical Biblical Commission itself voiced in more measured terms a certain ambivalence toward the historical-critical approach: "the fact is that at the very time when the most prevalent scientific method—the 'historical-critical method'—is freely practiced in exegesis, including Catholic exegesis, it is itself brought into question. To some extent, this has come about in the scholarly world itself through the rise of alternative methods and approaches. But it has also arisen through the criticisms of many members of the faithful, who judge the method deficient from the point of view of faith."[13] As for the plurality of methods and approaches involved in what it refers to as "scientific" exegesis (read *Wissenschaft*), the Biblical Commission acknowledges the critique of some who suggest,

> Instead of making for easier and more secure access to the living sources of God's word, it makes of the Bible a closed book. Interpretation may always have been something of a problem, but now it requires such technical refinements as to render it a domain reserved to a few specialists alone. To the latter some apply the phrase of the Gospel: "You have taken away the key of knowledge; you have not entered in yourselves and you have hindered those who sought to enter" (Lk 11:52; cf. Mt. 23:13).[14]

Making the case for a return to what he calls the theological interpretation of Scripture, Stephen Fowl presents the dilemma of the historical-critical approach in the following terms:

> One of the long-term results of historical critical methods of reading was to separate the practice of reading the Bible in a manner geared toward historical reconstruction from the practice of developing a theologically significant reading. By the time it came to dominate biblical study in America [*sic*], historical criticism had largely become separated from the theological ends it was initially meant to serve. While most biblical scholars of both Testaments still continue to identify themselves as Christians, they generally are required to check

their theological convictions at the door when they enter the profession of biblical studies.[15]

Furthermore, in Fowl's judgment, business as usual in the theological disciplines has become fragmented, with biblical scholars and systematic theologians working

largely in isolation from one another and often for very different ends. As a result, the work of professional biblical scholars is often seen by professional theologians as both too technical and too irrelevant for their own interests. Further, professional biblical scholars tend to find the interests of, for example, systematic theologians abstract and ill suited to their professional interests in the Bible.[16]

The assault on the historical-critical approach has not been limited to the voices of those who have found fault with its rationalist disdain for premodern interpretive strategies or with its diachronic dismantling of the church's "received understanding" of the Scriptures. Feminist biblical scholars and theologians and practitioners of contextual interpretations of the Bible have also challenged the pretense to objectivity of the historical-critical approach, and they have unmasked it as a set of contextual discourses that reflects the interests and the presuppositions of economically privileged Western European Christian male readers.[17] If *all* interpretation is contextual, as I believe it is, it must follow that the notion of "centrist" biblical exegesis is illusory and that other strategies must be sought for bringing biblical scholars and systematic theologians into productive conversations.[18]

AT THE GALILEAN BORDER: OF FENCES AND NEIGHBORS

Relatively little deliberate attention has been devoted either by Latino/a theologians or biblical scholars to the exploration of the grammar for interdisciplinary conversations with each other. To be sure, there is a growing body of contextual biblical interpretation by Latino/a Catholics and Protestants, and Latino/a biblical scholars have been participants in collaborative projects to reconfigure systematic theology *latinamente*, but thus far there is nothing that approximates the project of O'Collins and Kendall that offers guidelines for using the Bible theologically *latinamente*.[19] If and when we arrive at the point where such guidelines might be sketched, and at the point where we agreed to abide by such guidelines, their configuration is sure to be quite different from the uncomplicated business-as-usual genre of the ten principles formulated by O'Collins and Kendall.

I would like to consider one specific example of the use of the Bible in U.S.

Latino/a theology, focusing on a seminal work by the "father" of Latino/a theology, Virgilio Elizondo's *Galilean Journey: The Mexican American Promise.*[20] The choice of this book as a point of entry into a discussion of the place of biblical scholarship in conversation with Latino/a theologies has mainly to do with the abiding influence it has exerted among Latino/a Catholic systematic theologians—an influence convincingly documented in the dollars and cents of the publishing world by the appearance of a revised and expanded edition in 2000, seventeen years after the publication of the first edition in 1983. The abiding influence of *Galilean Journey* for Latino/a systematic theology is evident, for example, in Roberto Goizueta's *Caminemos con Jesús.* Goizueta writes, "In his groundbreaking work, *Galilean Journey*, for example, Virgilio Elizondo has demonstrated that an important aspect of Jesus' poverty was his Galilean roots. Not only was Jesus the son of a carpenter, but he was from Nazareth, from the borderlands, hardly the center of civilized life. Coming from an area where different cultures, races, religions and languages constantly mixed, Galileans were impure 'half-breeds'—in a word, mestizos."[21] In support of this observation, Goizueta provides the following lengthy quotation from *Galilean Journey*:

> At the time of Jesus, Galilee was peopled by Phoenicians, Syrians, Arabs, Greeks, Orientals and Jews. . . . A natural ongoing biological and cultural mestizaje was taking place. The Jews were scorned by the Gentiles and the Galilean Jews were regarded with patronizing contempt by the "pure-minded" Jews of Jerusalem. The natural mestizaje of Galilee was a sign of impurity and a cause for rejection . . . from the time of Solomon the land of Galilee had come to be known as the land of Cabul, which in itself meant "like nothing" or "very displeasing." The connotation remained and the inhabitants of the region came to be looked down on and considered good for nothing. . . . In the wisdom of God, it is precisely here in this impure, culturally mixed, freedom-loving, rebellious region that God made the historical beginning of his visible reign on earth. One cannot follow the way of the Lord without appreciating the scandalous way of Jesus the Galilean.[22]

Without further comment, Goizueta then declares, "The power of U.S. Hispanic popular Catholicism derives precisely from the fact that, in its narratives, symbols and rituals, God is identified with the half-breed, the racially and culturally marginalized. Jesus is a Galilean, and Mary is *la Morenita*."[23] Goizueta follows the same trajectory in his contribution to *Beyond Borders: Writings of Virgilio Elizondo and Friends.* In an essay entitled "A Christology for a Global Church," Goizueta declares, "Beyond the Christ of the kings and princes, beyond the Christ of the theologians and philosophers, beyond the Christ of the clerics and bishops, is the Christ of Juan Diego. This Christ is found not primarily in Jerusalem but in Galilee." At second hand, Goizueta contends that recent scholarship on Galilee "corroborate[s] the insights that Virgilio Elizondo presented in his doctoral thesis nearly a quarter century ago."[24]

Even more recently, in his well-received presentation of a Latino/a theological anthropology undertaken in deliberate dialogue with the work of Karl Rahner, Miguel H. Díaz also nods with reverence in the direction of Elizondo's *Galilean Journey*. Díaz writes, "For Elizondo, Galilee and the Galileans—the persons with whom Jesus identified, and the place associated with these persons—become the central loci of divine and human revelation." Díaz goes on to observe that while Elizondo "understands the *mestizo* identity of the Galileans as the unexpected cultural reality of encountering grace, he sees in their social marginalization a locus for understanding the preferential nature of this encounter. Beyond the latter, Elizondo understands the marginalizing experiences of the Galileans as something that predisposes them to receive God's grace."[25] Like Goizueta, Díaz illustrates his conclusion with a citation from Elizondo that discloses Elizondo's debt to the Latin American liberationist notion of the hermeneutical privilege of the poor:

> The apparent nonimportance and rejection of Galilee are the very bases for its all-important role in the historic eruption of God's saving plan for humanity. The human scandal of God's way does not begin with the cross, but with the historico-cultural incarnation of his Son in Galilee. The Galilean Jews appear to have been despised by all and, because of the mixture of cultures of the area, they were especially despised by the superiority-minded Jerusalem Jews. Could anything good come out of such an impure, mixed-up and rebellious area? Yet it is precisely within this area of multiple rejection that the restlessness for liberation and the anxiety for the kingdom of God was the greatest.[26]

Díaz affirms, "Elizondo's understanding of the Galilean identity of Jesus makes known what the Kingdom is like, and how to enable its presence in the world. . . . The Kingdom, suggests Elizondo in his observations above, becomes known in the face of 'Galileans.' And in communities that have embraced socio-cultural mixture, rather than purity."[27]

Elizondo himself took advantage of the opportunity provided by the publication of the revised and expanded edition of *Galilean Journey* to reflect on the genesis of the book as his doctoral dissertation presented at the Institut Catholique in Paris in 1978 with the title *Mestissage, violence culturelle, annonce de l'évangile*, a project at which Elizondo arrived after significant pastoral experience and in response to the urgings of Professor Jacques Audinet. Elizondo himself reminisces:

the Galilean identity of Jesus

After much reading, searching with my thesis committee, prayer, and long walks in the parks of Paris, all of a sudden the direction of my thesis became clear. The element that would connect all the materials I had gathered and provide the key point of theological interpretation would be the closest friend and companion of our people: *El Nazareno*, Jesus of Nazareth in Galilee. This was not so obvious to my thesis committee, but as they grasped what I was trying to do, they too became very excited. Yes, that was it: I would present our socio-cultural reality together with its cultural expression, then do a cultural reading of the gospel matrix (every reading is a cultural reading), and then offer a gospel interpretation of our Mexican-American reality and challenge. The journey of the Galilean Jesus through his particular history and culture would offer a point of departure for interpreting our own reality.[28]

Oh how wistfully familiar that process of brainstorming and negotiation with one's doctoral committee sounds to those of us who have been through those arcane rites of passage into the guild! Elizondo continues:

I knew a lot about Jesus' time in history but came to some exciting new insights as I discovered more and more about his cultural reality, the cultural reality of Galilee. It turned out to be very much like the Mexican Southwest of the United States. Since his Galilean identity and the Galilean identity of the disciples is so often mentioned, and especially at the core moments of the gospel narrative, it must have special significance. . . . The christologies I knew, written from the dominant cultures, had made no special mention of Galilee. But for me, the Galilean identity of Jesus became the most important interpretive key for my thesis, as it would continue to be in all my subsequent work.[29]

Let us be completely clear: Elizondo himself has never claimed to be a trained exegete. In *Galilean Journey*, his work took shape in conversation with what he and the professors who reviewed his doctoral dissertation regarded as reputable biblical exegetes. He explains, "We take the exegetical studies of biblical experts seriously, but we do not attempt to simply reproduce or broadcast them; we want to bring out their concrete salvific implications."[30] That being the case, we must reckon squarely with the well-founded critique of his work by Mary Boys. In *Has God Only One Blessing? Judaism as a Source of Christian Self-Understanding*, Boys—who is herself not an exegete but a practical theologian (the Skinner and McAlpin Professor of Practical Theology at Union Theological Seminary)—observes, "Unfortunately, some liberation theologians have gone considerably beyond what is known about Galilee in the first century in order to embellish their thesis about Jesus' identification with marginal people. Scholarship simply does not support the sweeping generalizations they draw."[31] For Boys, Elizondo's *Galilean Journey* is a banner instance of these tragic excesses. Consider, for example, the following quotation from *Galilean Journey*:

> Galileans maintained a refreshing originality in Judaism. It was a combination of the commonsense, grass-roots wisdom of practical expertise, their more open and personal relations with foreigners, and their relative distance from Jerusalem. Their hospitable and fertile land gave them a warmer, more optimistic outlook on life than the Judean Jews had. Distance from Jerusalem and daily contact with foreigners were characteristic of the Galilean Jew. The intellectual preoccupation of Jerusalem, with its various schools, hardly reached Galilee. The Galilean faith in the god of the fathers was thus more personal, purer, simpler, and more spontaneous. It was not encumbered or suffocated by the religious scrupulosities of the Jewish intelligentsia.[32]

Whether intentionally or otherwise, in these lines Elizondo lapses into a ruralist romanticism verging on anti-intellectualism—a rare and unfortunate combination for a volume that began as a doctoral dissertation! That odd anti-intellectualism *cum* anti-Judaism is a persistent motif in *Galilean Journey*. Elizondo writes: "Jerusalem was also the site of the greater rabbinical schools where Jews went to study so that eventually they could become 'doctors.' The scribes—that is, the degreed intellectuals—considered themselves to have a monopoly on knowledge and its power. They alone were the authorized interpreters of the law. They dominated the masses through a type of intellectual moralism inasmuch as they imposed their knowledge as God's way."[33] Baser still is the barely concealed stereotype of greedy Jewish businesspeople implied by Elizondo's remark that "If for no other reason than commerce, the Jews were friendly and accommodating to non-Jews."[34]

As for Jesus, Elizondo contends,

> The practices and teachings of Jesus struck a heavy blow at the fundamental convictions of the Jewish people of the time. He appeared to prostitute everything that the Jewish establishment had come to hold as sacred and that had become the basis for the survival and salvation of the people. Jewish authorities had worked hard to keep the community whole and pure. Now, in the name of the same God and kingdom, the unauthorized Galilean was challenging the very basis of the theological edifice that crowned their theocratic endeavors.[35]

Elsewhere in *Galilean Jesus*, Elizondo himself arrives at an important insight: "White Western supremacy permeates our way of life to such a degree that even good persons act in racist ways without even realizing that they are being racist. . . . Racism and ethnocentrism are interwoven in literature, entertainment, institutions, marriage relations, finances, and even religious symbolism."[36] To this list we must sadly add biblical and theological scholarship as well. At the heart of Elizondo's inadvertent anti-Judaism is his uncritical embrace of Western European exegetical discourses that were themselves irreparably racialized. This has been demonstrated convincingly in Shawn Kelley's important book, *Racializing Jesus: Race, Ideology and the Formation of Modern Biblical Scholarship*, which explores the ways in which racism and racialized discourses played key roles in the development of biblical scholarship in the nineteenth and twentieth centuries.[37]

A look at Elizondo's bibliography is instructive, for it includes Ernst Lohmeyer's work *Galiläa und Jerusalem* (Göttingen: Vandenhoeck & Ruprecht, 1936). In that work, according to Susannah Heschel, Lohmeyer "developed the theory of a two-site origin of early Christianity: Galilee, where a universalistic, son-of-man eschatology prevailed, and Jerusalem, dominated by nationalistic, Jewish eschatology."[38] Here, then, are the twisted roots of Elizondo's "Galilee principle" and his "Jerusalem principle." Four years after Lohmeyer's book appeared, Walter Grundmann suggested in *Jesus der Galiläer und das Judentum* (Leipzig: Georg Wigand, 1940) "that Jesus' rejection of the Jewish title of 'messiah' in favor of the title 'Son of man' proved his Galilean, and thus his Aryan, origin."[39] If it is true that *Galilean Journey* laid the foundation for Latino/a theologies in the United States, and if the Latino/a theologians who are indebted to Elizondo truly share his genuinely liberationist vision, then it is high time that we take a closer and more careful look at its hidden assumptions and at the unexamined implications of its discourse about *mestizaje*.

SUMMING UP

The example of Elizondo's use of biblical scholarship in *Galilean Jesus* clearly demonstrates that there is more to the give-and-take between biblical scholars and practitioners of other theological disciplines than the Pontifical Biblical Commission suggested:

> On the one hand, systematic theology has an influence upon the presuppositions with which exegetes approach biblical texts. On the other hand, exegesis provides the other theological disciplines with data fundamental for their operation. There is, accordingly, a relationship of dialogue between exegesis and the other branches of theology, granted always a mutual respect for that which is specific to each.[40]

For better and for worse, both intentionally and unintentionally, exegetes bring more than data to the table for the consideration of the "other theological disciplines," and that fact so complicates the rules of engagement between biblical studies and theological scholarship that it leads one to wonder whether good fences do indeed make for good neighbors. Exegesis has never been *just* exegesis pure and simple. Looking across the disciplinary divide with suspicion in the light of what we have learned, systematic theologians might well be tempted to part company with exegetes and to regard the increasing distance between themselves and biblical scholarship as a matter of salutary insulation. I would venture to disagree.

While the increasing inter- and intradisciplinary specialization is surely here to stay, good fences make for good neighbors only when well-maintained gates grant easy access of each to the other side. Responsible biblical scholarship and responsible theological research call for—and call each other to—transparency and accountability.[41] Rather than accepting at face value—and often at second or third hand—the claims of biblical scholarship, systematic theologians who turn to the Bible as the "soul of theology" would do well to bear in mind the contextuality of all discourses as they read the discourses of biblical scholarship with a measure of care and caution. For their part, biblical scholars would do well to call systematic theologians to operate within the framework of what Fernando Segovia has called a hermeneutics of otherness and engagement as a prolegomenon to reading with (or alongside, or even against) exegetes and other readers (academic, pastoral, professional, and otherwise) of biblical texts.[42]

If the Latino/a practice of *teología de conjunto* is to be more than an empty aspiration, then the conversations in which we participate among ourselves must be as frank and candid as they are civil and respectful. If by *teología de conjunto* we understand a paradigm of theological discourse that rejects the competing academic models of debates as zero-sum games, then constructive self-critical discourse makes us all winners—even those with whom we must disagree. If, as Latino/a biblical scholars and theologians, ours is an ecclesial vocation—and it surely is—then the Scriptures themselves provide common ground for our committed discourses, for in them the church finds sustenance: "The Church has always venerated the divine Scriptures just as she [*sic*] venerates the body of the Lord, since, especially in the sacred liturgy, she unceasingly receives and offers to the faithful the bread of life from the table both of God's word and of Christ's body" (*Dei Verbum* 21).[43]

2

The Bible and Liberation: Between the Preferential Option for the Poor and the Hermeneutical Privilege of the Poor

GUSTAVO GUTIÉRREZ COMES TO QUEENS

When the Second General Conference of the Latin American Episcopate convened at Medellín in 1968, I was a young boy, trying to figure out how much different a place the world had become after the assassination of Martin Luther King, Jr., on April 4, 1968, and then of Robert F. Kennedy on June 6, 1968—just days before my own birthday. I had no idea then of what was happening at Medellín, even though that gathering was to shape the direction in which theology would move throughout the hemisphere and beyond, even though, all these years later, as a Latino biblical scholar I recognize the profound indebtedness of Latino/a biblical scholarship and theologies to that historic assembly. That being said, I remember vividly my very first encounter with liberation theology, and that came thanks to my mother.

If you had known my mother, you would not be surprised at all. When I was in high school, she brought a book into our home in Queens, New York, that was written by a Peruvian priest named Gustavo Gutiérrez. As she so often did, after devouring the book herself, my mother insisted that I read it so that we could talk about it at table, and so I did. I can't say that I understood very much of it, but she did a credible job of helping me to understand at least as much as a bookish teenager could manage. I still have that copy of *A Theology of Liberation*, and I can't help but thinking that, all these many years after Medellín, my own personal and professional trajectory as a Latino biblical scholar owes something to that first encounter.

GIVING VOICE TO THE PREFERENTIAL OPTION

The bishops who gathered at Puebla in 1979 for the Third General Conference of the Latin American Episcopate (CELAM) looked back eleven years to the Second General Conference of CELAM at Medellín and noted the following:

> Since Medellín in particular, the Church, clearly aware of its mission and loyally open to dialogue, has been scrutinizing the signs of the times and is generously disposed to evangelize in order to contribute to the construction of a new society that is more fraternal and just; such a society is a crying need of our peoples. Thus, the mutual forces of tradition and progress, which once seemed to be antagonistic in Latin America, are now joining each other and seeking a new, distinctive synthesis that will bring together the possibilities of the future and the energies derived from our common roots. And so, within this vast process of renewal that is inaugurating a new epoch in Latin America, and amid the challenges of recent times, we pastors are taking up the age-old episcopal tradition of Latin America and preparing ourselves to carry the Gospel's message of salvation hopefully and bravely to all human beings, but to the poorest and most forgotten by way of preference.[1]

It was at Puebla that the "preferential option for the poor" emerged as the now familiar expression that captures succinctly and effectively this key contribution of the church in Latin America to Catholic social teaching by focusing sharply on the church's commitment to and solidarity with those on the margins of society. As Carmen Nanko-Fernández points out, after it was coined at Puebla, the expression quickly made its way into papal teaching. For example, Nanko-Fernández calls attention to the use of the phrase by Pope John Paul II in his July 10, 1980, address to the bishops of Brazil at Fortaleza:

> You know that the preferential option for the poor was strongly proclaimed at Puebla. It is not a call to exclusiveness, it is not a justification for the bishop to omit to announce the word of conversion and salvation to one or another group of persons on the pretext that they are not poor. After all, what is the context that we do give this term? . . . It is a call to special oneness with the small and weak, those that suffer and weep, those that are humiliated and left on the margin of life and society.[2]

At Puebla, the Latin American bishops pointed back to Medellín as a key point of departure for the train of thought that led to the development of the preferential option for the poor as a key principle of Catholic social teaching. It was at Medellín that the bishops declared that they could not remain indifferent "in the face of the tremendous social injustices existent in Latin America, which keep the majority of our peoples in dismal poverty, which in many cases becomes inhuman wretchedness. A deafening cry pours from the throats of millions of men [*sic*], asking their pastors for a liberation that reaches them from nowhere else."[3] It was with the outcry of these many millions ringing in their ears that the bishops recognized with new understanding Jesus' call to solidarity with the poor:

> The Lord's distinct commandment to "evangelize the poor" ought to bring us to a distribution of resources and apostolic personnel that effectively gives preference to the poorest and most needy sectors. . . . We ought to sharpen the awareness of our duty of solidarity with the poor, to which charity leads us. This solidarity means that we make ours their problems and their struggles.[4]

This chapter takes a close look at the relationship between two distinct but very closely interrelated principles that can trace their lineage back some forty years to Medellín, the relationship between an ethical principle and a hermeneutical principle: the "preferential option for the poor," on the one hand, and the "hermeneutical privilege of the poor," on the other. I submit that in some significant measure, the conversion to solidarity with the poor of the Latin American bishops that found its expression at Medellín was set in motion by the new ways in which they came to understand the message of the Bible.

In its turn, that conversion toward the preferential option for the poor gave rise to the principle of the "hermeneutical privilege of the poor." In July 1968, the month before the Medellín conference convened, Gustavo Gutiérrez delivered a presentation entitled "*Hacia una teología de la liberación*," "Toward a Theology of Liberation," in which he sketched the broad lines of a shift that is both ethical and hermeneutical, that has to do with how we read the Bible and how our reading calls us to act. Gutiérrez confessed,

> We have deeply interiorized a framework for interpreting the Bible: as Christians we must understand everything the Old Testament says about the temporal order as belonging to the spiritual plane. This spiritual outlook would begin with the New Testament. Thus we translate "to preach good news to the poor" as meaning that we should tell the poor in spirit that they should hope in God. "To preach liberation to captives" means to speak to the captives about sin. "The recuperation of sight by the blind" means that they do not see God. "Freedom to the oppressed" means those oppressed by Satan.

In reality all these expressions have a meaning that is direct and clear. For example, let us take "to proclaim a year of grace." This becomes clear if we refer to Leviticus 25:10, which says that a just society must be established. *Populorum Progressio* says the same thing: When it is left simply to economic laws freely to organize human life, then we begin to have rich and poor. If the economy is given free rein, the distance between them increases. That is what happened in the past, in the time of Leviticus. For that reason, the "year of grace" was created, when all would have to go back to the starting point, when all would leave aside what they possessed and go back to the starting point.

We have said that everything in the Old Testament was purely secular and thus required transformation into a more religious framework, but this is not true. Certainly there is a religious significance, but the messianic promise means something integral and global, which affects the whole person. If we understand salvation as something with merely "religious" or "spiritual" value for my soul, then it would not have much to contribute to concrete human life.[5]

There can be no doubt that for Latin American Catholics, the renewal of the church that was a late-twentieth-century concretization of the principle *ecclesia semper reformanda* was prompted by a *recursus ad fontes*, by a *ressourcement* at the grassroots level that called for a profound reorientation with respect not only to the foundational value of the Bible for Christian belief and practice, but also with respect to the readers of the Bible whose interpretations should be foregrounded. In his essay "'Listening to What the Spirit Is Saying to the Churches.' Popular Interpretation of the Bible in Brazil," Carlos Mesters reminisced, "1968 was the year of the world revolution of youth, the military coup in Brazil, the meeting of the Latin American bishops' conference at Medellín, and the systematization of the theology of liberation. It was also the time when this new step in popular interpretation became more clearly visible."[6]

Reflecting on the foundational role of the Bible as read in basic ecclesial communities, Mesters identified a twofold dynamic, suggesting on the one hand that "There are communities, which, motivated by reading the Bible, place themselves at the service of the people and enter the struggle for justice," while on the other hand, "Other communities emerge directly out [*of*] the struggle and, as a result of that struggle, begin to read the Bible."[7] What gave rise to this reading strategy? For Mesters, the CELAM gathering at Medellín was one among several crucial factors that encouraged ordinary readers to turn to the Bible. Thus, according to Mesters, "The Bible comes to be seen," by ordinary readers among the poor of Brazil, "as the mirror or 'symbol' of what they live today. It is at that point, from this new connection between the Bible and life, that the poor make the discovery, the greatest of all discoveries: 'If God was with that people then, in the past, then he is also

with us in the struggle we are waging to free ourselves. He hears our cries.'
This is the seed of the theology of liberation."[8]

The shift involved a clear move from the ethical principle of solidarity
with the poor to the principle of the hermeneutical privilege of the poor.
According to Mesters, "the Bible itself has shifted its place and moved to the
side of the poor. One could almost say that it has changed its class status.
This is important."[9] In similar terms, Paulo Fernando Carneiro de Andrade
suggests that "The poor discover in the Bible not just a history of earlier
times but their own life, as if in a mirror. For the poor who read the Bible
in the base communities, there is such a connaturality between their lives
and the stories in the Sacred Scriptures that they recognize themselves in the
Scriptures."[10]

Mesters is honest enough to admit that Medellín was only one among
several factors that gave rise to popular interpretation of the Bible among
basic Christian communities in Brazil and elsewhere in Latin America.
Another contributing factor was, at least indirectly, apologetic, a matter of
Catholic mobilization against what Mesters calls "Protestant missionary
energy." He writes, "What helped to bring the Bible to the poorest was the
missionary energy of the Protestant churches. Many Catholics started to
read the Bible in order to be able to answer the Protestants and so overcome
their inferiority complex."[11] In fact, Mesters's exuberant declaration echoes
centuries-old voices of the Reformation when he writes, "The Bible was
taken out of the people's hands. Now they are taking it back. They are
expropriating the expropriators: 'It is our book! It was written for us!' It had
always been 'Father's book,' it seemed. Now it is the people's book again."[12]

READING PRIVILEGES

The ethical imperative of the preferential option for the poor led elite
readers like Mesters—a Dutch-born Carmelite priest who was trained as
an exegete—to reconsider the relationship between academic exegesis
and popular reading. In this vein, the formulation of the principle of the
hermeneutical privilege of the poor came to suggest that ordinary readers
might in fact be better equipped to understand the Bible than biblical
scholars. Elsa Tamez frames the hermeneutical privilege of the poor in the
following terms:

Every liberation reading from the perspective of Latin American
women must be understood within the framework that arises from the
situation of the poor. In a context of misery, malnutrition, repression,
torture, Indian genocide, and war—in other words, in a context of
death—there is no greater priority than framing and articulating
the readings according to these situations. The poor (men, women,

black, Indians) comprise the large majority, and it is because of their discontent that repression and mass killings generally take place. They are in a privileged place, hermeneutically speaking, because we conceive of the God of life and One who has a preferential option for the poor. Besides, the mystery of God's reign is with them because it has been revealed to them (Matt. 11.25).[13]

Pablo Richard contends that "The indigenous peoples, with their millennial history, with their cultural and religious tradition, and recently with their own native method of evangelization and their native theology, are much better prepared to read and interpret the Bible than the Western European Christian who has a millennial history of violence and conquest, impregnated with the erudite, liberal and modern spirit."[14] Elsewhere he writes, "The Bible was not written with a colonial, patriarchal, and anti-body spirit but with the Spirit of the poor and the oppressed."[15] For Richard, this calls for a reconsideration of the value of academic exegesis and of the role of the professional exegete with respect to communities of ordinary readers:

To be sure, the exegesis of the last one hundred years has produced works of enormous importance and relevance; many exegetes, both women and men, have emerged as authentic teachers of the faith and prophets. However, the dominant *spirit* of this exegesis has been, without a doubt, the spirit of modernity—marked by positivism, rationalism, liberalism, individualism, and existentialism. Exegesis normally takes place in closed academies, where the search for power and prestige has been informed by the spirit of competition and the economy of the marketplace.[16]

Addressing the question of whose understanding of the Bible is to be privileged, Justin Ukpong underscores the ways in which Western elite academic readings have asserted exclusive authority: "In classical Western readings, the epistemological privilege is given to the academy, for it is only the interpretations of trained experts that are regarded as valid within the academy. Non-expert interpretations of ordinary people are regarded as uninformed as therefore inconsequential for ascertaining the true meaning of the biblical text."[17]

In the context of the hermeneutical privilege of the poor and of the reading practices of grassroots readers, the rehabilitation of reading strategies that had often been dismissed as naïve and disparaged as precritical called for professional exegetes in Latin America—most of whom received their training in European and North American academic settings—to remap their relationships with communities of ordinary readers, to understand themselves not as teachers or as mediators but as listeners and fellow learners. Transposing liberationist hermeneutics from its Latin American beginnings into his own South African context, Gerald West underscores the importance of the ethical dimension of this shift:

> In their emphasis on epistemology and the experience of oppression and the struggle for liberation and life, liberation theologies ask a question not normally asked in Western theology: who are the primary interlocutors of theology? Who are we talking about and collaborating with when we read the Bible and do theology? Liberation theologies not only pose this question, they also give a specific answer: the poor and marginalized. . . . Furthermore, an option for the poor is more than an ethical choice. Solidarity with the poor also has consequences for the perception of social reality, insisting that the experience of the poor and marginalized is a necessary condition for biblical interpretation and theological reflection. Theologies of liberation require that we not only make "an option for the poor," but that we also accept the "epistemological privilege of the poor." This involves an epistemological paradigm shift in which the poor and marginalized are seen as the primary dialogue partners in reading the Bible and doing theology.[18]

West rightly calls attention to

> two potential problems which constantly recur when biblical scholars participate in Bible reading with local communities of the poor and marginalized: biblical scholars either romanticize and idealize the contribution of the poor and marginalized or they minimize and rationalize that community's contribution. Both an uncritical "listening to," that romanticizes and idealizes the interpretations of the poor and marginalized, and an arrogant "speaking for," that minimizes and rationalizes the interpretations of the poor and marginalized, must be problematized.[19]

For himself and for other socially engaged biblical scholars, West proposes a position of "reading with," which "takes seriously the subjectivity of both the biblical scholar and the ordinary poor and marginalized 'reader' of the Bible, and all that this entails for their respective resources, categories and contributions."[20] In a similar vein, Ukpong proposes an inculturation hermeneutics for which "reading with" locates "the primacy of the reading activity . . . not among individual theologians working in isolation but in concert with communities of ordinary people."[21] Thus, "Reading 'with' means that the reading agenda is that of the community and not that of the trained readers. The trained readers do not direct or control the reading process or seek to 'teach' to the community the meaning of the text they have already known."[22] Because of the dialogical character of "reading with," Ukpong suggests, "the academic reader accesses the resources of popular readings of the Bible, and academic scholarship is informed and enriched by resources outside its own circle, while the ordinary readers acquire the perspective of critical reading."[23]

READING AND REPRESENTING

As appealing as one may find proposals such as those of West and Ukpong with respect to their reconfiguration of dialogue between academic readers and ordinary readers of the Bible through emancipatory reading practices that emerge from their understanding of the hermeneutical privilege of the poor, some words of caution are in order. Grateful though he may be, inasmuch as "liberation hermeneutics has valiantly and almost single-handedly helped to maintain liberation at the centre of theological discussion," R. S. Sugirtharajah offers a pointed critique: "Liberation hermeneutics is postmodern in its desire to take the Other—the poor, women, indigenous and all the marginalized peoples—seriously. In doing so, it rightly overrides the Enlightenment concern with the non-believer, and focuses on the non-person. But this does not preclude reifying the poor, and it functions within the Enlightenment paradigm of dichotomous thinking—rich/poor, oppressed/oppressor and have/have nots."[24]

In a similar vein, Carmen Nanko-Fernández rightly critiques the language that has been used to unpack the principle of the preferential option for the poor when she observes that "The marginalization of the poor and vulnerable is further evident in the language used to communicate this moral imperative. . . . The impression often given is that the poor exist to enlighten or evangelize or raise the consciousness of the non-poor."[25] She insists that "Consistent references to the poor and vulnerable in the third person further increase marginalization while diminishing agency," setting up a "dichotomous 'us' and 'them' that undermines talk of solidarity."[26] Thus, it is quite safe for academic readers of the Bible to write with great sincerity of their engagement with "the poor," who are "ordinary readers" of the Bible, and who are said to have much to teach "us," even though that very language perpetuates the othering and instrumentalization of those dialogue partners in reading the Bible who happen to be academically undocumented, so to speak.

TOO MUCH READING?

Yet another critique of liberation hermeneutics comes from a different direction. Sugirtharajah argues that "For liberation hermeneutics, the project of liberation remains within the bounds of Christianity and its construction is informed by Christian sources. Liberation hermeneutics sees liberation as something lodged and located in biblical texts, or in ecumenical and Christian Church documents, and as something that can be extracted from these textual records."[27] Thus, in addition to its "homogenization of the poor," Sugirtharajah suggests that liberationist hermeneutics falls short in virtue of its "incessant biblicism."[28] Here, in some sense, the observation made by Mesters and noted earlier in this discussion returns to haunt us, namely, that "What helped to bring the Bible to the poorest was the missionary energy of the Protestant churches. Many Catholics started to read the Bible in order to be able to answer the Protestants and so overcome their inferiority complex."[29] Did this apologetic impetus reduce the bandwidth available to liberationist hermeneutics to the boundaries of the biblical canon in an effort to address *sola Scriptura* on its own terms?

In this respect, the work of Nancy Cardosa Pereira offers an important corrective. She acknowledges that "The journey of the theology of liberation from/with the Bible was a tremendous effort to free Christianity of its ideological commitments to the politics of domination"; yet "To understand the role of the Bible in Latin American culture it is necessary to walk the second mile and to talk about popular religion or, to be more exact, the religion of the poor."[30] To illustrate what is involved, she cites a statement from Atabaque, the Black Pastoral Agents:

> The Bible is one source among many. Sometimes it is not even the main one. For the poor and the black, the stories of the saints and of miracles stand side by side, for example, with the sung and danced stories of the *Terreiro* of Candomblé. The Bible of the *terreiro* is a story that is danced and sung. It is not written, it cannot be read . . . but it is also a story of salvation and liberation.[31]

Thus, as Cardoso Pereira affirms, "Black Pastoral Agents can proclaim an image of God that is and is not in the Bible. The Bible is a source of light for dialogue and solidarity, but it cannot exist as the Book, the Word or the Truth. It will be accepted in dialogue, not in exclusivity. . . . The authority of the sacred has shifted to a dialogue with a plurality of living traditions."[32]

Here the challenge to a narrow view of liberationist hermeneutics comes from those who would be numbered among the academically undocumented.

CONCLUSION

As this chapter ends, I want to suggest that we drink from our own wells just a bit (if I may be forgiven for misappropriating and repurposing the title of Gustavo Gutiérrez's book by that title).[33] I would like to suggest that we have very near at hand some important resources for addressing Sugirtharajah's well-framed critique of a narrowly framed liberationist hermeneutics. The first such resource is one that helps us avoid the homogenization of the poor, and this is the repeated emphasis of Latino/a theologies on the vital significance of *lo cotidiano*, of lived daily experience, for theological reflection. Lived daily experience is always situated, always specific, always concrete. It is always *someone's* lived daily experience, irreducible to the anonymity of abstraction. It takes place in ordinary time; it is always incarnate, embodied, of-this-world, and yet it points beyond itself, open to encountering and engaging the experiences of others in all their differences and in all their shared resonances.

A second nearby resource might help us to avoid the narrow biblicism of a restrictive liberationist hermeneutics, and this resource comes from what some might regard as a surprising direction, namely, the 2008 Twelfth Ordinary General Assembly of the Synod of Bishops in Rome, with its attention focused on the theme "the Word of God in the life and mission of the church." During the assembly, it was asserted with some insistence that Catholics are *not* a people of the Book, and that it might be more accurate to affirm that we *are* people of the Word, and, even more specifically, people of the Word-made-flesh. Because we are peoples of the Word-made-flesh, we are invited to affirm that there is no flesh that does not bear the mark of the *Logos* (John 1:3 NRSV, "All things came into being through him, and without him not one thing came into being"). The "canon" of the Word-made-flesh embraces those who are excluded, minoritized, and marginalized. Here, then, I would suggest, we find the hermeneutical edge of the preferential option for the poor.[34]

3

Latino/a Biblical Studies
as Public Theology and the Case
of U.S. Immigration Reform

On May 12, 2008, Immigration and Customs Enforcement (ICE) agents of the U.S. Department of Homeland Security raided the Agriprocessors meatpacking plant in Postville, Iowa, a raid that resulted in the arrest of nearly three hundred Latin American workers who, in a matter of just four days, were convicted on federal charges of document fraud.[1] To commemorate the anniversary of the Postville raid, Bishop John C. Wester, then-chairperson of the United States Conference of Catholic Bishops' Committee on Migration, issued the following statement, with its insistent appeal to the Bible:

> May 12, 2009 marks the one-year anniversary of what was, at the time, the largest work site immigration enforcement action in history. Since that raid in Postville, Iowa, larger raids have occurred, but the precedent set at Postville and the accompanying compassionate response by that small Iowa community and its people of faith underscore the humanitarian costs of workplace immigration raids as well as the need for reform of our nation's immigration policies.
>
> As religious leaders, my brother Catholic bishops and I understand and support the right and responsibility of the government to enforce the law. We strongly believe, however, that worksite enforcement raids do not solve the challenge of illegal immigration. Instead, they lead to the separation of U.S. families and the destruction of immigrant communities. The result of the Postville raid was family separation, immense suffering, denial of due process rights and community division.
>
> *Our religious and social response to such harm to our God-given human dignity is based on Scriptures, which call believers to welcome the newcomers among us, to treat the alien with respect and charity, and to provide pastoral and humanitarian assistance to individuals and their families.*

The Postville action of a year ago is a disturbing reminder of the need to repair the nation's broken immigration policies.

I ask all Catholics, the greater faith community, and persons of good will to commemorate the Postville raid of May 12, 2008, by remembering in their prayers those hurt by the raid and to work for comprehensive immigration reform so that others will not face similar pain and cruelty in the future.[2]

Such appeals to the Bible have become crucial to the pastoral efforts of church leaders to persuade their communities about the imperatives that flow from the Scriptures with regard to social ethics and public policy. Where are biblical scholars in all of this? To what extent have biblical scholars partnered with pastors to take to the public square to advocate on behalf of immigrants and others whose human dignity is being threatened?

The fact is that biblical scholars are rarely cast as public intellectuals, and those few high-profile cases where the members of this guild make it to the television screen are the exceptions that prove the rule. Thus, University of North Carolina professor Bart Ehrman made it to the *New York Times* bestseller list not by speaking out on immigration reform but by such savvy public relations moves as an appearance on "The Colbert Report" on April 9, 2009 (Holy Thursday!) to tout his book *Jesus Interrupted: Revealing the Hidden Contradictions in the Bible (And Why We Don't Know about Them)* (New York: Harper One, 2009).[3] Princeton University's Elaine Pagels, for her part, made it to the headlines by telling us that the Gospel of Judas "contradicts everything we know about Christianity."[4] Ehrman himself complains,

> Scholars of the Bible have made significant progress in understanding the Bible over the past two hundred years. . . . Yet such views of the Bible are virtually unknown among the population at large. In no small measure this is because those of us who spend our professional lives studying the Bible have not done a good job communicating this knowledge to the general public and because many pastors who learned this material in seminary have, for a variety of reasons, not shared it with their parishioners once they take up positions in the church.[5]

READING THE BIBLE IN PUBLIC

Let me make it clear that when I use "biblical scholar" and "public intellectual" in the same sentence, I am not referring to the sort of star quality that the scholars like Ehrman and Pagels have achieved by engaging in high-profile (and high-profit) popularization. I am referring to the responsibilities that fall squarely on the shoulders of those who "spend our professional lives studying the Bible" by virtue of the prominent place that the Bible occupies both in the pulpit and in the public square. A growing number of biblical scholars have begun to insist on this, engaging in a reorientation of the academic discipline of biblical studies that follows from what amounts to an examination of conscience. Vincent Wimbush frames the matter in terms that are worth citing at length:

> Biblical scholars have for the most part functioned not so much as the detached objective critics that many have claimed to be but as a certain specialized subcategory of "tribal theologians." The creation and practice of a dizzying number of sophisticated methods and approaches notwithstanding, and the occasional larger sociocultural controversy and hysteria surrounding the Bible notwithstanding, and with acknowledgment that there are in every era those who are rare birds, biblical scholars on the whole do not exactly capture the imagination of thoughtful persons in society. Nor have they generally been associated with, or represented sustained radical challenge— political, epistemic, academic, or otherwise. I am suggesting here that there is some flaw in those persons attracted to such studies; I am saying that low-profile apolitical identification, stance, orientation, and association are expected of the biblical scholar—that, sadly, these are the terms of membership. Those moments when church and society have been troubled by biblical scholarship have been few and brief.[6]

This indictment is accompanied by an interesting diagnosis on Wimbush's part. He suggests that this is the outcome of "a fetishization of or obsessive-compulsive focus on the Bible as (collection of) texts. This focus on texts has rendered and kept the study of the Bible essentially an elitist and sociopolitically conservative phenomenon and practice, the special purview of a technically trained and/or ordained or appointed professional corps of interpreters as diviners."[7] The reorientation Wimbush calls for is a project that concentrates "not on the meaning *of* texts but on meaning *and* texts, upon the *meaning of meaning-seeking* in relationship to texts."[8] Thus, for Wimbush, "interest should be shifted away from the pursuit of the meaning of any particular text to the meaning of a particular interpreting community's orientation and practices and what those orientations and practices reveal about the communities."[9]

Elisabeth Schüssler Fiorenza draws on the field of empire studies (a relative newcomer on the scene) to call for a transformation of biblical studies as a practice that

> cannot only be deconstructive but must also search for traces of a scriptural rhetoric that can inspire the resistance to empire. This project is especially important for those religious people for whom the

bible is key in understanding the world and G*d. Hence, scriptural and the*logical emancipative work always has to have two focal points: the Roman Empire as the context and location of Christian scriptures, on the one hand, and contemporary forms of empire and global possibilities for resistance, on the other. To that end, it becomes necessary to reconceptualize the sub-discipline of biblical the*logy not as a confessional dogmatic discipline, but as a rhetorical-emancipative inquiry into biblical and contemporary religious world-constructions and their political deployments today. Such a critical biblical the*logy is not only needed for intra-Christian discourses but also for cultural-political ones.[10]

In the United States, resituating biblical scholarship from merely intra-Christian discourses to broader cultural-political ones makes it possible for the discipline to engage the Bible and its readers in a space already staked out by Christian evangelicals, who have employed the Bible in the service of a variety of explicit and implicit political agendas not only in the church, but in the public square as well.[11] Schüssler Fiorenza is conscious of the influence of Christian evangelicalism:

In a time when people experience real economic and social insecurities, religious fundamentalism in general and Christian Evangelicalism in particular address this pervasive insecurity. However, they do not actually give people security but provide the means to manage such insecurity. With Foucault, [Nancy] Fraser understands Evangelicalism "as a care-of-self-technology that is especially suited to neo-liberalism, insofar as the latter is always generating insecurity."[12]

Schüssler Fiorenza challenges biblical scholars to embrace a constructive task, one that involves drawing attention to the ways in which "Christian scriptures are impregnated not only with the language of empire, but also with the logic of radical equality, inclusivity, citizenship, and decision-making power for all members of the Christian community."[13] Thus understood, the Bible can become an exceptionally powerful resource in the service of justice, and engaged biblical scholars can set aside the trappings of "tribal theologian" and take up a demanding extramural agenda:

Since *ekklēsia* is not primarily a religious but a political term, such a change would position biblical scholarship in the public sphere of the *cosmo-polis* and transform it into a critical discourse that is dedicated to producing knowledge that will further the well-being of all the inhabitants of the planet today. Biblical studies, understood as such a critical discourse, could build rhetorically on the ancient Greek democratic notions of *polis* and *ekklēsia*, but would need to change them from signifying exclusion and privilege to signifying radical democratic equality. If Biblical studies were positioned in the space of the *ekklēsia*, redefined in egalitarian inclusive terms, they could speak both to the publics of religious bodies, such as church, synagogue or mosque, and to the publics of civic society at large.[14]

In a discussion of Schüssler Fiorenza's work, Yale University's John J. Collins, writes that "Among biblical feminists, her work is exceptional both in its overtly political character and in the vehemence of its rhetoric."[15] Does that sound like a compliment? One wonders what Professor Collins might have to say about Latino/a biblical scholars, yet by the end of his book the puzzlement remains, because (and perhaps fortunately) he does not refer to any of us. In a chapter entitled "Exodus and Liberation in Postcolonial Perspective," he does mention the usual suspects from Latin America (in order of their appearance in the footnotes: Leonardo and Clodovis Boff, Gustavo Gutiérrez, Enrique Dussel, J. Severino Croatto, George V. Pixley), but no reference to Latino/a biblical scholars appears anywhere in the book.[16]

While it might be said, in Collins's defense, that his attention was drawn mainly to scholars in his own subdiscipline of biblical scholarship (he is the Holmes Professor of Old Testament Criticism and Interpretation at Yale Divinity School), it might also be observed that Latino New Testament scholar Fernando F. Segovia has contributed at least as much to the discussion of postcolonial theory and biblical interpretation as New Testament scholar Stephen Moore has to postmodern biblical criticism, yet Moore *does* make it into Collins's footnotes while Segovia does not.[17]

I mention Fernando Segovia here both because of his very explicit embrace of an activist approach to sociopolitically engaged biblical studies and because of the candor with which he shares his own experience as a postcolonial biblical scholar born-and-made.[18] The following anecdote recounted by Segovia is especially telling:

> Quite recently, at dinner at a committee meeting of one of the various professional societies to which I belong, I happened to sit next to a well-known and established scholar. This was a gentleman, many years my senior, perfectly cast in the social mold of the traditional learned scholar—the *homo eruditus* oblivious to and distrustful of matters theoretical, with a view of all theory as outside the realm of history; largely unaware of as well as unconcerned by any major shifts in either discipline or academy; thoroughly self-absorbed in his own work. After speaking at length about his most recent accomplishments, he asked unexpectedly about my own research interests. When I explained my growing interest in the competing ideologies of the early Christian texts in the face of the Roman imperial situation that they faced and within which they had been produced, he asked politely whether I

thought such a connection was really important. When I responded that I thought the connection was not only important for the ancient world but also for both the modern world and the contemporary world, since the development of criticism had paralleled the imperial expansion, contraction, and transformation of Europe and the United States, he discreetly dropped any further inquiries about my work and proceeded to outline at considerable length his own research agenda for the future.[19]

Do I detect an understated note of what Carmen Nanko-Fernández has called "pastoral hostility" on Segovia's part?[20] I also want to underscore Segovia's autobiographical discussion of what it means to him to be "born" and "reborn"—using the language of John 3—as a Latino critic. He explains,

To be sure, I was "born" a Latino critic, insofar as I was a member of such a constituted minority racial-ethnic grouping. At the same time, I was "reborn" a Latino critic upon consciously appropriating the community ties, marginalized status, and minoritarian agenda associated with such a designation. Thus, I would readily avow, I would not qualify as a Latino/a scholar in my initial phase in the academy and the profession, although "born" as such of "flesh and blood," but only in my later phase, as a result of a process of conscientization, whereby I was "reborn" as such in "spirit and truth." Indeed my reaction to any description of myself in that beginning phase of my academic and professional life as a Latino critic would be one of disavowal—unacceptable as well as misleading.[21]

Many of us—myself included—can resonate with Segovia's narrative of personal and professional conscientization, marked as many of us are by academic and professional socialization in graduate studies and early in our careers that made it necessary to "play the game" according to rules not of our own making in order to earn our stripes as credentialed professionals in our discipline and in order to survive in the academic marketplace.[22] Indeed, Segovia points to two concrete examples among well-respected biblical scholars: On the one hand, he speaks of Moisés Silva as one example of a biblical scholar "born" Latino who has "never identified himself . . . as a Latino critic and has never taken part in Latino/a endeavors." On the other hand, he mentions Sharon Ringe as a colleague "who has allied herself openly and wholeheartedly with Latino/a criticism and ventures," her Union Theological Seminary training under Raymond Brown notwithstanding.[23]

In what he describes as a "first sortie" toward articulating a Latino/a American biblical criticism, Segovia identifies several key critical goals. With respect to the purpose of such criticism, he suggests that "the task of Latino/a biblical criticism appears as radically situated and perspectival: emerging from a particular world of material and cultural exclusion; cognizant of a wider world in the throes of social and cultural devastation; and pledged to a world of freedom and justice, dignity and well-being for all."[24] Such a politically engaged stance, disturbing though it may have been to Segovia's erudite dinner companion, is fully consonant with the intentional positioning of this scholarship within the setting of the university (including the divinity school!), understood as—in the words of Ignacio Ellacuría—"inescapably a social force: it must transform and enlighten the society in which it lives."[25]

Cognizant of the need to build bridges of mutual understanding, solidarity, and common cause among minoritized biblical scholars in the United States, Segovia worked together with Randall C. Bailey and Tat-siong Benny Liew to organize a project entitled "Reading the Bible as Black, Asian American and Latino/a Scholars in the U.S." Begun in 2003 with the support of a generous grant from the Wabash Center for Teaching and Learning in Theology and Religion, the project bore fruit in the volume entitled *They Were All Together in One Place? Toward Minority Biblical Criticism*, co-edited by the three project organizers, eight other biblical scholars, and three scholars from outside the discipline of biblical studies.[26] The aim of the project was to take some first steps "to work out a disciplinary coalition or alliance with transformation in mind," a transformation both with regard to the explicitly intercontextual and interdisciplinary nature of the project as an undertaking in biblical studies, and also with regard to the extramural implications of such coalition-building, beyond the boundaries of academic discourses in biblical and theological studies.[27]

What Segovia is proposing, together with other minoritized biblical scholars, is not merely about the reshaping of our academic discipline, for that would make precious little difference beyond the narrow confines of the academy. It is instead a matter of working to impact society. Thus, in the words of María Pilar Aquino, "a significant segment of the university population seeks after a knowledge that will support social transformation toward the protection of dignity and the rights of all people."[28]

THE BIBLE AND THE BORDER

All this serves as a framework for understanding what makes it imperative for biblical scholars to take an active role among those in the church and in the academy who have been and continue to be engaged in advocating for just and comprehensive reform of immigration policies, in defending the human dignity of migrants and refugees, of all those who are displaced from their homelands. Intramurally, this involves our being deliberate about the critical questions we frame, the reading strategies we employ, and about the venues we choose for our scholarly publications. Extramurally, this is a matter of being intentional in engaging the various and overlapping communities of interpretation with whom we read, not only in the academy with our colleagues and students, but also in the church and in the community at large.[29]

In this respect, the recent book by M. Daniel Carroll R. is an especially important and timely contribution. *Christians at the Border: Immigration, the Church, and the Bible* is not written with an audience of biblical scholars in mind.[30] Well known and respected among biblical scholars for his important work on the book of the prophet Amos, Carroll aims *Christians at the Border* at English-speaking Latino/a and non-Latino/a Christians for whom the Bible continues to matter a great deal, especially to evangelical Protestants.[31] He explains,

> My intention is to try to move Christians to reconsider their starting point in the immigration debate. Too often discussions default to the passionate ideological arguments, economic wrangling, or racial sentiments that dominate national discourse. Among Christians, my experience has been that there is little awareness of what might be the divine viewpoint on immigration. It is neither exhaustive nor comprehensive. Rather, it is designed as a primer for a more biblically and theologically informed approach to the topic.[32]

Beginning with a chapter that sketches the history of immigration from Latin America to the United States, Carroll goes on to make his case in two chapters that focus on the Hebrew Bible (chapter 2: "Immigrants, Refugees, and Exiles," and chapter 3, "The Law and the Sojourner") and one chapter that offers guidance from the Christian Testament (chapter 4, "Welcoming the Stranger"). Patient and expository in style, Carroll's book is blessedly free from jargon, and most of the biblical scholarship he cites comes from such publishers as Baker, Eerdmans, Zondervan, and InterVarsity— pedigrees likely to receive nods of approval from the evangelical readers who are this book's main intended audience. Perhaps just as important is Carroll's political astuteness in garnering endorsements for the book from people such as Dallas Theological Seminary New Testament professor Darrell Bock, Wheaton College Old Testament professor Daniel I. Block, National Association of Evangelicals president Leith Anderson, and Fuller Theological Seminary's Juan Francisco Martínez, among others. A preface by National Hispanic Leadership Conference president Samuel Rodríguez and an afterword by Evangelicals for Social Action president Ronald J. Sider round out a roster of endorsers that establish Carroll's impeccable evangelical credentials.

Thus, it becomes possible for him to tackle Romans 13:1-7 ("Everyone must submit himself to the governing authorities, for there is no authority except that which God has established. The authorities that exist have been established by God. Consequently, he who rebels against the authority is rebelling against what God has instituted, and those who do so will bring judgement upon themselves," NIV) in ways that derail a simplistic appeal to that text by those who would argue, "What is it about 'illegal' that you don't understand?"[33] Carroll patiently explains with an impeccably constructed inner-biblical argument that appeals to evangelicals' deep respect for the authority of Scripture:

> Many Christians read Romans 13 with the assumption that all the nation's laws are inherently good and just. To obey them is then not only pleasing to God, it is common sense. What can be missed is that Romans 12, which prefaces Paul's words concerning human government, contrasts the mind-set and life of Christians with what they encounter in society. Romans 12 exhorts believers not to be shaped by the "pattern of this world"; they should serve others, show love and have compassion, and help their enemies (Rom. 12:3-21).[34]

Carroll concludes firmly that

> To quote Romans 13 on the immigration issue without nuance or biblical and historical depth simply will not do. . . . Discussion on legality cannot be limited just to questions about complying with the present laws. If the laws are problematic theologically, humanely, and pragmatically . . . the call to submit to the authorities in Romans 13 can be processed in fresh and constructive ways.[35]

Christians at the Border is not the sort of book that would have scored points for Carroll during his tenure and promotion process, for, in his own words, "This book is not an academic tome full of specialist jargon and bewildering charts."[36] Likewise, this is not the sort of book that would have been likely to earn Carroll a cameo on "The Colbert Report." It was not Carroll's intention to advance the discipline of biblical studies intramurally by means of this book. Yet, this is the sort of important volume that only someone of Carroll's stature as a scholar and reputation in the evangelical Christian community could have published.

Furthermore, it is his distinguished track record in the evangelical community and his allies from various sectors of that rather diverse community that got him into Baker Academic's catalogue in the first place, and that gives his argument a toehold among readers who might have avoided the book if it had appeared under another publisher's imprint. It is a carefully crafted and astutely launched work of biblical scholarship *extra muros* as public practice that performs an urgent service to the church and to society. It may not sell as many copies as Ehrman's *Jesus Interrupted*, but I hope it will make more of a deep-down difference.

Gilberto Ruiz's essay "A Migrant Worker at Work: John's Christology of

Migration and Its Implications" is a markedly different sort of contribution to the discussion than is Carroll's. By proposing a Johannine Christology of migration, he stands much of the usual deployment of the Bible on its head with respect to the immigration reform. He does so by inviting us to consider the Johannine Jesus as a migrant. This differs from the direction of the argument set forth by Carroll in his chapter "Welcoming the Stranger," which foregrounds Jesus' own conduct toward "outsiders," as well as the response of the synoptic Jesus to the question, "Who is my neighbor?" (Luke 10:29), and the judgment passed on the basis of conduct vis-à-vis "the least of these brothers of mine" (Matt 25:31-46).[37] The ethical force of Gilberto Ruiz's argument builds on a strong link between Johannine Christology and Christian ethics, an original twist that translates *imitatio Christi* into pointedly Johannine terms:

> Just as the Johannine Jesus is in solidarity with believers in the world since he has entered the world and experienced this alienation for himself, our own experience of disconnectedness means all believers must be in solidarity with (im)migrants, who experience a double-alienation, the existential alienation experienced by believers in the world and the social alienation that comes with being a foreigner in a foreign society.[38]

This argument is on target both from the standpoint of Christian ethics and from that of Johannine studies.[39] As Gilberto Ruiz rightly notes, with a nod to Fernando Segovia, "Giving John's Christology of migration its due importance is thus an act against the long history of treating John as a text that promotes disengagement from worldly matters and is exclusively concerned with the spiritual edification of individuals."[40] He provides a necessary corrective from within biblical studies that has crucial extramural implications for the ways in which we deploy biblical arguments in our advocacy for immigration reform.

Countering the predominant reading of the Johannine Jesus' reassurance that he goes to prepare a place in his Father's house for his disciples, Gilberto Ruiz refuses to read this as a warrant for a soteriology that diminishes the importance of being *in* the world. Instead, he offers it as an imperative so that it is incumbent on Christians to "prepare a place for our (im)migrant sisters and brothers," a place in an otherwise inhospitable world.[41] He likewise takes an important step *away* from the "othering" rhetoric by which well-intentioned theologians and pastoral agents unwittingly objectify and dehumanize immigrants by framing biblical imperatives in terms of what "we" should do for "them."[42]

Different as Gilberto Ruiz's essay may be from Daniel Carroll's, both scholars approach the biblical text well disposed to enlist it as a potent rhetorical ally in efforts to promote immigration reform. While Carroll notes that "there is no direct teaching on immigration in the Gospels," it is also true for Carroll that Jesus' "proactive consideration of those who were marginalized in his society" is a model for his followers to imitate.[43] So too for Gilberto Ruiz; the Fourth Gospel calls on believers in the migrant Word-made-flesh to do as Jesus did, to participate in his work of preparing a place for our brothers and sisters.[44] Neither scholar is unaware of the complexities of the material with which he is working, and neither pretends that the Bible speaks with a single voice to readers who search its pages in search of guidance on immigration or other pressing issues.

JESUS BEHAVING BADLY? REREADING MARK 7:24-30 WITH SHARON RINGE

With that complexity in mind, I want to focus attention on one exceptionally challenging text that we would be hard pressed to read as though the conduct of Jesus offers an example to be imitated. This is Mark 7:24-30, the encounter between Jesus and the Greek Syrophoenician woman in the region of Tyre (an episode that has a parallel in Matthew 15:21-28). This pericope has received more than its share of attention, especially because Jesus' response to the woman's request for healing is so disturbing: "Let the children be fed first, for it is not fair to take the children's food and throw it to the dogs" (Mark 7:27).[45] For the purposes of the present discussion, it is worth underscoring that this pericope narrates the encounter with two ethnic "others": Jesus, who leaves Galilee to enter Tyrian territory in verse 24 and who leaves the region of Tyre at the conclusion of this episode in verse 31, and the woman who is identified not by her own proper name but as a Greek and a Syrophoenician.

Among the many fellow readers of this text, Sharon Ringe is the one with whom I would like to converse, focusing on her contribution to the scholarship on this text in "A Gentile Woman's Story, Revisited: Rereading Mark 7.24-31."[46] The title of the essay represents a significant revision of an earlier treatment of this text that Ringe published in 1985.[47] At the end of her more recent essay, Ringe explains, "My earlier struggles with this text had a happier outcome. I was able to find in the woman of the story a positive role model, and in the portrait of Jesus an initially sexist, but finally teachable man, one able to learn about the meaning of his messiahship from this woman (whom I took to be among the most marginalized of the society). This time I find the pictures of her and of him more ambiguous."[48]

Ringe's move away from her earlier reading of this text, she tells us, has much to do with the enrichment of her own scholarly perspective:

I was aware of having learned much since the early 1980s, especially about cultures and customs in first-century Palestine and in the early church, and about the experiences of women in those contexts. Then as now, such factors as class, ethnicity, demographic context, education, health, age, and family circumstance made for a richly textured fabric of experiences whose variations needed to be examined closely. I had not done that, being largely captive to the fiction of being able to analyze biblical texts from a unitary perspective of gender.[49]

The rereading she proposes in the later essay is informed by a candid foregrounding of her own reading context, by a nuanced understanding of the first-century social context that forms the historical and literary matrix of the pericope, and by her entering into conversation with a broad range of interpreters of the pericope who constitute her reading community. Ringe calls attention to three intersecting aspects of her identity that shape her experience of the text:

First, as a woman I am fascinated by the prominence of the woman in the narrative. The fascination is one of repulsion, then attraction. . . . As a Christian I am troubled by the picture this passage paints of Jesus. . . . The final issue of my identity that intersects the story is my professional interest in postcolonial reading strategies, which is shaped by my existential concern with the issue of dominance and subordination as that is affected by both gender and ethnicity. . . . As a reader I find myself resonating with the woman on the question of gender, but with Jesus on the question of ethnicity.[50]

In Mark's narrative, this is Jesus' first venture to "the region of Tyre," but his reputation has preceded him there: "hearing all that he was doing, they came to him in great numbers from Judea, Jerusalem, Idumea, beyond the Jordan, and the region around Tyre and Sidon" (Mark 3:8). About the social context of the "region of Tyre," Ringe notes,

Typical of most borderlands, this area was ethnically mixed. Though Tyre itself was populated principally by Gentiles, the surrounding territory included Jews as well. The result was an often uncomfortable collision of ethnic, religious, and cultural differences, with resulting suspicions and prejudices, between city dwellers and residents of the villages. This ethnically mixed region was also the site of economic tension, principally between the wealthier urban trading centers and the poorer farming communities that were captive to the needs and desires of the city dwellers, such that in times of poor harvests, when food was scarce everywhere, the requirements to supply the needs

of city dwellers meant that the farmers themselves would go hungry.
The urban-rural tension with its economic factors combined with the
cultural, ethnic, and religious tensions to make the region a miniature
version of the larger context of Roman-occupied Palestine.[51]

While the explicit references to the arrival of Jesus in Tyrian territory in
verse 24 and to his departure from that region in verse 31 suggest that these
issues are at work in the first-century world behind the text, Ringe suggests
that other dynamics are at work in the world of the Markan narrative itself.
With respect to gender and ethnicity, the woman and Jesus are "outsiders"
to each other, it is clear that

> The narrative does not present such a neutral, balanced view . . .
> because the encompassing Gospel narrative makes Jesus the norm, and
> she inhabits the margin of the page. Despite the woman's prominence
> in the story, it is told as part of the Gospel of which he is the focus, and
> not as her story. Similarly, while the setting of the story suggests she is
> a member of the dominant group in that place, the Gospel narrative
> makes Jesus the insider and her the one whose inclusion is contested.[52]

While Jesus is in her part of the world geographically, in the world of the
narrative she is part of his story. Whatever the power dynamics may have
been between two such figures in the "region of Tyre," in the literary world
of the Gospel narrative, it is Mark who has the upper hand. In this regard,
Ringe explains that the narrator's introduction of Jesus' interlocutor in verse
26 according to her Greek ethnicity and her Syrophoenician provenance
"interrupts the flow of the story and by its literary awkwardness calls
attention to itself."[53] Ringe suggests that the identification of the woman in
this way portrays her "as part of the group in that region whose policies and
lifestyle would have been a source of suffering for her mostly poorer, rural,
Jewish neighbors."[54]

In fact the text of Mark 7:24-30 provides us with no direct evidence of the
woman's economic standing. Gerd Theissen, to whose work Ringe refers,
suggests that the woman's characterization as a Greek (*Hellēnis*) indicates
her belonging to an upper class, inasmuch as Hellenization first impacted
persons of higher social and economic status.[55] Theissen finds subtler
evidence of the woman's economic standing in verse 30, where the woman's
daughter, freed from the demon, is lying on the bed. Here Mark uses *klinē*
("bed") instead of *krabbatos* ("mat"), which is used elsewhere in Mark (2:9,
9, 12; 6:55). That the woman's daughter lies on a bed rather than a simple
mat suggests a certain level of affluence and also that she lives in an urban
setting.

For Theissen, that Jesus encounters a Greek Syrophoenician woman in
the region of Tyre also calls attention to the close economic relationship

between city and countryside. The material evidence of archaeological excavations underscores the orientation of northern Galilee to the cities on the Phoenician coast. Theissen explains, "Tyre was a wealthy city that needed to buy agricultural produce from the hinterland. . . . The Galilean hinterland and the rural territory belonging to the city (partly settled by Jews) were the 'breadbasket' of the metropolis of Tyre."[56] Thus, in times of crisis, "the rural Jewish population in the hinterland of the Hellenistic cities shared the general fate of the whole country: in the struggle over food waged between city and country, they usually get the short end of things."[57] This, Theissen concludes, frames Jesus' response to the woman's request in terms of the "associative field conditioned by the historical situation" as "First let the poor people in the Jewish rural areas be satisfied. For it is not good to take poor people's food and throw it to the rich Gentiles in the cities."[58]

In the literary context of Mark's Gospel, Jesus' concern to provide food for the hungry is emphasized in the two feeding miracles between which—in some sense—the encounter with the Syrophoenician woman is sandwiched (6:30-44 and 8:1-9), and each of these concludes with a mention of the abundant leftovers.

Economic tensions between city and countryside notwithstanding, Jesus' response remains incongruous: the woman is asking *not* for food but for the healing of her sick daughter. As Ringe points out, "it is not the response that would be anticipated from any practitioner of healing when confronted with a situation of need."[59] Ringe contrasts Jesus' response to the Syrophoenician woman with another parent's similar request: in Mark 5:22 it is Jairus, "one of the leaders of the synagogue," who prostrates himself before Jesus (just as the Syrophoenician woman does in 7:25) and asks that Jesus heal his sick daughter. Jairus's request meets with a positive response on Jesus' part. The contrast between the two episodes leads Ringe to conclude that Jesus rejects the woman's request "as an inappropriate one to make in the light of the disproportionate share of the region's resources her people had been exploiting."[60] This assumes, not inappropriately in the light of Mark 5:30, that Jesus' healing power is limited, and so his first concern is to exercise a preferential option for the poor by attending to their needs first.

Jesus' harsh response is not where the story ends, for his Syrophoenician interlocutor uses the words he directed against her to win the day. First, "the woman demonstrates how to avoid being trapped by another's characterization as enemy . . . instead of confronting the insult, she turns the offensive label into a harmless one, and uses it to her advantage." Second,

> She confronts the assumptions about the meaning of her identity that appear to undergird Jesus' saying. His words label her as contemptible, a 'dog.' . . . Instead of presenting a list of credentials to argue that the label is unfair . . . her reply relinquishes the place of privilege his response attributes to her, and her "word" moves her into the place of

receiving only what is left over—the place where the poor of the region have always been.[61]

It is "because of this word" of hers (Mark 7:29) that Jesus accedes to her request—performing what is in Mark's Gospel the only healing miracle that does not involve a face-to-face encounter between Jesus and the one in need of healing.

Sharon Ringe's persuasive reading of Mark 7:24-30 effectively moves the conversation about this text away from "the common attempts by interpreters to make the passage in Mark address in some way the legitimization of the church's mission to the Gentiles."[62] The persuasiveness of the reading Ringe offers is further advanced by its open-endedness, both by the fact that important questions remain unresolved and by the expansion of her reading circle to include readers of this pericope from contexts different from her own: Hisako Kinukawa, Elaine Wainwright, Leticia Guardiola-Saenz, and Kwok Pui-lan.[63] This reading-with simultaneously broadens Ringe's field of vision and sharpens her focus on crucial issues of gender and ethnicity in this text.

For example, in Japanese feminist Hisako Kinukawa's reading of Mark 7:24-30 in the light of racial exclusivism in Japan (discrimination against "the seven hundred thousand 'Koreans living in Japan'—Ainus, Okinawans, and the outcast village people as 'inside others'"), Ringe recognizes "the significance of the role of 'inside others' in the story—those seen as foreigners in their own land, for my own reading context contains many such groups of (apparently) permanent insiders, according to the ethnic and racial norms of the dominant culture."[64]

Reading with Mexican-American Leticia Guardiola-Saenz, Ringe appreciates the ways in which Guardiola-Saenz's reading of Matthew 15:21-28 attends to "assumptions about the roles and behaviors of women among the 'dispossessed' groups that color various interpretations of this story." Ringe finds her reading especially "helpful in unmasking the romantic and fundamentally harmful view of the Other (and especially the female Other) as winning favor by submissive behavior in the presence of a male from the dominant group."[65]

She is likewise led to reflect on the ways in which the Markan text inverts the insider/outsider relationships that would have existed in the first-century CE eastern Mediterranean socioeconomic context. In the world behind the text, it is Jesus who is the outsider and the woman who belongs to the dominant group; in the world of the text, it is Mark's Jesus who is the dominant figure, and the woman who is an anonymous outsider, identified only in terms of her ethnicity. Reading with Kwok Pui-lan, Ringe is led to reaffirm that that "'Other' is not a unitary category, either of experience or interpretive lens, but rather one that includes 'the Other within the Other.'"[66]

No reading of the story can make the harsh words attributed to Jesus go away, even if the economic and political circumstances in which they are pronounced sets them into historical context. Reading this text with Sharon Ringe and with her expanded reading community, I too am "brought up short" by the humiliation that the Syrophoenician woman experiences from Jesus.[67]

MARK'S MIGRANT JESUS

By no means is Mark 7:24-30 the sort of text I would marshal to sway the hearts and minds of Christians to advocate for immigration reform.[68] That would be irresponsible on any number of accounts. At the same time, though, reading Mark's narrative of the encounter between the Greek-speaking Syrophoenician woman *en voz alta* and in the company of other readers brings to the surface a number of insights that—at least indirectly—help us to appreciate the complexity of the immigration debate.

To begin with, in this episode, Mark's Jesus is a border crosser. By making his way into the region of Tyre, he finds himself in a location where he is *other* in multiple ways to the dominant sectors of society and to his Syrophoenician interlocutor in particular. Commentators who take note of Jesus' movement into Tyrian territory both in terms of the historical conditions or world behind Mark's text and in terms of Mark's agenda often speak of this move across the border in overly straightforward terms. Taking a cue from what immediately precedes this passage in Mark 7:1-23, many suggest that Jesus' reorientation of purity regulations sets the stage for 7:24-30, which is then said to be "about the transcendence of Jewish particularism, and looks forward to the increasingly Gentile church of Mark's own day."[69]

What I find puzzling about this conclusion is the clear indication at the beginning of the pericope that Jesus "did not want anyone to know he was there" (Mark 7:24). Matthew's version makes a much bigger deal of the border crossing, with Jesus accompanied by his entourage of disciples, and with the encounter between the woman and Jesus occurring outdoors (Matt 15:22-25). In Matthew's version, Jesus' very presence "in the district of Tyre and Sidon" makes a difference even before his encounter with the woman, whereas for Mark, it is the encounter itself that matters, and the devil—so to speak—is in the details.

Second, as for the details, whatever else may be said about Mark's twofold identification of the woman as a *Hellēnis* and as a Syrophoenician, it serves as an indication that Jesus spoke Greek. This is the conclusion at which Stanley Porter arrives:

The first example of a passage in which Jesus may well have spoken Greek is Mark 7:25-30, when Jesus travels to the area of Tyre . . . the description of the woman in the Gospel makes sure the reader knows that the woman was a Greek-speaker despite her birth. Otherwise the reference is gratuitous. There is no indication of an interpreter being present. Although there is insufficient corroborative evidence to know whether Jesus' words here are his own, the context clearly indicates the likelihood that Jesus spoke in Greek to the gentile woman, even if he is bested by her in their battle of wits.[70]

This altogether-too-easily overlooked detail points to yet another level of complexity in the Markan version of the episode, namely, the interrelationship between language and ethnic identity, as complex in antiquity as it continues to be in the present.[71] While the indication that Mark's migrant Jesus speaks Greek is significant in and of itself, what complicates matters still further is that because his interlocutor is doubly identified as ethnically Syrophoenician (*Syrophoinikissa tō genei*) and a Greek speaker *both* are speaking what is in effect a second language. They speak the *koinē* Greek, which was the political and commercial *lingua franca* of the first-century Mediterranean, a language that frames both characters as colonized others in the sociopolitical context of the Roman Empire.[72]

A third consideration that rereading Mark 7:24-30 brings to the surface is that such reading calls us to be attentive to the ways in which "others" are either romanticized or vilified by virtue of the otherness that is attributed to them.[73] Mark's migrant Jesus knows little about his interlocutor, never asking even her name or the circumstances of her request. He knows only that she is Syrophoenician, and on this basis he uses the *koinē* language that they have in common to vilify her, calling her a dog.

Yet, Mark's Gospel itself and many of its readers give the benefit of the doubt to Jesus (though he behaves badly), and the Gospel leaves the woman a nameless recipient of Jesus' reluctant beneficence. It is not only in the Bible and among its readers that such othering occurs: elsewhere I have suggested that "statements by church leadership regarding immigration reform" with the best of intentions, too often fall into the trap of speaking about immigrants—in the third person plural speaking about 'them.'"[74] When we use the Bible in ways that focus on "the immigrant" as the object of our attention, however noble our attentions and however on target our summons to justice might be, we are implicated in the systematic othering that perpetuates the very injustice we seek to correct.

CONCLUSIONS: READING *EN VOZ ALTA*

In a February 2007 *Boston Globe* column, James Carroll wrote,

Are you moving your lips as you read this? Do you put your forefinger under each word as you decipher it? Is your tongue between your teeth, perched on your lower lip? Those are physical characteristics of the very young reader. Why did your teachers cure you of such external manifestations of the mental work of reading? As you learned to read, in fact, you recapitulated the historic evolution of this activity, a shift from the physical realm to the utterly interior space of contemplation; from rote and imitation to invention. Reading, as you do it now, is internal. Your eyes move, but nothing else does.

In the ancient world, texts were read aloud, not silently. The mind grasped the meaning of words as much through the ear as the eye, and the full body was engaged in the act. This was made necessary by the technology of text. The scroll and codex were rare objects, unavailable to most people, so groups gathered to hear them read. Even when alone, readers read aloud. On the page, the words were not separated, as here, and there was no punctuation, which meant that the reader had to depend on prior knowledge to make sense of the run-on letters. That knowledge was gained by having heard others read before. Vocalizing was the way in which text could initially be understood, and memorization was the way that understanding could be passed on.[75]

Of his teacher Ambrose of Milan, Saint Augustine wrote,

When he read, his eyes moved down the pages and his heart sought out their meaning, while his voice and tongue remained silent. Often, when we were present—for no one was forbidden to enter, it was not his custom to have whoever came announced to him—we saw him reading to himself in silence—who would dare annoy a man so occupied? (Augustine, *Confessions* 6.3.3)[76]

Such silent reading as amazed the young Augustine represented a shift away from what was the much more common practice in Greco-Roman antiquity, the practice of reading texts aloud. This older practice is attested in the New Testament itself. The narrator of the book of Revelation, for example, opens the Apocalypse with these words: "Blessed is the one who reads aloud the words of the prophecy, and blessed are those who hear and who keep what is written in it" (Rev 1:3). 1 Timothy 4:13 instructs, "Until I arrive, give attention to the public reading of scripture, to exhorting, to teaching," and Colossians 4:16 insists, "when this letter has been read among you, have it read also in the church of the Laodiceans; and see that you read also the letter from Laodicea." Such reading took place in the context of the *ekklēsia* as the community gathered for worship, and so, reading out loud was also a matter of reading-with.

I would suggest that the time has come for us to return to this practice, to move away from an academic practice of private reading to a practice of reading *en voz alta,* which is a corollary of our commitment to practices of *teología en conjunto* that contribute to the struggle for justice. I also want to suggest that Daniel Carroll, Gilberto Ruiz, and Sharon Ringe, with whose reading practices I have entered into conversation in this chapter, provide us with especially useful entrées into reading *en voz alta* that attend responsibly to the sort of engaged scholarship that Fernando Segovia delineates: "the task of Latino/a biblical criticism appears as radically situated and perspectival: emerging from a particular world of material and cultural exclusion; cognizant of a wider world in the throes of social and cultural devastation; and pledged to a world of freedom and justice, dignity and well-being for all."[77]

From Vincent Wimbush, Elisabeth Schüssler Fiorenza, and Fernando Segovia we have learned that the re-orientation of biblical scholarship toward communities and their practices of meaning-making can keep us from lapsing into the sort of academic esotericism that fetishizes texts and reduces biblical scholars to irrelevance as "tribal theologians." Schüssler Fiorenza urges us to transform biblical scholarship "into a critical discourse that is dedicated to producing knowledge that will further the well-being of all the inhabitants of the planet today," a critical discourse that can speak in telling ways to such urgent issues of public policy as the need for just and comprehensive immigration reform.[78]

From our conversation with Daniel Carroll, we learn that those with whom we engage in reading *en voz alta* may not only always be—indeed should not always be—readers who are like-minded. If we restrict our reading-with to reading communities of the like-minded, we might as well be reading silently and to ourselves. Given the abiding authority of the Bible for evangelical Christians, Carroll's patient and even-tempered approach shows great respect for readers whom biblical scholars might be inclined to ignore at best, and rail against at worst.

In conversation with Gilberto Ruiz's reading of the Johannine Jesus as migrant, we encounter an effective challenge to readings of the Fourth Gospel that focus on the individual rather than on the community, to readings that focus on salvation as flight from the world rather than with-us-ness of the Word-made-flesh.

Reading in dialogue with Sharon Ringe underscores the dangers of reading from a unitary perspective. Reading Mark 7:24-30 with Sharon Ringe and with the expanded reading community she convenes also makes it clear that our own practice of reading-with *en voz alta* must include a broad range of voices, especially those whose voices have been minoritized and thereby reduced to whispers from the margins by those who effectively control reading practices in the academy, in the churches, and in society at large.[79]

If reading is done *en voz alta*, it follows that while some read, others are listening with open minds. When such reading takes place *en conjunto*, it must follow that each voice listens respectfully to every other voice, with equal attention to the whole range of intonations, idioms and accents, subtlest nuances, and to the loudest and most insistent shouts. Finally, the candor with which Sharon Ringe admits the need to revisit her earlier treatment of Mark 7:24-30 makes it clear that no reading is definitive, no reading is once-and-for-all. As she confesses, so too must we: "This reading then, claims no definitive answers, but only a place in a conversation that must continue."[80]

PART II

Looking to the Texts

4

Abram and Sarai Cross the Border:
A Reading of Genesis 12:10-20

Years ago, I spent more than a few sleepless nights during the last weeks of my work as parochial vicar at the Roman Catholic Church of Our Lady of Loreto in the East New York section of Brooklyn, New York, wondering whether I was doing the right thing by leaving inner-city ministry in that Latino/a and African American community to return to graduate school for a doctoral degree in biblical studies. I had to ask myself over and over again whether I was escaping from the daily grind of *la lucha* into the pages of the Bible. R. S. Sugirtharajah insists, "The task of postcolonialism is to insure that the yearnings of the poor take precedence over the interests of the affluent; that the emancipation of the subjugated has primacy over the freedom of the powerful; and that the participation of the marginalized takes priority over the perpetuation of a system which systematically excludes them."[1]

That imperative prodded my conscience over and over again at a meeting in Miami that began the train of thought from which this chapter emerges. That meeting brought together a group of Latino/a biblical scholars and pastoral agents, Roman Catholic and Protestant, to explore the possibility of producing a *Biblia del Inmigrante*. This was to have been an edition of a Spanish translation of the Bible intended to provide spiritual sustenance for the many thousands of Latin Americans who cross the border from Mexico to the United States, a compact volume that was to be made available at little or no cost on both sides of the border. Besides study aids and explanatory material, the projected *Biblia del Inmigrante* was to include practical information that would be useful for Spanish-speaking immigrants making their way in the United States. The project did not make it very far, for the proposed *Biblia del Inmigrante* was never published; and perhaps it is just as well, for reading the Bible at the border is no simple matter. Indeed, such reading raises as many vexing questions as it provides answers.

As this chapter considers concerns that were set in motion by my involvement as a consultant to that well-intentioned project, I turn first of all to several key statements on immigration issued over the last several years

by the leadership of my own Roman Catholic faith community to see the
ways in which these statements appeal to texts from the Hebrew Bible. I am
especially interested in the ways in which these documents make reference
to texts from the Hebrew Bible in the effort to argue in favor of just and
comprehensive reform of immigration policies, and to ground the church's
efforts to serve the needs of the growing immigrant community. I then turn
from biblical imperatives to a narrative, to a provocative and challenging
text that I offer as a case study for reading *with* people on the move, a text
that provides a mirror from antiquity to the challenges that immigrants and
refugees continue to face.[2]

BIBLICAL IMPERATIVES AND THE WORLD
IN FRONT OF THE TEXT

In May of 2004, the Vatican's Pontifical Council for Migrants and
Refugees published an instruction entitled *Erga migrantes caritas Christi*,
"The Love of Christ towards Migrants."[3] That instruction, addressed
mainly toward Catholic pastoral agents entrusted with the responsibility of
attending to the needs of migrants and refugees, considered the pressing
present reality of people on the move—some two hundred million around
the world—so as to formulate effective pastoral strategies for meeting their
needs. After an introduction that sketches "The Migration Phenomenon
Today" (*Erga migrantes* 1-11), Part 1 of the instruction, "Migration, Sign of
the Times and Concern for the Church" (*Erga migrantes* 12-32) begins with
a treatment of "Migration as Seen with the Eyes of Faith" (*Erga migrantes*
12-13) that suggests that migration should be seen

> in the light of those biblical events that mark the phases of humanity's
> arduous journey towards the birth of a people without discrimination
> or frontiers, depository of God's gift for all nations and open to man's
> eternal vocation. Faith perceives in it the journey of the Patriarchs,
> sustained by the promise as they moved towards the future homeland,
> and that of the Hebrews, freed from slavery, as they crossed the Red
> Sea in the Exodus, that formed the People of the Covenant. Again, in
> a certain sense, faith finds in migration an exile, in which every goal
> reached in fact is relative. In migration faith discovers once more the
> universal message of the prophets, who denounce discrimination,
> oppression, deportation, dispersion and persecution as contrary to
> God's plan. At the same time they proclaim salvation for all, witnessing
> even in the chaotic events and contradictions of human history, that
> God continues to work out his plan of salvation until all things are
> brought together in Christ (cf. Eph 1:10). (*Erga migrantes* 13)

The instruction invites believers to see in the present realities of people on the move not an obstacle to the accomplishment of God's will but an unfolding of God's purposes "even in the chaotic events and contradictions of human history." It is under the heading of "Migration and the History of Salvation" that the instruction very briefly considers migration in the Hebrew Bible:

> Israel traced its origins back to Abraham, who in obedience to God's call left his home and went to a foreign land, taking with him the divine Promise that he would become the father "of a great nation" (Gn 12:1-2). Jacob, a wandering Aramean, "went down into Egypt with a small household and lived there as an alien. But there he became a nation, great, strong and numerous" (Dt 26:5). After its long servitude in Egypt Israel received its solemn investiture as the "People of God" during its forty-year "Exodus" through the desert. The hard test of migration and deportation is therefore fundamental to the story of the chosen people in view of the salvation of all peoples: Israel knew the return from exile (cf. Is 42:6-7; 49:5). With these memories it could take new heart in its trust in God, even in the darkest moments of its history (Ps 105 [104]: 12-15; Ps 106 [105]: 45-47). With regard to the foreigner living in the country, the Law enjoins the same commandment on Israel as applies to "the children of your people" (Lv 19:18), that is, "you must . . . love him as yourself" (Lv 19:34). (*Erga migrantes* 14)

It is clearly not the intention of this instruction to provide a comprehensive survey of how the Hebrew Bible deals with immigrants, refugees, and other people on the move. It does seek to underscore the biblical witness to Israel's story as the story of a people on the move: "The hard test of migration and deportation is therefore fundamental to the story of the chosen people." This story begins with Abraham, to whom God commands, "Go from your country and your kindred and your father's house to the land that I will show you" (Gen 12:1). The subsequent biblical citations in this paragraph of the Vatican instruction include a reference to Deuteronomy 26:1-11, the offering of first fruits to be made by those who have settled in the land.[4] This offering was to be accompanied by the following response:

> A wandering Aramean was my ancestor; he went down into Egypt and lived there as an alien, few in number, and there he became a great nation, mighty and populous. When the Egyptians treated us harshly and afflicted us, by imposing hard labor on us, we cried to the LORD, the God of our ancestors; the LORD heard our voice and saw our affliction, our toil, and our oppression. The LORD brought us out of Egypt with a mighty hand and an outstretched arm, with a terrifying

display of power, and with signs and wonders; and he brought us into
this place and gave us this land, a land flowing with milk and honey.
(Deut 26:5-9)

It is this experience of living as aliens in Egypt that is the ground of
solidarity on which the precepts of the Holiness Code call Israel to treat
aliens, in the last biblical citation noted in *Erga migrantes* 14, that is,
Leviticus 19:34: "The alien who resides with you shall be to you as the citizen
among you; you shall love the alien as yourself, for you were aliens in the land
of Egypt: I am the LORD your God."

In 2003, a year before the Pontifical Council for Migrants and Refugees
published *Erga migrantes caritas Christi*, the Roman Catholic bishops
of Mexico and the United States published a joint pastoral letter entitled
Strangers No Longer: Together on the Journey of Hope, a symbolic and
substantive contribution to the discussion on immigration from Latin
America into the United States. The bishops explained,

> We speak as two episcopal conferences but as one Church, united in
> the view that migration between our two nations is necessary and
> beneficial. At the same time, some aspects of the migrant experience
> are far from the vision of the Kingdom of God that Jesus proclaimed:
> many persons who seek to migrate are suffering, and, in some cases,
> tragically dying; human rights are abused; families are kept apart; and
> racist and xenophobic attitudes remain.[5]

Here too, as in the subsequent Vatican instruction, the bishops take a
moment to present reflections on "Migration in the Light of the Word of
God," with two paragraphs devoted to migration in the Old Testament (24
and 25) and two paragraphs to the New Testament (26 and 27). With regard
to people on the move in the Old Testament, the bishops observed:

> Even in the harsh stories of migration, God is present, revealing himself.
> Abraham stepped out in faith to respond to God's call (Gn 12:1). He
> and Sarah extended bounteous hospitality to three strangers who were
> actually a manifestation of the Lord, and this became a paradigm for
> the response to strangers of Abraham's descendants. The grace of
> God even broke through situations of sin in the forced migration of
> the children of Jacob: Joseph, sold into slavery, eventually became the
> savior of his family (Gn 37:45)—a type of Jesus, who, betrayed by a
> friend for thirty pieces of silver, saves the human family.
>   The key events in the history of the Chosen People of enslavement
> by the Egyptians and of liberation by God led to commandments
> regarding strangers (Ex 23:9; Lv 19:33). Israel's conduct with the
> stranger is both an imitation of God and the primary, specific Old

Testament manifestation of the great commandment to love one's neighbor: "For the Lord, your God, is the ... Lord of lords, the great God, mighty and awesome, who has no favorites, accepts no bribes, who executes justice for the orphan and widow, and befriends the alien, feeding and clothing him. So you, too, must befriend the alien, for you were once aliens yourselves in the land of Egypt" (Dt 10:17-19). For the Israelites, these injunctions were not only personal exhortations: the welcome and care of the alien were structured into their gleaning and tithing laws (Lv 19:9-10; Dt 14:28-29).[6]

In an era of rampant human trafficking, the Joseph story takes on a special poignancy. Likewise, in an era of ever-increasing xenophobia and intolerance toward undocumented immigrants, the precepts of Leviticus and Deuteronomy should stir the consciences of those who themselves "were once aliens," whether a generation ago or centuries ago.[7] The Roman Catholic bishops of Arizona referred to the very same texts (Deuteronomy 10 and Leviticus 19 in their own 2006 pastoral letter on migration, "You Welcomed Me," addressing themselves to their fellow Arizonans, residents of a state that "has become the focal point of the immigration debate in recent years,"[8] and where then-governor Janet Napolitano vetoed a bill passed by the Arizona legislature that would have criminalized undocumented immigrants in her state.

There can be no doubt that the Roman Catholic bishops of the United States have taken a high-profile stance in the current public policy debate in the United States regarding immigration reform, with none more prominent than Cardinal Roger Mahony, who at the beginning of Lent 2006 made clear his opposition—as archbishop of Los Angeles—to the Border Protection, Anti-Terrorism and Illegal Immigration Control Act (HR 4437) then being debated by the House of Representatives.[9] Mahony made equally clear his intention to instruct the priests of the archdiocese to disobey the law inasmuch as its provisions called for service providers (not excluding religious workers) to ascertain the immigration status of their clients. This courageous stance received applause from such unexpected quarters as the *New York Times*, where the lead editorial of the March 3, 2006 issue carried the headline "The Gospel vs. H.R.4437." The editorial went on to praise what it called Mahony's "declaration of solidarity with illegal immigrants":

It has been a long time since this country heard a call to organized lawbreaking on this big a scale. . . . If current efforts in Congress make it a felony to shield or offer support to illegal immigrants, Cardinal Mahony said, he will instruct his priests—and faithful lay Catholics—to defy the law. . . . Cardinal Mahony's declaration of solidarity with illegal immigrants, for whom Lent is every day, is a startling call to civil disobedience, as courageous as it is timely. We hope it forestalls the day when works of mercy become a federal crime.[10]

Not everyone was moved to applause. In the pages of the *National Review*, George Neumayr wrote that Cardinal Mahony, "Contrary to his faux-pious rhetoric, he is speaking not for the Catholic Church but for himself, using, in a textbook example of clericalism, the prestige and trappings of his episcopal office to advance nothing more than his personal opinion in favor of open borders."[11] Congressional Representative Peter King, the co-sponsor of HR 4437, called for his church's bishops to stay out of politics and "spend more time protecting little boys from pedophile priests." A self-confessed "blue collar Catholic," King mused about his opposition to the church's stance on immigration: "It's quite possible this could end up helping me politically. Maybe it shows that God's on my side."[12] This is the same Peter King who in 2004, according to *Newsday* reporter Glenn Thrush, "dismissed the Vatican's criticism of the U.S. military's human rights abuses at Iraq's Abu Ghraib prison, saying they were 'nothing compared to what nuns and priests did to Catholic kids for decades.'"[13]

It is unmistakably clear that there is still a lot of preaching to the choir that needs to take place (since the "choir" includes Catholics like Peter King and Minuteman co-founder Jim Gilchrist), that many more Catholic Christians need to take to heart their church's embrace of the imperative of Leviticus 19:34: "The alien who resides with you shall be to you as the citizen among you; you shall love the alien as yourself, for you were aliens in the land of Egypt: I am the LORD your God."

On the basis of statements from Rome and from leaders in the United States, it is clear that the Catholic Church's stance on immigration reform has deep roots in the biblical imperatives that flow from Israel's consciousness as a people "who were once aliens in the land of Egypt." In the world in front of the biblical text, that ethical consciousness is shaped by centuries-long patterns of immigration to the United States, constituted as a "nation of immigrants" with a national mythology that continues to tap into biblical narratives for its language and its substance.[14] Thus, the solidarity with recently arrived immigrants called for by church leaders is framed as fitting recognition of a shared heritage of migration at a greater or lesser distance in time.

It must be noted, though, that the language of statements by church leadership regarding immigration reform too often falls into the trap of speaking about immigrants—especially the undocumented—in the third person plural, speaking about "them" in ways that do not take account of the fact that Hispanics (including both Latin American immigrants and U.S.-born Latinos/as) represent 71 percent of the U.S. Catholic population growth since 1960, that some 39 percent of Roman Catholics in the United States are of Latin American origin (Latin American immigrants and U.S.-born

Latinos/as), and that more than 20 percent of Roman Catholic parishes in the United States are majority Latino/a.[15] When church leadership comes to reckon with statistics like these, there can be no doubt that "they" are "us,"[16] and that the solidarity they call for is not only *ad extra* and at a distance but *ad intra* as well. From this emerges the important insight that dealing with the Bible and immigrants calls us to engage not only in reading *about* immigrants but also in reading *as* immigrants and reading *with* immigrants.

PEOPLE ON THE MOVE IN THE HEBREW BIBLE

Dianne Bergant explains, "Two Hebrew words are used by the biblical authors to distinguish those who belong to other nations. Though the words are sometimes used interchangeably, *nokrî* usually refers to transient foreigners and *ger* to sojourners or resident aliens."[17] Francisco García-Treto suggests,

If we were to summarize in a single phrase the clear thesis of these biblical traditions [regarding migration], it would be, simply, that the *ger* is protected by Yahweh. The ancient Hebrew Tradition is clearly different from the xenophobic attitudes that were prevalent in antiquity. . . . The *ger*, the alien who lives among the people of Israel, could have been completely deprived of dignity and even of the most basic right to justice, since the *ger* lacked the two traditional elements that, at the purely human level, were the foundation of dignity and right in Israel: hereditary property, and the protection of family and kinship. The biblical tradition, however, surprises us by including the *ger* as the object of a particular predilection on Yahweh's part, and therefore to be included, jointly with the native, in the rites that expressed the community's solidarity, as well as among those to whom the law grants a special protection.[18]

Commenting on García-Treto's observations, Justo González notes that "the *ger* even serves a specific religious function in Israel, reminding the people that Israel too was alien in the land of Egypt, and remains forever alien in a land that ultimately belongs only to God."[19] According to García-Treto,

The biblical tradition . . . reiterates that Israel not only was, but still is, an "alien" people. Solidarity with the dispossessed is not only an external attitude, but the deepest reality of Israel's existence as people of Yahweh. References such as Deuteronomy 28:8 remind Israel that it too was a *ger* in Egypt, but even more relevant are others such as the one in Leviticus 25:23, where Yahweh admonishes the people: "The

land shall not be sold in perpetuity, for the land is mine; with me you
are but aliens and tenants."[20]

This dynamic suggests that the reading strategy I am offering, that is, the
practice of not only reading *about* immigrants, but also reading *as* immigrants
and reading *with* immigrants holds promise. As we proceed, I would like
to offer a case study for the practice of reading *as* immigrants and reading
with immigrants. The text I offer for consideration is Genesis 12:10-20, the
episode in the patriarchal narrative where a famine in Canaan forces Abram
to seek refuge as a resident alien in Egypt (Genesis 12:10): "Now there was a
famine in the land. So Abram went down to Egypt to reside there as an alien,
for the famine was severe in the land"), in effect as a temporary economic
migrant. The selection of this text as a case study does not imply either that
this text is especially appropriate for reading *with* twenty-first-century people
on the move or that it ought to be understood as prescriptive or normative
for the conduct of twenty-first-century people on the move. Nor do I mean
to suggest that this text furnishes an appropriate model for navigating the
challenges of living in a land that is not one's own—quite the contrary![21]

Yet, by selecting this text as a case study I *do* mean to suggest that the
characterization of people on the move in the Hebrew Bible is substantially
more complex and substantially more nuanced than one might be led to
believe on the basis of the somewhat limited range of texts from the Hebrew
Bible that are referenced in recent official Roman Catholic documents
regarding migrants and refugees. To be sure, the biblical imperatives that
find a place in these documents to renew in the present day the ancient call
for justice toward migrants ring deeply true.[22] At the same time, the range of
biblical narratives involving characters who are people on the move testifies
to the pervasiveness across history of the challenges of moving across borders
and to the difficulty of the ethical choices and tactical decisions people make
in order to survive in lands far from their own.

ABRAM AND SARAI CROSS THE BORDER: GENESIS 12:10-20

Now there was a famine in the land. So Abram went down to Egypt to
reside there as an alien, for the famine was severe in the land. When he
was about to enter Egypt, he said to his wife Sarai, "I know well that
you are a woman beautiful in appearance; and when the Egyptians
see you, they will say, 'This is his wife'; then they will kill me, but
they will let you live. Say you are my sister, so that it may go well with
me because of you, and that my life may be spared on your account."
When Abram entered Egypt the Egyptians saw that the woman was
very beautiful. When the officials of Pharaoh saw her, they praised
her to Pharaoh. And the woman was taken into Pharaoh's house. And

for her sake he dealt well with Abram; and he had sheep, oxen, male donkeys, male and female slaves, female donkeys, and camels. But the LORD afflicted Pharaoh and his house with great plagues because of Sarai, Abram's wife. So Pharaoh called Abram, and said, "What is this you have done to me? Why did you not tell me that she was your wife? Why did you say, 'She is my sister,' so that I took her for my wife? Now then, here is your wife, take her, and be gone." And Pharaoh gave his men orders concerning him; and they set him on the way, with his wife and all that he had.

In *The Art of Biblical Narrative*, Robert Alter identifies this text as a type scene, for it is one of the three instances in Genesis in which "a patriarch is driven by famine to a southern region where he pretends that his wife is his sister, narrowly avoids a violation of the conjugal bond by the local ruler, and is sent away with gifts."[23] Abram and Sarai are involved in two such scenes, Genesis 12:10-20 and 20:1-18, and Isaac and Rebekah in Genesis 26:1-16. In her commentary on Genesis in *The Women's Bible Commentary*, Susan Niditch writes of these wife–sister tales:

Three times in Genesis when a patriarch and his wife are "sojourning,"—traveling as resident aliens—in a foreign land, the ruler of the country is told that the wife is a sister of the patriarch. In two versions he takes her to be his own woman, and each time the couple is eventually found out. Despite the similarities, the three stories possess quite different nuances and voices. It is assumed in all three versions that a brother has more power to exchange his sister than a husband his wife. The patriarchs are portrayed as assuming that the foreigners would not hesitate to kill a husband in order to get a woman but that they would engage in normal marital exchange with a brother. The story that makes the most sense in a crass, male-centered way is the version in 12:10-20, where it is clear that Abram has more to gain as the brother of an unmarried, protected woman than as the husband of a "used" one.[24]

I will focus on the first of these scenes, Genesis 12:10-20.[25] Gordon Wenham points out the clearly concentric structure of the tale:

A   Exposition: Entry (v. 10)
    B   First Scene: Abram's Speech (vv. 10-13)
        C   Second Scene: The Ruse at Work (vv. 14-16)
    B[1]   Third Scene: Pharaoh's Speech (vv. 17-19)
A[1]   Conclusion: Exit (v. 20)[26]

From the very outset of the story, it is clear that Abram and Sarai are economic refugees from Canaan, crossing the border into Egypt to escape a deadly famine. The concentric structure of verses 10–20 frames Abram's journeying to Egypt to live there as a resident alien between mentions of the famine in the land—the second time making explicit reference to the severity of the famine. The mention of Abram's journey into Egypt comes abruptly, following quickly after the vision at Shechem, described in verse 7: "Then the LORD appeared to Abram, and said, 'To your offspring I will give this land.' So he built there an altar to the LORD, who had appeared to him." His intention to sojourn in Egypt as a resident alien as a result of the famine raises considerable doubt, generating significant narrative tension that is only resolved at the conclusion of the story. Having left his homeland in pursuit of God's promise, would his hopes be dashed by the very barrenness of a land that would prove more curse than blessing? Would he end his days as an alien sojourning in a land far from his own?

It is not unimportant for the development of the narrative that Abram gives voice to his fears about the dangers that lie ahead just as he is about to cross into Egyptian territory. As Wenham writes,

> Escaping the danger of famine in Canaan, Abram fears that in Egypt he will run another sort of risk. As an immigrant there he would lack the support and protection afforded by the wider family network. The danger of immigrants being exploited is frequently harped on in the law, e.g., Exod 22:20 (21); 23:9. Why Abram should have felt secure in Canaan but exposed in Egypt is not explained, though of course strange environments often do give rise to unfounded fears.[27]

To twenty-first-century interpreters reading *as* immigrants and reading *with* immigrants, there is nothing unfounded at all about the fears involved in border crossings. The physical dangers to which those who cross the border between Mexico and the United States are altogether terrifying, and the fear of deportation once across the border is no less preoccupying. Claus Westermann successfully sketches the geopolitical dimensions of such perils—albeit in another era and another place—describing yet another instance of well-founded fear elsewhere in Genesis:

> As one who has to beg for food, Abraham has no rights. We meet this same feeling, of being delivered to a far superior power without protection, once more in the case of Joseph's brothers on their way down to Egypt. Real experience lies behind this—that of a small group confronted by a superpower. The mighty colossus engenders the feeling of utter powerlessness on the part of the lesser one. It is in this situation in the ancient world that the ruse everywhere has its place. The ruse is the only weapon left for the powerless given over to the mighty.[28]

Giving voice to his fear about the danger he will face when they enter Egyptian territory, Abram asks Sarai to say that she is his sister, "so that it may go well with me because of you, and that my life may be spared on your account" (v. 13). For her part, Sarai says nothing at this point, nor do we hear her voice at any point in the story. In verse 20, Pharaoh addresses Abram to ask, "Why did you say, 'She is my sister,' so that I took her for my wife?" Yet Niditch suggests that Abram and Sarai are actually "co-tricksters," pointing out that Abram uses "coaxing language" in his request, "Please say you are my sister." Niditch warns,

> This is no woman-affirming tale. Sarai is an exchange item to be traded for wealth. She is shown as accepting this role, as are all the women in Genesis. She and Abram play out their roles in a particular social structure, but do so as marginals. Facing famine in their own land, they flee to Egypt, where they have insecure status. There they use deception to improve their situation at the expense of those who have authority over them.[29]

The intertwined dynamics of power and gender that are at work in Sarai's silent compliance with Abram's request come full circle in the story's second speech, where it is Abram who is reduced to silence, giving no response to Pharaoh's question, "Why did you say, 'She is my sister,' so that I took her for my wife?" (v. 20). Yet Pharaoh sends Abram away with all his possessions— his newly acquired wealth and his wife besides—and the patriarch leaves Egypt and returns "to the place where his tent had been at the beginning, between Bethel and Ai, to the place where he had made an altar at the first; and there Abram called on the name of the LORD" (13:3). Genesis 13:3 forms an inclusion with 13:8-9, framing the story of Abraham as a transnational temporary migrant from Canaan to Egypt and back again.

Nahum Sarna prefers to call the story in Genesis 12:10-20 "The Kidnapping of Sarah," suggesting that Pharaoh's officials "carry her off to the royal palace. Only divine intervention protects her honor and she returns to her husband unviolated."[30] It is evident from verse 16 that what happened was anything but a kidnapping. As Niditch points out, Sarai was an "exchange item to be traded for wealth."[31] Happily-ever-after ending or not, this episode in the Abraham story is deeply disturbing. Sarna writes,

> The biblical heroes are not portrayed as demigods or perfect human beings. They are mortals of flesh and blood, subject to the same temptations and possessed of the same frailties as are all other human beings. Abram, the man of implicit faith in God's word, is fearful of the evil of which people are capable. In order to save his own life, he appears to place his wife's honor in jeopardy through misrepresentation

of their relationship. Sarai's collusion may be looked upon as an act of self-sacrifice on behalf of her husband—but how is Abram's conduct to be judged? Ramban comments as follows: "Know that our father Abraham inadvertently committed a great sin by placing his virtuous wife in a compromising situation because of his fear of being killed. He should have trusted in God to save him, his wife and all he had, for God has the power to help and to save."[32]

By turns, commentators lament Abram's failure to trust in God, or else they point to the version of the story in Genesis 26 to suggest that Abram was actually telling the truth by having Sarai identified as his sister (Gen 26:12: "she is indeed my sister, the daughter of my father but not the daughter of my mother; and she became my wife"). Some of the commentators who favor the latter option then invoke some indirect evidence for practices in surrounding cultures that sanctioned some sort of endogamous marriage to one's sister.[33]

Whether or not she was complicit in Abram's ruse, Sarai finds herself doubly victimized by powerful males in this story: first by her own husband, whose fear and desire for self-preservation take priority over her welfare, and second by the Pharaoh, the foreign sovereign whose attendants acquire her for their master's house in a transaction in which—to put it as bluntly as possible—Abram receives far more livestock than he loses by surrendering Sarai: "sheep, oxen, male donkeys, male and female slaves, female donkeys, and camels" (Gen 12:16). In the end, Abram the trickster leaves Egypt safe and sound, with all of his newly acquired wealth *and* Sarai as well (Gen 12:20).

CONCLUSION

What happens when we read about Sarai's experience of crossing the border into Egypt along with Gloria Anzaldúa? In *Borderlands/La Frontera*, Anzaldúa writes the following about what faces those who cross the border between the United States and Mexico:

Living in a no-man's borderland, caught between being treated as criminals and being able to eat, between resistance and deportation, the illegal refugees are some of the poorest and the most exploited of any people in the U.S. It is illegal for Mexicans to work without green cards. But big farming combines, farm bosses and smugglers who bring them in to make money off the "wetbacks'" labor—they don't have to pay federal minimum wages, or ensure adequate housing or sanitary conditions.

The Mexican woman is especially at risk. Often the *coyote* (smuggler) doesn't feed her for days or let her go to the bathroom. Often he rapes her or sells her into prostitution. She cannot call on county or state health or economic resources because she doesn't know English and she fears deportation. American employers are quick to take advantage of her helplessness. She can't go home. She's sold her house, her furniture, borrowed from her friends to pay the *coyote* who charges her four or five thousand dollars to smuggle her to Chicago. She may work as a live-in maid for white, Chicano or Latino household for as little as $15 a week. Or work in the garment industry, do hotel work. Isolated and worried about her family back home, afraid of getting caught and deported, living with as many as fifteen people in one room, the *mexicana* suffers serious health problems. *Se enferma de los nervios, de alta presión.*

La mujer, la mujer indocumentada, is doubly threatened in this country. Not only does she have to contend with sexual violence, but like all women, she is prey to a sense of physical helplessness. As a refugee, she leaves the familiar and safe home-ground to venture into unknown and possibly dangerous terrain.

> This is her home
> This thin edge of
> barbwire.[34]

What happens when we read Genesis 12:10-20 *with* women who have crossed the border from Mexico into the United States? The very first words we hear from the mouth of the border-crosser Abram are the words of fear he whispers to his wife in Genesis 12:11-13, and it is Sarai who becomes the victim of her husband's fear when that fear is the force that keeps him from seeing her as spouse or as sister but as no more than livestock that can assure him a prosperous future in spite of famine. For twenty-first-century border crossers, there is ample cause for fear. Thousands have died in the years since the Clinton administration launched Operation Gatekeeper to seal the border between Tijuana and San Diego.[35] A 2006 report issued by the United States Government Accountability Office found that "Since 1995, the number of border-crossing deaths increased and by 2005 had more than doubled," and "the annual number of border-crossing deaths increased from 241 in 1999 to a total of 472 deaths recorded in 2005." Further, "deaths among women increased from 9 percent of all deaths in 1998 to 21 percent of all deaths in 2005."[36]

The moral clarity of the regulations in the Hebrew Bible regarding the treatment of aliens becomes considerably more muddled as these aliens themselves become implicated in the tension between disclosure and non-disclosure, between the truth and trickery that are essential to survival in the borderlands, the life-and-death tension at the barbed-wire boundary between truth and trickery where the collateral damage is considerable, and where the most vulnerable also become the most expendable. The stories of people on the move in the Hebrew Bible are colored not in simple black and white, but in subtle and complex shades.

In the world in front of the text, the stories of people on the move across the border between Mexico and the United States in the twenty-first century are stories too often written in their own sweat, and in their own blood. For the responsible reader of the Bible, who recognizes with Sugirtharajah that "Postcolonial hermeneutics has to be a pragmatic engagement, an engagement in which praxis is not an extra option or a subsidiary enterprise taken in the aftermath of judicious deconstruction and reconstruction of the texts," there must be no flight from these stories into the pages of the ancient text.[37]

5

Symbolism on the Street: Reading Prophecy as Performance in Ezekiel 12:1-16

The word of the LORD came to me: Mortal, you are living in the midst of a rebellious house, who have eyes to see but do not see, who have ears to hear but do not hear; for they are a rebellious house. Therefore, mortal, prepare for yourself an exile's baggage, and go into exile by day in their sight; you shall go like an exile from your place to another place in their sight. Perhaps they will understand, though they are a rebellious house. You shall bring out your baggage by day in their sight, as baggage for exile; and you shall go out yourself at evening in their sight, as those do who go into exile. Dig through the wall in their sight, and carry the baggage through it. In their sight you shall lift the baggage on your shoulder, and carry it out in the dark; you shall cover your face, so that you may not see the land; for I have made you a sign for the house of Israel.

I did just as I was commanded. I brought out my baggage by day, as baggage for exile, and in the evening I dug through the wall with my own hands; I brought it out in the dark, carrying it on my shoulder in their sight.

In the morning the word of the LORD came to me: Mortal, has not the house of Israel, the rebellious house, said to you, "What are you doing?" Say to them, "Thus says the Lord GOD: This oracle concerns the prince in Jerusalem and all the house of Israel in it." Say, "I am a sign for you: as I have done, so shall it be done to them; they shall go into exile, into captivity." And the prince who is among them shall lift his baggage on his shoulder in the dark, and shall go out; he shall dig through the wall and carry it through; he shall cover his face, so that he may not see the land with his eyes. I will spread my net over him, and he shall be caught in my snare; and I will bring him to Babylon, the land of the Chaldeans, yet he shall not see it; and he shall die there.

I will scatter to every wind all who are around him, his helpers and all
his troops; and I will unsheathe the sword behind them. And they shall
know that I am the LORD, when I disperse them among the nations and
scatter them through the countries. But I will let a few of them escape
from the sword, from famine and pestilence, so that they may tell of all
their abominations among the nations where they go; then they shall
know that I am the LORD (Ezek 12:1-16).

READING EZEKIEL FROM THIS HYPHENATED PLACE

For a number of Latino/a theologians, the Babylonian Exile has begun to
acquire something of the resonance that the Exodus holds for Latin American
liberation theologians. This is because, as Cuban-American theologian
Justo González writes, "For whatever reasons, we find ourselves in a land
not our own—in some cases, in a land that was our own, but is no longer.
In that land, we must find a way to live, to survive, and to be faithful."[1]
Fernando Segovia, another Cuban-American, has written poignantly of his
own "Narrative of Origins: The Journey of Exile" that brought him from
Cuba to the United States in July 1961:

> I recall the preparations for the journey itself. The efforts to get me
> out of the country . . . the frantic search for a missing passport . . .
> the surprise call on a Friday to the effect that I would be leaving on the
> following Monday, alone—as so many others did, though in the end
> a seat came open for my mother as well. The final weekend of visits
> to family, friends, places—the exchange of goodbyes, *sotto voce* in
> case somebody might wish to do us harm; the preparation of the one
> piece of baggage per-person allowed, a sack that came to be known
> as *el chorizo* (the sausage) and that was stuffed with clothing for an
> unspecified period of time in the unknown *el norte*.[2]

This experience is not my own, for I am not a member of the Cuban
diaspora, but I am an Antillean cousin, as it were, with a Puerto Rican
heritage. Even more specifically, I am a Nuyorican, a member of that
peculiar hybrid group that rides the frequent flyer hyphen between San Juan
and New York.[3] In an essay entitled "Puerto Rican Identity Up in the Air,"
Alberto Sandoval Sánchez writes,

> Growing up in San Juan, I always heard relatives and friends saying,
> "Mi primo se va p'allá fuera," "Mi hija vive allá fuera hace años,"
> "Mi hermana viene de fuera el domingo." . . . *Fuera* meant New York,
> New Jersey, Philadelphia, Florida, Illinois, California. *Fuera* was and
> still is a euphemism for migration. *Fuera* is that space at a distance

from the speaker, that location outside, away from the island that is always conducive to spatio-geographical demarcations such as *Allá* and *Acá*, "over there" and "over here." Since mass air migrations of Puerto Ricans started in the late 1940s, the migrant's myth has been to return, to come back to the island; as the song "En mi viejo San Juan" says, "Me voy . . . pero un día volveré, a buscar mi querer a soñar otra vez en mi viejo San Juan." Unfortunately, the myth of the eternal return to the place of origin is anything but a reality; as the song says, "Pero el tiempo pasó y el destino burló mi terrible nostalgia." What was supposed to be a round-trip ticket became a one-way ticket. . . . Irse pa' fuera" was a life journey that implied walking on the edge of loneliness, alienation, isolation, loss of identity, and ultimately death.[4]

Such is the bittersweet betwixt-and-between that provides an overture to this reading of Ezekiel 12:1-16.[5] Ezekiel was among the eight thousand or so people who were deported from Judah in 597 BCE when Nebuchadrezzar laid siege to Jerusalem and took King Jehoiachin captive. Active from 593 to 571 BCE, Ezekiel was, along with his somewhat older contemporary Jeremiah, a prophet who, in Walter Brueggemann's words, "ministered across the discontinuity, that is before and after 587," when Jerusalem fell and the temple was destroyed.[6] The specific challenge this chapter engages is the search for appropriate categories for considering the coherence and consistency of the material in Ezekiel 12 and the similar sign-action material in Ezekiel 4:1-5:17. After setting out some of the issues involved in treating Ezekiel 12:1-16 and other symbolic actions in the book, I will examine the approach proposed by Bernhard Lang and suggest that, with some readjustment, it furnishes a useful framework for understanding this material.

EXTRAORDINARY TEXTS AND ORDINARY READERS

Whatever the impact of Ezekiel's sign-actions may have been on their earliest audiences, they have vexed and disturbed many subsequent generations of hearers and readers of the book. For example, Maimonides writes, in his *Guide for the Perplexed*,

The ordinary reader believes that the acts, journeys, questions and answers of the prophets really took place, and were perceived by the senses, and did not merely form part of a prophetic vision. . . . In the description of the vision in which Ezekiel is brought to Jerusalem, we read as follows: "And when I looked, behold a hole in the wall. Then he said unto me, Son of man, dig now in the wall; and when I had digged in the wall, behold a door," etc. It was thus in a vision that he was commanded to dig in the wall, to enter and see what people were doing there, and it was in the same vision that he digged, entered through the hole, and saw certain things, as is related. Just as all this forms part of a vision, the same may be said of the following passages: "And thou take unto thee a tile," etc., "and lie thou also on thy left side," etc., "Take thou also wheat and barley," etc., "and cause it to pass over thine head and upon thy beard." It was in a prophetic vision that he saw that he did all these actions which he was commanded to do. God forbid that God would make his prophets appear an object of ridicule and sport in the eyes of the ignorant, and order them to perform foolish acts. . . . Weak-minded persons believe that the prophet relates here what he was commanded to do, and what he actually did, and that he describes how he was commanded to dig in a wall on the Temple mount although he was in Babylon, and relates how he obeyed the command, for he says, "And I digged in the wall." But it is distinctly stated that all this took place in a vision.[7]

Maimonides was by no means either the first or the last commentator to wrestle with the peculiar practices portrayed in the narrative of Ezekiel. Commenting on Ezekiel 12:17-20, where the prophet is commanded, "Mortal, eat your bread with quaking, and drink your water with trembling and with fearfulness" (Ezek 12:18), Peter Craigie explains, "The prophet's hand would be shaking so that water spilled before reaching his lips and the bread was fumbled at the mouth. By his actions, he was demonstrating to his audience the fearful condition of the inhabitants of Jerusalem, who would dine in trembling in the twilight of their city's doom."[8] Evaluating Ezekiel's behavior, Craigie adds, "Had Ezekiel been a seminary student of homiletics, he would doubtless have failed the course on this performance. The prophet-preacher must surely be dynamic and strong, inspiring his audience. He must surely draw them by a positive personality, not appeal to them by trembling theatrics."[9]

This material in Ezekiel that may have perplexed Maimonides' readers and earns an unsatisfactory grade from Craigie, clustered in 4:1-5:17 and then in 12:1-20, is ordinarily understood form critically under the rubric of the report of a symbolic action, often following a tripartite pattern of (1) command to perform the act, (2) report of the act, and (3) response of the audience/interpretation.[10]

J. Lindblom regards this material quite favorably, setting out what amounts to a quasi-sacramental understanding of the genre and its function:

It is a *verbum visibile*, a visible word . . . as a divine word, the word uttered by a prophet had an effective power. The same is true of a visible word. . . . Such an action served not only to represent and make evident a particular fact, but also to make this fact a reality. . . . The effect . . . upon the onlookers was consequently not only to present visibly what the prophet had to say, but also to convince them that the events . . . would really take place. They were also intended to arouse the emotions of fear or hope. . . . What was done reinforced powerfully what was said.[11]

To this reader of Ezekiel, at least, Lindblom's explanation falls a bit short, because it privileges word over deed, construing prophetic action as subordinate and subservient to prophetic proclamation: what they said matters more than what they do. However, by calling attention to the intention of prophetic actions, that is, "to arouse the emotions of fear and hope," Lindblom's oblique allusion to the Aristotelian notion of tragic *katharsis* moves the discussion an important step forward, in a direction taken up more recently by Bernhard Lang in his essay "Street Theater, Raising the Dead and the Zoroastrian Connection in Ezekiel's Prophecy."[12]

In that study, Lang argues that these symbolic acts "should be understood as public, street-theater-like performances," while admitting that when he "presented this view of prophetic symbolism to academic audiences, the immediate reaction was not entirely favorable. 'There must be more to the symbolic acts,' insisted one colleague, arguing that I was seeking to minimize the difference between modern western thought and 'Hebrew mentality.'"[13] I find Lang's approach promising, for it suggests that the tools at our disposal for understanding the narratives of this prophet's sometimes perplexing actions can be expanded beyond the constraints of form-critical concerns, with their attendant presuppositions.

Indeed, understanding the Ezekiel of these reports of symbolic action as a performance artist substantially repaints the portrait of this priest-prophet "among the exiles by the River Chebar" (Ezek 1:1). In addition, there is genuine hermeneutical value in doing what Lang's colleague accused him of doing. From the standpoint of contextual biblical interpretation, "reading from this place,"[14] this reconfiguration reduces the effective distance between the world of the prophet and the worlds of Latinos/as living far from their lands of origin in the urban areas of the United States where both staged and impromptu street theater are features of everyday life.

In the performance scripted in 12:1-16, Ezekiel mimes the experiences of his fellow exiles: "prepare for yourself an exile's baggage, and go into exile by day in their sight; you shall go like an exile from your place to another place in their sight. Perhaps they will understand, though they are a rebellious house" (12:3). As I read this text of Ezekiel, I cannot help but recall the words of Fernando Segovia's narrative of exile: "the preparation of the one piece of baggage per-person allowed, a sack that came to be known as *el chorizo* (the sausage) and that was stuffed with clothing for an unspecified period of time in the unknown *el norte*."[15] For those who have experienced the hurried packing of an exile themselves—whether Ezekiel's fellow deportees from

Judah in the deportation of 597 BCE or twentieth-century CE Cubans who fled their homeland, memory confers on the prophet's pantomime a jarring and unmistakable eloquence.

Lang challenges the assumption, common among biblical scholars since the 1920s, that the symbolic actions of the prophets are bound up with a magical worldview. Taking on Georg Fohrer's *Die symbolische Handlungen der Propheten*, Lang surfaces three interrelated assumptions that provide the underpinning for Fohrer's consideration of the genre:

> First, the symbolic acts are derived from a common Near-Eastern or even international repertoire of magic. . . . Secondly, the internal structure of the symbolic acts involved certain assumptions that must be seen in the context of a "primitive mentality." . . . Finally, the symbolic act does not exclusively serve as a medium of instruction. The act pre-imitates the future, that is, it influences and shapes future events simply by being performed. . . . The self-fulfilling magical act is the blueprint for a course of events that cannot be changed.[16]

Lang concludes that "what Fohrer and others have put together is a rather uninspired collection of outdated fragments of anthropological theory."[17] A more serious weakness of Fohrer's analysis, Lang contends, is his miscellaneous accumulation of Near Eastern parallels to the prophetic symbolic acts—parallels Fohrer cites in support of his position that the symbolic actions tap into traditional magical ritual gestures. Lang maintains instead that the symbolic acts

> never belong to a known and pre-established repertoire of gestures and customs, but are invented for the occasion. The prophet is his own author of the script; no script is provided by the culture in which he works. He is an imaginative and creative performer rather than the magician who relies on traditional rituals others cannot or do not dare to use. The prophetic acts belong to the history of teaching aids and provocative street theater rather than to the phenomenology of magic.[18]

Recognizing further that not all symbolic acts are alike, Lang offers a fourfold typology of symbolic acts:

1. teaching aids: "actions that visualize an aspect of the prophetic message or preaching. . . . We are justified in referring to them as teaching aids or provocative one-man street theater."
2. performative gestures: "To this group belong such gestures as Elijah's throwing of his cloak over young Elisha."

3. symbolically conceived acts: "Sometimes a prophet understands events of his biography or of everyday life in a symbolic way."
4. magical acts: "The prophet may also act as a magician. His acts are then based on the illusion of the self-fulfilling wish."[19]

Lang places most of Ezekiel's symbolic acts under the first heading, classifying them as teaching aids and suggesting that street theater furnishes a promising framework for understanding them. In proposing this alternative model for understanding prophetic symbolic acts, Lang explains that "The street can become the stage for small and informal groups, and often individuals supplement their speeches and handing-out of leaflets by mimes and props."[20]

Recalling the flourishing of street theater in Germany during the student revolts of 1968, Lang cites the remarks of A. Bornkessel on the objectives of street theater:

> Street theater wants to inform a wide, heterogenous audience about political issues that are important yet officially disguised in a euphemistic rhetoric or actually distorted. Making the didactic efficacy its exclusive criterion, it is in a radical way oriented toward the audience. It is geared toward activating the audience to making comments, to argue, and eventually to learn the lesson and act accordingly.[21]

Lang contends that "The public demonstrations of biblical prophets share the basic characteristics, and especially the objective, of the modern political street theater performed by the unofficial, self-appointed opposition."[22] The spontaneity, originality, and audience-oriented didactic objectives of twentieth-century CE street theater are what recommend this genre to Lang as a point of contact with Ezekiel's narratives of symbolic action.

STREET THEATER, PERFORMANCE, AND SCRIPT

As suggestive and stimulating as Lang's hypothesis appears to be for the interpretation of the symbolic-action narratives in Ezekiel, his treatment of this material as street theater raises at least as many questions as it answers. The first of these has to do with Lang's undifferentiated understanding of street theater: while Lang successfully distinguishes among several types of symbolic acts (teaching aids, performative gestures, symbolically perceived acts and magical acts), he offers no such distinction among various forms of street theater. Introducing "the wild array of configurations that radical street performance in the twentieth century has taken," Jan Cohen-Cruz offers a fivefold typology:

1. Agit-prop: Attempts to mobilize people around partisan points of view that have been simplified and theatricalized to capture by-passers' attention directly or by way of the media. Popularly identified with the whole domain of street theater, this represents but one approach to the form.
2. Witness: Publicly illuminating a social act that one does not know how to change but must at least acknowledge. The site of such performance usually relates directly to the event being scrutinized.
3. Integration: The insertion of a theatrically heightened scenario into people's everyday lives to provide an emotional experience of what otherwise might remain distant.
4. Utopia: The enactment of another vision of social organization, temporarily replacing life as it is, and often performed with public participation.
5. Tradition: The use of a communally shared cultural form bespeaking common values, beliefs, and connections, to address a current concern.[23]

The prophet Ezekiel was no 1968-style left-wing student militant; hence, the narratives of symbolic actions found in Ezekiel 4:1-5:17 and 12:1-20 have more to do with witness and integration than with agit-prop.[24] Thus, when Ezekiel 12:1-16 is understood as street theater, the prophet's pantomime, Janus-like, looks to the past and the future simultaneously. His gesture recalls the experience of his fellow exiles so as to announce what was yet to befall Jerusalem, the eventual fall of the city to Nebuchadrezzar's armies and the second deportation of its population: "I am a sign to you: as I have done, so shall it be done to them; they shall go into exile, into captivity" (12:11). Here, according to Moshe Greenberg,

> The purpose is . . . to convince his audience that the destruction of Jerusalem and the exile of its inhabitants are inevitable. It is not meant to enable the Jerusalemites to avert their fate, for their repentance is not called for or considered; no room is made for mitigating the doom. The message was to the exiles, whose sympathy with Jerusalem and hopes of speedy repatriation justified this stigmatization as "the rebellious house."[25]

Commissioned as a prophet-in-exile to address the exiles, Ezekiel is not addressing the inhabitants of Jerusalem about the fate that is to befall them. The performance scripted in chapter 12 is scripted for an audience of those already deported about the place and the people to whom they are bound by all that the exile's baggage of memory contains.

Ellen F. Davis calls attention to a second critique of Lang's presentation, suggesting that, despite the distance he establishes between his views and those of Fohrer, he shares Fohrer's assumption that the narratives of symbolic actions are to be understood literally as records of actual performances. To begin with, "in some cases such an interpretation . . . stretches the limits of credulity (the 430 days of bondage)." Furthermore, Ezekiel 4:4-8 also raises the issue of audience impact: "Lying bound for more than a year is something entirely different from a street theatre production; the cost of such a lengthy 'performance' may be considered far in excess of its impact."[26] Davis prudently suspends judgment, suggesting that "It is best to remain agnostic about whether any of the sign actions was actually performed. One can only say that, while a number of them present great difficulties for a literal interpretation, they are all comprehensible and effective as literary devices."[27]

In this vein, some studies suggest that the gap between prophet-as-performer and prophet-as-writer is not so wide as it was once thought to be. Davis maintains, "it is likely that Ezekiel composed his oracles in writing, yet in a manner deeply imbued with the forms and practices of traditional oral prophecy."[28] Indeed, while writing was a feature of prophecy from the eighth century on,

> Ezekiel greatly exceeded his predecessors in the degree to which he exploited the potential inherent in writing. . . . Ezekiel's was a fundamentally literate mind, i.e., his patterns of thought and expression were shaped by habits of reading and writing. Therefore, it was through him that Israelite prophecy for the first time received its *primary* impress from the new conditions and opportunities for communication created by writing.[29]

The swallowing of the scroll in Ezekiel's visionary call narrative (2:8-3:3) serves as an eloquent metaphor[30] for the role Davis suggests that this prophet took on.[31] In the light of these caveats and corrections, what remains of Lang's suggestion that Ezekiel's sign acts should be understood as performances analogous to street theater is the crucial and reciprocal connection between performance and script. Whether or not the sign actions were ever actually performed, the narratives themselves constitute a sort of script that has its own relative autonomy. Performance theorist Richard Schechner underscores the distinctions between—and the interpermeability of—performance and script:

> Drama is the domain of the author, composer, scenarist; script is the domain of the teacher, guru, shaman, master; theatre is the domain of the performer; performance is the domain of the audience. Clearly, in many situations, the author is also the guru and the performer; in some situations the performer is also the audience. The boundary between the performance and everyday life is arbitrary.[32]

In the case of the narratives of symbolic actions in Ezekiel, it might therefore be said that the literary activity of composing this material itself constitutes a sort of performance, the sort of "street theater," as it were, where the page itself becomes the stage, and Ezekiel's readers are the audience.

Ezekiel's audiences themselves are assigned an important role in the script of 12:1-16, not only in hope expressed in the stage directions given in 12:3, "Perhaps they will understand, though they are a rebellious house," but also in 12:9, where they are given a speaking part as their response to the prophet's enactment: "Mortal, has not the house of Israel, the rebellious house, said to you, 'What are you doing?'" This verse, with the explanation of the symbolic action that follows in verse 11, establishes an implicit distinction between the audience in the script and subsequent audiences who hear and read the script in its entirety. For readers and hearers outside the script of Ezekiel 12, the meaning of Ezekiel's action is already disclosed in verse 6, "For I have made you a sign for the house of Israel," whereas the audience within the script is left to wonder until the delivery of the prophet's lines in verse 11, "Say, I am a sign for you."

REWRITING THE SCRIPT: DIACHRONICITY, COHERENCE, AND CONSISTENCY

Turning again to the text of Ezekiel 12:1-16, further perplexity results from inconsistencies that many interpreters have resolved by resorting to what Greenberg describes as "literary surgery."[33] Here, too, the tension between performance and script comes to the surface. By its very nature, performance is ad hoc and ephemeral, here now, gone tomorrow. On the other hand, texts have a remarkable staying power, surviving by undergoing editing and adaptation over time. This appears to have been the case for Ezekiel 12. Zimmerli explains that "the narrative of the sign action 12:1-16, in which Ezekiel announces the deportation of the Jerusalem citizens, has undergone some reworking with features of a second action which dealt with the personal fate of Zedekiah at the downfall of Jerusalem."[34]

As for the events that precipitated this reworking, 2 Kings 25:4-7 describes what became of King Zedekiah, who sought to escape the desperate final siege of Jerusalem, only to be captured by the Babylonian army and brought before the King of Babylon: "They slaughtered the sons of Zedekiah; they bound him in fetters and took him to Babylon" (2 Kgs 25:7). Even if we did not have Ezekiel 12:10, "Say to them, 'Thus says the Lord God: This oracle concerns the prince in Jerusalem and all the house of Israel in it,'" Ezekiel 12:13 provides an unmistakable echo of Zedekiah's fate: "I will spread my net over him, and he shall be caught in my snare; and I will bring him to Babylon, the land of the Chaldeans, yet he shall not see it; and he shall die there."[35] Even Greenberg, whose holistic approach makes him hesitant to resort to question the integrity of the text, admits that this constitutes a "later reinterpretative touch."[36]

Insights from performance theory suggest another possible path through the obvious diachronic inconsistencies and incoherence of Ezekiel 12:1-16. If the composition of a script can itself be understood as a mode of performance, if writing itself constitutes a sort of enactment, then the same can be said of the adaptation and elaboration of this script that took place subsequent to the events of 587 BCE. Thus, on the one hand, the inconsistencies and incoherences that surface in Ezekiel 12:1-16 testify to the relative fixity of the text.[37] On the other hand, the emendation of the script of Ezekiel 12 to reflect the events of 587 BCE attests to a degree of flexibility that allows for sensitivity to the changing needs and expectations of changing audiences/readers/hearers.

FINALE: PERFORMANCE AND PERMANENCE

Among the challenges that remain for the analysis of the narratives of symbolic action is the relationship between this material and other material in Ezekiel. Are these narratives to be understood principally as "a form of preaching," as Zimmerli and others have suggested?[38] Do they, as Louis Ramlot suggests, "serve to illustrate, underscore and confirm the word, especially when they convey a dramatic message about the future of an individual or the people as a whole? These acts are performed to present the message of the prophets in a more forceful way."[39] Are they to be seen, as Lang understands them, as "teaching aids" that "visualize an aspect of the prophetic message or preaching"?[40] Kelvin Friebel's study considers them as being primarily forms of nonverbal communication.[41] If the visual, nonverbal dimension is foregrounded, then the relationship between this material and the abundant and elaborate vision report material in Ezekiel takes on new significance.

Only a few verses before Ezekiel receives and ingests the proffered scroll, he receives the following commission:

> Mortal, I am sending you to the people of Israel, to a nation of rebels who have rebelled against me; they and their ancestors have transgressed against me to this very day. The descendants are impudent and stubborn. I am sending you to them, and you shall say to them, "Thus says the Lord GOD." Whether they hear or refuse to hear (for they are a rebellious house), they shall know that there has been a prophet among them. (2:3-5)

These words are echoed in 12:2-3: "Mortal, you are living in the midst of a rebellious house, who have eyes to see but do not see, who have ears to hear but do not hear; for they are a rebellious house." Precisely because the prophetic word is reconfigured as text in Ezekiel, and performance as script, "God's word is no longer frustrated by the intransigence of any generation; it can wait until such time as it may be heard."[42] Unlike the ad hoc and ephemeral performances of street theater, their impact dependent on the willingness of an immediate audience to see and hear and remember, Ezekiel's narratives of symbolic action—whether or not they were ever performed—remain available for subsequent audiences, audiences whose circumstances may or may not correspond to those exiled with Ezekiel by the River Chebar.

6

An Exile's Baggage: A Postcolonial Reading of Ezekiel 20

ECHOES OF EXILE

Edward Said has observed, "To think of exile as beneficial, as a spur to humanism or to creativity, is to belittle its mutilations. It is produced by human beings for other human beings; it has torn millions of people from the nourishment of tradition, family, and geography."[1] In the reminiscences of Cuban-American theologian Ada María Isasi-Díaz we hear the echoes of exilic lament across the centuries in the bittersweet poetry of Psalm 137:

It was the summer of 1961, in Santa Rosa, California, when I first read Psalm 137. I remember resonating with most of what the psalm says; I remember feeling it could appropriately voice the pain I was experiencing being away from my country against my will. After the Cuban Missile Crisis in 1962 I realized that my absence from Cuba was to be a long one. Shortly after there came the day when my visa status was changed from "tourist": I became a refugee. . . . I recall vividly the day I dared mention to a friend how much I identified with Psalm 137. Jokingly she answered me, "Are you going to hang up your guitar from some palm tree?" I knew that though she and many others around me intended no harm, in reality they were incapable of understanding the sorrow of my being away from *la tierra que me vió nacer* (the land that witnessed my birth).[2]

Decades later, tens of millions of people continue to shoulder the burdens of an exile's baggage, as deportation, flight from armed conflict, and forced migration—raw and real—are neither ancient history nor old news for political, religious, and economic refugees and asylum seekers around the world. The Office of the United Nations High Commissioner for Refugees reports that at the end of 2009, some forty-nine million people around the world were forcibly displaced.[3] These numbers do not include the millions

who are classified as economic migrants, persons in economic need who
leave their countries of origin in pursuit of a decent living elsewhere, among
them the many Latin Americans who risk their lives to cross the militarized
border between the United States and Mexico.

It is because the deep river of migrant and refugee tears continues to flow
across the centuries from ancient Mesopotamia into our own time that this
study of Ezekiel—himself deported from Jerusalem in 597 BCE—makes no
pretense to detachment or neutrality.[4] As Liisa Malkki notes, "There has
emerged a new awareness of the global social fact that, now perhaps more
than ever before, people are chronically and routinely displaced."[5] The
pressing reality of involuntary displacement and dislocation of so many in
our own time may be said to frame a moral challenge for biblical scholarship
generally and for the interpretation of exilic texts in particular. Daniel L.
Smith-Christopher frames that imperative in the following terms:

> All biblical books are products of a community of transmission, and
> the community of the book of Ezekiel is clearly a community struggling
> with mobile identities and transnational culture and theology. *That* is
> why Ezekiel's crisis is our crisis. And that is why we listen to Ezekiel
> today. It was economics, control, and power that dragged Ezekiel
> to Babylon, and it is economics, control, and power that create our
> current situation.[6]

While I am sympathetic to Smith-Christopher's take on Ezekiel, I find that
Fernando Segovia's hermeneutics of engagement and otherness sounds a
note of salutary caution, and I am inclined to believe that Smith-Christopher
himself would not disagree. Segovia argues,

> Rather than positing any type of direct or immediate entrance into
> the text, the hermeneutics of otherness and engagement argues for the
> historical and cultural remoteness of the text. Such a hermeneutics
> begins, therefore, by recognizing that the biblical text comes from a
> very different historical situation and cultural matrix, a very different
> experience and culture; that all texts, including the biblical texts, are
> contextual products; and that no text—not even the biblical text—is
> atemporal, asocial, ahistorical, speaking uniformly across time and
> culture.[7]

Likewise,

> [T]he reader is also to be regarded as socially and culturally conditioned,
> as other to both text and other readers. . . . Rather than seeking after
> impartiality or objectivity, presuming to universality, and claiming
> to read like anyone or everyone, the hermeneutics of otherness and

engagement argues for a self-conscious exposition and analysis of the reader's strategy for reading, the theoretical foundations behind this strategy, and the social location underlying such a strategy.[8]

Thus, while Ezekiel's crisis is *not* our crisis, *our* crisis may well move us to read Ezekiel's crisis with urgently interested eyes. This chapter suggests that postcolonial hermeneutics might provide us with one set of useful optics for this purpose. First, I will offer a sketch of postcolonial theory as it has begun to gain ground in biblical interpretation. Then, I will offer a reading of Ezekiel 20 through the lens of postcolonial criticism's attention to the dynamics of deterritorialization, assimilation, and resistance.

WHAT *IS* POSTCOLONIAL HERMENEUTICS AND WHY DOES IT MATTER ANYWAY?

Postcolonial hermeneutics, a relative newcomer in the discipline of biblical studies, appeared on the scene in the last decade through the efforts of scholars from the so-called Third World and scholars from the Third World diaspora with academic appointments in First World settings.[9] Arif Dirlik identifies the pedigree of postcolonialism in the following terms:

[P]ostcolonialism has its intellectual origins in the poststructuralist revolt against the very real limits of Eurocentric modernity (in both its liberal and Marxist versions), and has answered a very real critical need: not only in calling into question the obliviousness to the local of generalized notions of modernity, but also in calling attention to problems of a novel nature that have emerged with recent transformation in global political and social relations.[10]

Postcolonialism emerged when the subjects of empire—the British Empire in particular—began to *write back*, to borrow a phrase from the title of a key text of postcolonial theory.[11] Dirlik goes on to locate the rise of postcolonialism on the academic horizon, suggesting that

The term in its current usage acquired popularity in the late 1980's, and rapidly catapulted to the forefront of cultural studies, making an impact not only across academic disciplines, but through slogans such as "multiculturalism," in politics as well, especially the politics of academic institutions. The dynamic power moving the discourse of postcoloniality was the visible impact on cultural studies of intellectuals of Third World origin in First World institutions. . . . The emergence of postcolonialism to the forefront of consciousness has coincided over the last decade with the increasing visibility of the term "diaspora," which may well be the immediate social condition for a postcolonial consciousness. Diasporas have become a highly visible component of a global social landscape.[12]

R. S. Sugirtharajah, who is among those who have taken the lead in transposing postcolonial theory from (nonbiblical) literary criticism into biblical studies maintains that "The major achievement of postcolonialism is to inaugurate a new era of academic inquiry which brings to the fore the overlapping issues of empire, nation, ethnicity, migration and language," and he suggests, vis-à-vis biblical interpretation, that "postcolonialism is roughly defined as scrutinizing and exposing colonial domination and power as these are embodied in biblical texts and in interpretations, and as searching for alternative hermeneutics while thus overturning and dismantling colonial perspectives."[13]

Fernando Segovia offers a similarly broad description of the range of postcolonial studies: "I take the by now common designation of 'Postcolonial Studies' to signify the study of the realm of the geopolitical—the relationship between center and margins, metropolis and periphery, on a global political scale: the imperial and the colonial. Such a relationship I further see as encompassing both social and cultural 'reality'—social formation and cultural production."[14]

In some sense, the concerns of postcolonial criticism do not appear unfamiliar to more conventionally conceived biblical studies. In fact, as Stephen D. Moore suggests,

> Much traditional biblical scholarship reads like postcolonial criticism *avant la lettre*—or else badly done. That hallowed gateway to biblical criticism, for example, the "Old" or "New" Testament introduction (whether the textbook or the course), has derived much of its efficacy and allure from its ability to summon "exotic" empires from the shadows of the biblical texts and parade them before the student: Egypt, Assyria, Babylon, Persia, Greece, Rome. So much biblical scholarship is already a reflection on imperialism, colonialism, and the resistance they inevitably elicit.[15]

Sugirtharajah and others who have begun to employ postcolonial hermeneutics in biblical interpretation are not unaware of the controversies surrounding postcolonialism. The cynicism of Russell Jacoby is not atypical:

> "Oh it's something post-colonial," responded the gift giver to my friend's question about a birthday present, a piece of pottery with an unusual pattern. Was it a Mayan design? Or Persian? No, it was post-colonial—the latest catchall term to dazzle the academic mind. . . . If

you think history or sociology or anthropology has an identity crisis, try post-colonial studies. Its enthusiasts themselves don't know what it is. Indeed, this is part of its charm. Post-colonial studies is obsessed with itself. Few agree on where it came from, what it includes, or where it is going.[16]

Marxist critic Terry Eagleton's voice is prominent in the chorus of postcolonialism's cultured despisers, as he observes, "There must be surely be in existence somewhere a secret handbook for aspiring postcolonial theorists, whose second rule reads: 'begin your essay by calling into question the whole notion of postcolonialism.' (The first rule reads: 'Be as obscurantist as you can decently get away with without your stuff going absolutely unread')."[17]

Well aware of the hypnotic power of discourse for its own sake among academics, Sugirtharajah insists on the praxeological imperatives that impinge on the responsible postcolonial critic.[18] While the liberationist inclinations of postcolonial critics are clear, postcolonial critical practices are characterized by a very deliberate methodological eclecticism, an eclecticism that Sugirtharajah suggests is itself a strategic move:

> Postcolonialism's critical procedure is an amalgam of different methods ranging from the now unfashionable form-criticism to contemporary literary methods. It is interdisciplinary in nature and pluralistic in its outlook. It is more an avenue of inquiry than a homogeneous project. One of the significant aspects of postcolonialism is its theoretical and intellectual catholicism. It thrives on inclusiveness, and it is attracted to all kinds of tools and disciplinary fields, as long as they probe injustices, produce new knowledge which problematizes well-entrenched positions and enhances the lives of the marginalized.[19]

The eclecticism of postcolonial biblical criticism is neither random nor capricious. Postcolonial biblical critics neither conceal their own social locations, nor do they mask their ideological investment in and commitment to their constituencies. Sugirtharajah lays out three intersecting tasks for postcolonial biblical criticism:

> First, scrutiny of biblical documents for their colonial entanglements: the Bible as a collection of documents which came out of various colonial contexts—Egyptian, Persian, Assyrian, Hellenistic and Roman . . . needs to be investigated again. . . . It will revalue the colonial ideology, stigmatization and negative portrayals embedded in the content, plot and characterization. It will scour the biblical pages for how colonial intentions and assumptions informed and influenced the production of the texts. It will attempt to resurrect lost voices and

causes which are distorted or silenced in the canonized text. It will address issues such as nationalism, ethnicity, deterritorialization, and identity, which arise in the wake of colonialism.

The second task of postcolonial criticism is to engage in reconstructive reading of biblical texts. Postcolonial reading will reread biblical texts from the perspective of postcolonial concerns such as liberation struggles of the past and present . . . it will interact with and reflect on postcolonial circumstances such as hybridity, fragmentation, deterritorialization, and hyphenated, double or multiple, identities. One postcolonial concern is the unexpected amalgamation of peoples, ideas, cultures, languages, and religions.

The third task of postcolonial criticism is to interrogate both colonial and metropolitan interpretations. The aim here is to draw attention to the inescapable effects of colonization and colonial ideologies on interpretative works such as commentarial writings, and on the historical and administrative records which helped to (re) inscribe colonial ideologies and consolidate the colonial presence. . . . Postcolonial interpretation will also investigate interpretations which contested colonial interpretations and concerns. It will bring to the fore how the invaded, often caricatured as abused victims or grateful beneficiaries, transcended these images and wrested interpretation from the invaders, starting a process of self-discovery, appropriation and subversion.[20]

To the growing body of postcolonial studies, biblical criticism informed by postcolonial theory contributes a sense of depth by calling attention to histories of empire and colonization that predate (and that have directly and indirectly influenced) the development of European imperial and colonial initiatives in Africa, Asia, and the Americas beginning in the early modern era. While it makes little sense simply to set Queen Victoria's British Empire side by side with Nebuchadrezzar's Neo-Babylonian Empire, postcolonial biblical critics argue that quite a bit can be learned by using the critical tools crafted to investigate texts that emerged under the influence of the former to re-examine texts that emerged under the influence of the latter. It is easy to see how such categories as deterritorialization, diaspora, ethnicity, identity (including hyphenated, double, or multiple identities), hybridity, assimilation, and resistance might be useful tools for sorting out some of the entanglements of ancient texts with ancient empires. At the same time, the place of the Bible close to the religious heart of the European imperial and missionary enterprise makes biblical interpretation from a postcolonial vantage a valuable contribution to the intellectual history of the European colonization of Africa, Asia, and the Americas.

To illustrate some of the moves of postcolonial biblical interpretation, I offer two examples that suggest the wide range of approaches postcolonial critics have explored. First, I discuss Francisco García-Treto's reading of the Joseph story in Genesis 39-41 from the standpoint of the subfield of diaspora studies. Then I turn to Daniel L. Smith-Christopher's provocative postcolonial treatment of Ezekiel from the standpoint of the subfield of refugee studies. These two studies converge in their attention to the impact of exile as a consequence of empire and colonialism. "The very nature of exile," says Justo González, is "a life in which one is forced to revolve around a center that is not one's own, and that in many ways one does not wish to own. Exile is a dislocation of the center, with all the ambiguities of such dislocation. Thus the exiled poet sings about not singing. . . . 'How could we sing the LORD's song in a foreign land?'"[21]

In "Hyphenating Joseph: A View of Genesis 39-41 from the Cuban Diaspora," Francisco García-Treto offers a reading of the Joseph story mediated through Cuban-American cultural critic Gustavo Pérez Firmat's analysis of a new exile's process of adaptation to a new homeland, a three stage process of (1) substitution, (2) destitution, and (3) institution.[22] Substitution, the first stage, "consists of an effort to create substitutes or copies of the home culture."[23] For the Cuban-American diaspora, this substitution took the form of the creation of "little Havana" in Miami. In the Joseph story in *Genesis Rabbah* 86:5 (on Gen 39:3), we find that "In the early days of his captivity in Potiphar's house, Joseph goes about repeating (whispering) the Torah which he had learned in his father's house. This is his strenuous attempt to 're-member' his identity and culture, to keep 'God with him.'"[24]

Destitution, Pérez Firmat's second stage of exilic adaptation, occurs when "the awareness of displacement crushes the fantasy of rootedness."[25] Here, García-Treto suggests, "Among the many factors that can bring about an awareness of being displaced, none is perhaps more frequent or disturbing in the experience of exiles than the experience of being 'put in one's place' by the prejudices and stereotypes of the dominant culture."[26] García-Treto suggests that in the Joseph story this stereotyping happens in several ways. For Potiphar's wife, Joseph is stereotyped as a sexual object, while for Pharaoh's baker, Joseph is "a Hebrew lad there with us" (Gen 40:12). García-Treto speculates, tongue in cheek, "Did the Egyptians have equivalents of the 'Latin lover' or of the 'hot-blooded *señorita*' stereotypes for Hebrews?"[27]

The third stage, institution, is the construction of a hybrid, hyphenated self. Joseph becomes a Hebrew-*hyphen*-Egyptian, "so thoroughly at home, at least in the externals of Egyptian culture, that by the denouement of the story his constructed identity functions as a successful disguise to fool his own brothers."[28]

In his moves back and forth from the world behind and of the text to the world in front of the text, it is ultimately the praxeological dimension of postcolonial biblical hermeneutics that drives García-Treto's reading.[29] He concludes that the Joseph story "is the story of many diasporas, over many centuries and across many borders . . . a story of survival and success, of reunion and reconciliation, in a word, of salvation."[30] García-Treto's study of Genesis 39-41 takes up what Sugirtharajah identifies as the second task of postcolonial biblical criticism, as a rereading of the Joseph story from the perspective of his own hyphenated identity as a member of the Cuban-American diaspora.

The clever title of Daniel L. Smith-Christopher's study, "Ezekiel on Fanon's Couch: A Postcolonialist Dialogue with David Halperin's *Seeking Ezekiel*," offers a clue to Smith-Christopher's approach. The Afro-Caribbean anticolonial activist, philosopher, and psychiatrist Frantz Fanon (1925-1961) is widely regarded by postcolonial theorists as "a romantic hero of decolonization."[31] Born in Martinique and trained as a psychiatrist in France after the Second World War (in which he fought as a member of the Free French), Fanon's experiences both in France and in Algeria sensitized him to the crisis of colonialism. His first book, *Peau noire, masques blancs* (*Black Skin, White Masks*) focused on the psychology of oppression.[32] In *L'an V de la révolution algérienne* (*A Dying Colonialism*) and *Les damnés de la terre* (*The Wretched of the Earth*) he advocated revolutionary resistance to French colonialism in Algeria.[33]

Smith-Christopher writes, "Though Fanon is often remembered for his political philosophy, he was also a pioneer in the exploration of the psychological impact of colonization and of the sociopolitical context of psychological illness."[34] It is through this door that Smith-Christopher returns to revisit the question of Ezekiel's psychological condition. Critical of the Freudian approach adopted by David J. Halperin's *Seeking Ezekiel: Text and Psychology*,[35] Smith-Christopher argues that

> tendencies to read the psychological state of Ezekiel totally apart from the social and psychological experiences he suffered are symptoms of the same avoidance in other biblical scholarly analyses—an avoidance of the Exile as a real event where human beings deeply suffered. Any psychological assumptions about Ezekiel derived apart from serious attention to the Exile are thus tantamount to blaming the victim.[36]

Therefore, "when Halperin ignores the social circumstances and realities of the Exile in order to read Ezekiel as struggling with sexuality, he is blaming the victim."[37]

For Smith-Christopher, understanding the sociopolitical context of the Exile and of Ezekiel's condition as a deportee to Babylon is key to understanding the prophet's peculiar behavior, especially the bizarre sign-acts: "What appears to have driven Ezekiel to act out the horrors of conquest—the scattering of refugees in fear, the butchering of prisoners captured, and the taking of exiles? The answer is what drives thousands of traumatized human beings to relive memories that can literally drive them to despair, alcoholism, silence, and suicide."[38] Smith-Christopher finds a more coherent framework for considering Ezekiel's condition in the symptomatology and literature of post-traumatic stress disorder, insisting that this "forces us to ask serious questions about the adequacy of any psychological assessment of Ezekiel that does not appreciate the historical and social implications of the siege of Jerusalem, the deportations, and the executions by the Babylonian armies in the Exile."[39] Thus, in Smith-Christopher's reading, Ezekiel carried painfully heavy baggage into exile, baggage that readers unpack in the text of the book as it witnesses to the impact of the Exile.

Smith-Christopher's study stands as a contribution to postcolonial biblical criticism not so much in view of his deliberate nod in the direction of Frantz Fanon but especially as it demonstrates the entanglement of the book of Ezekiel with its sociopolitical context in the Neo-Babylonian imperial project, that is, with the forced dislocation of Ezekiel in 597 BCE from Jerusalem to Tel-Abib by the river Chebar.[40] Smith-Christopher's study of Ezekiel, like García-Treto's study of Genesis 29-31, is driven mainly by praxeological concerns. He reads Ezekiel "the refugee prophet" side by side with Homi K. Bhabha's assessment of the human costs of globalization: "The demography of the new internationalism is the history of postcolonial migration, the narratives of cultural and political diaspora, the major social displacements of peasant and aboriginal communities, the poetics of exile, the grim prose of political and economic refugees."[41] It is his acute consciousness of this reality that ultimately led Smith-Christopher to articulate a biblical theology of exile in his book by that very title.[42]

BETWEEN ASSIMILATION AND RESISTANCE: A POSTCOLONIAL APPROACH TO EZEKIEL 20[43]

What you are thinking will never happen: "We shall become like the nations, like the tribes of the countries, worshipping wood and stone."
—Ezek 20:32

Identity, hybridity, assimilation, and resistance are commonplace in the idiom of postcolonial criticism. Frantz Fanon puts the issue before us more forcefully: "Colonisation is not satisfied merely with holding a people in its grip and emptying the native's brain of all form and content. By a kind of perverted logic, it turns to the past of oppressed people, and distorts, disfigures and destroys it."[44] This is the perversely effective logic of the Neo-Babylonian imperial practice of forced deportation, of which the prophet Ezekiel was himself a victim. As Daniel Block notes,

Mesopotamia had long been the benefactor of forced Israelite immigration. According to neo-Assyrian records hundreds of thousands of citizens from the northern kingdom had been dispersed throughout the empire. . . . Nebuchadrezzar continued this policy with the Judeans, bringing the cream of the population to Babylon and settlements nearby. These deportation policies were driven by several objectives: (1) to break down bonds of nationality and resistance; (2) to destroy political structures by removing civil and religious leaders; (3) to provide conscripts for the Babylonian army; (4) to bolster the economy of Babylon.[45]

Some scholars, at least since Martin Noth, have gone to considerable lengths to downplay the impact of the deportation on the Judeans exiled to Babylon. Noth contended that "the exiles were not 'prisoners' but represented a compulsorily transplanted subject population *who were able to move about freely in their daily life*, but were presumably compelled to render compulsory labor service."[46] Bustenay Oded declares,

There is no clear and explicit evidence that the Mesopotamian exiles lived under conditions of suppression or were subjected to religious persecution at any time during the years 586-583 BCE. . . . One gets the impression that they had a certain internal autonomy and that they enjoyed the freedom to manage their community life (Ezek. 33.30-3). . . . The exiles had the benefit of personal freedom.[47]

With respect to religion as a marker of the persistence (or otherwise) of the identity of the deportees from Judah, Oded maintains that

many of them did not lose their national identity and their special religious nature, and they persisted in maintaining the link with their homeland, with Jerusalem and with the dynasty of David. The Assyrians as well as the Babylonians customarily permitted national-ethnic groups, exiles or not, to express their national and religious identity, obviously without national independence.[48]

Hans Barstad's sarcasm is downright disturbing:

When reading the commentators on the biblical texts relating to these events, one sometimes gets the Sunday school feeling that they regard the Babylonians as an evil people who came to destroy the true believers in Judah out of sheer wickedness, and that the bringing of Judeans into exile was a mean punishment or base revenge following the uprising of the Judean king. It is high time that we start thinking about the whole matter from a rather different perspective. The Neo-

Babylonian empire represented a highly developed civilization, with an advanced political and economic structure. . . . Already at an early stage the economy of the Mesopotamian countries had turned into an aggressive and expansionist one, soon to be followed also by territorial expansion. The conquest of the neighbouring countries became necessary in order to secure control of vital trade routes, and taxes and tribute were needed for the consolidation of the empire.[49]

We cannot help but ask, "Was Neo-Babylonian imperialist adventurism just the necessary price of doing business, in which the fate of the Judean exiles constituted easily dismissed collateral damage?" We need to recall that although they belonged to the elite classes of the Judean population, Ezekiel and the other Judeans by the Chebar were in fact forced deportees, and not voluntary expatriates. That being the case, Ezekiel 20:32 can be recognized—through a postcolonial optic—as an unmistakable expression of destitution, Pérez-Firmat's second stage of exilic adaptation, in which "the awareness of displacement crushes the fantasy of rootedness." Pérez-Firmat elaborates: at this point exiles feel "that the ground has been taken out from under them, that they no longer know their place, that they have in fact lost their place. Rather than nostalgic, they now feel estranged and disconnected."[50]

Translators and exegetes alike are of two very different minds when it comes to Ezekiel 20:32. Moshe Greenberg renders this verse, "And what has entered your minds shall never, never be, your thinking, 'We will become like the nations, like the families of the earth, serving wood and stone.'"[51] He finds here an echo of 1 Samuel 8:20, the adamant refusal of the elders of Israel to listen to Samuel's warning against their insistent request for a king to govern Israel: "[W]e are determined to have a king over us, *so that we also may be like other nations.*" Therefore Greenberg holds that Ezekiel 20:32 expresses "the wish of the people, not their despair" and that "It is this defiant wish that arouses God's indignation (here, vs. 33)," whereas to despair God "responds with encouraging exhortation (33:10ff.; 37:12ff.)."[52]

Walther Zimmerli takes the other side. He recognizes that the phrase "like other nations" is "as a rule interpreted as a cohortative" and that the phrase "has usually been understood as the expression of a definite idolatrous decision."[53] While aware of this, Zimmerli holds that "it is more correct to find in v. 32, in accordance with 33:10; 37:11, the expression of a deep despair. . . . If the judgment of being scattered among the nations . . . [by YHWH] is already an accomplished fact (v. 23) . . . is any hope left of any other future than dispersion among the nations with all its bitter religious consequences?"[54] Thus, Zimmerli renders 20:32 as follows: "It will never happen, what has arisen (as a thought) in your spirit, that you say 'We shall become like the nations, like the families of the (heathen) lands and worship wood and stone.'"[55]

Leslie C. Allen's rendering of 30:32 is also in line with this: "The thought that is in your minds will never happen, the prospect of your being like other nations, like the communities of foreign countries, worshiping wood and stone."[56] The practice of "worshiping wood and stone" is mentioned in Deuteronomy 4:28; 28:36, 64; 29:16; 2 Kings 19:18; and Isaiah 37:19. Adrian Graffy argues that the phrase "is necessary to complete the sense and should not be deleted as a deuteronomic addition."[57] It would seem quite a stretch to take "We shall become like the nations, like the tribes of the countries, worshipping wood and stone" as a cry of defiance or as anything but an expression of the most abject despair. Its resonances echo in the sentiments of Lamentations 1:3: "Judah has gone into exile with suffering and hard servitude; she lives now among the nations, and finds no resting place; her pursuers have all overtaken her in the midst of her distress."

Stepping back for a moment to consider Ezekiel 20:32 in its immediate literary context, I note, with Graffy, that while "Ezekiel 20 has sometimes been considered a unit," most commentators "find it necessary to divide the chapter."[58] Graffy suggests that the break should be made before verse 32 and that verse 32 marks the beginning of a disputation speech that continues until verse 44. The disputation begins by taking up a quotation attributed to Ezekiel's fellow exiles, a pattern that is also found in 12:27, 33:10, and 37:11. Graffy observes that "all the quotations in disputation speeches attributed to the exiles in Ezekiel express despair and hopelessness, whereas those of the people left in Jerusalem have a confident, arrogant tone" (11:3, 15; 12:22; 18:2; 33:24).[59] He also insists that despite the echoes of 1 Samuel 8:20, the tone we find in Ezekiel 20:32 "is similar to that found in Ezek 25,8, where Moab insults Judah by describing her as 'like all the nations,'" and that in Ezekiel 20:32, "The people despondently accept this as a fact. They consider they have lost their special place among the nations."[60]

Following the quotation in 30:32 we find a programmatic refutation in verse 32 that is introduced with an oath: "As I live, says the Lord GOD, with strong hand and arm outstretched I will rule over you." The refutation then proceeds in three parts (vv. 34-38, 39-42, 43-44), each of which concludes with the recognition formula "you will know that I am YHWH." The divine response to the despair of the deportees is a direct challenge to Nebuchadrezzar's sovereignty.

Fittingly enough, in verses 34-38 the reestablishment and emphatic reaffirmation of sovereignty over the exiles by their deity takes place through a deterritorialization that is likened to the Exodus from Egypt:

> I will bring you out from the peoples and gather you from the lands where you are scattered. . . . I will bring you into the wilderness of the peoples and I will enter into judgment with you there face to face. Just as I judged your ancestors in the wilderness of the land of Egypt, so I will judge you, says the Lord GOD. . . . I will lead you into the obligation of the covenant . . . and you will know that I am YHWH.

Contra Greenberg, who suggests that "the wilderness of the peoples" is the "Syro-Arabian desert, bounded by various peoples,"[61] the reference need not be geographically localized. "The desert is important here simply as the typological counterpart to the first 'desert of Egypt,'"[62] the desert in which the identity of Israel in covenant with its God first took shape.

The promised deterritorialization into "the wilderness of the peoples" where divine sovereignty over the deportees is to be reaffirmed is followed in verses 39-42 by a reterritorialization, the reestablishment of the deportees in their deity's own land:

> On my holy mountain, the mountain height of Israel, says the Lord GOD, there all the house of Israel, all of them, shall serve me in the land; there I will accept them. . . . As a pleasing odor I will accept you, when I bring you out from the peoples, and gather you out of the countries where you have been scattered; and I will manifest my holiness among you in the sight of the nations. (Ezek 20:40-41)

At this point, the disputation speech addresses the despair of the deportees with an unmistakable expression of resistance against the Neo-Babylonian imperial ideology. David Stephen Vanderhooft cites a neo-Babylonian inscription in which Nebuchadrezzar is presented as protector of humanity:

> (As for) the widespread peoples whom Marduk, the lord, gave into my hand . . . I continually strove for their welfare. (In) a just path and correct conduct I directed them ... I stretched a roof over them in the wind, (and) a canopy in the tempest. I brought all of them under the sway of Babylon. The yield of the lands, the abundance of the mountain regions, the produce of the countries, I received within it (Babylon). Into its eternal shadow I assembled all the peoples for good.

Vanderhooft then explains:

> This passage and its parallels emphasize the idea that the king is the protector of all humanity. Thus, the gods grant the king rulership over the "widespread peoples," a phrase that refers to all populations under royal control. The king is thus able to better their circumstances; he is, in short, their divinely appointed protector and benefactor, not their conqueror. The modern historian might argue that this is merely a pious fraud, designed to blunt the crassness of the more important concern, also expressed here: namely, the material exploitation of conquered populations for the benefit of a ruling elite. The notion of the king as protector of humanity, however, deserves attention as an important aspect of the imperial theory.[63]

Furthermore,

> [A]ccording to the imperial ideology, the conquest . . . of non-Babylonian populations is not to their detriment, since the Babylonian elite views "the eternal shadow of Babylon" as a restorative one. Similarly, there is no reference in Nebuchadnezzar's inscriptions to the king placing his yoke (*nīru*) upon conquered people, as there so often is in Assyrian royal inscriptions. Rather, Nebuchadnezzar asserts that he gathers the people into Babylon's shadow *tābiš*, "for good, peacefully."[64]

The disputation speech of Ezekiel 20:32-44 is especially striking in the face of claims like these, claims that could easily have led the deportees to the level of despair that the saying in 20:32 expresses. The Neo-Babylonian imperial ideology established clear and unmistakable distinctions between the metropolitan center and the conquered subject peripheries, mapping their relationships in ways that reflected the exploitative flow of labor and goods *from* Judah (and elsewhere) *to* Babylon. The prophetic refutation of the despairing saying of 20:32 utterly rejects the Babylonian configuration of metropolis and peripheries out of hand, to present the Judean deportees with an alternate, resistant worldview: "As a pleasing odor I will accept you, when I bring you out from the peoples, and gather you out of the countries where you have been scattered; and I will manifest my holiness among you in the sight of the nations. You shall know that I am the LORD, when I bring you into the land of Israel, the country that I swore to give to your ancestors" (Ezek 20:41-42). This promise anticipates the elaborate restoration vision of chapters 40-48, which includes the detailed mapping of the land "for inheritance among the twelve tribes of Israel (47:13).[65] All this casts doubt on the label Greenberg assigns to Ezekiel 20:1-44, namely, "threat of a new Exodus," and suggests instead that it might be more fitting to see here the *promise* of a new Exodus.

To fill out this postcolonial take on Ezekiel 20:32 just a bit more, I offer two further interrelated observations, both of which touch on the relationship between 20:32-44 and the first part of the chapter, 20:1-31. In that respect, I agree with Graffy's position that 20:32-44 has its own integrity as a disputation speech as well as with his explanation that the "lack of a full introduction to the disputation speech suggests that it was intended to be closely related to what precedes, perhaps to balance the negative tone of vv. 1-31 with brighter prospects."[66] On the basis of the relationship between the two parts of Ezekiel 20, a look at the beginning of the chapter may prove instructive, first with respect to the date and, second, regarding the audience: "In the seventh year, in the fifth month, on the tenth day of the month, certain elders of Israel came to consult the LORD, and sat down before me."

Commentators note that the oracle is dated to 591 BCE, according to the pattern in Ezekiel whereby events are identified with Jehoiachin's exile as the *terminus a quo*. The "seventh year" is the seventh year since the deportation of Jehoiachin, two years after the first such date of Ezekiel's inaugural vision (1:2).[67] The first siege of Jerusalem in 597 BCE is a constant reference point for the exiled priest-prophet, and the dated oracles are a clear indication of how deep the scars of this event were (see 2 Kgs 24:10-20). Recall the autobiographical remarks of Fernando Segovia, quoted at the beginning of this paper, the still-vivid memories of September 10, 1961, several decades after the fact, as he said, "I still recall that journey as if it had taken place but yesterday or last week, although I was only thirteen at the time."[68]

The occasion of the oracle in Ezekiel 20:1-32 is the arrival of "certain elders of Israel" in the presence of the prophet "to consult the LORD." The inclusion in verses 3 and 31, "As I live, says the Lord GOD, I will not be consulted by you," indicates that the elders are the audience for verses 1-31, and suggests (in the absence of any indication to the contrary) that they continue to be the audience for verses 32-44. This is the third time in the book that the elders approach Ezekiel (also see 8:1; 14:1), and it is also the third time that they face condemnation for the sin of idolatry (in 8:11-12 they are observed *in flagrante delictu*).[69]

While the accusation can be understood under the rubric of the self-destructive rhetoric of blaming the victim, it might also be suggested that the sin of devotion to deities other than the national deities received such intense condemnation because it already represented an assimilationist behavior that threatened the distinctiveness of the people's identity.[70] Thus, the remedies proposed in the refutation portion of the disputation speech (20:33-44) emphasize the recognition formula ("you will know that I am YHWH," 20:38, 42).

While the struggle over identity, between assimilation and resistance, was an issue before 597 BCE, the deportation of Ezekiel and the elders of Judah and the collapse of any viable notion of national autonomy and self-determination made it an even more urgent matter. The pre-deportation polemic against the worship of gods other than the national deity becomes escalated into a discourse of subaltern resistance for a population of involuntary deportees. While Oded may speak confidently about the survival of "the national religious identity" during the Exile "because of the celebration of such traditional customs as Sabbath observance . . . and circumcision and because of the activity of prophets like Jeremiah, Ezekiel, and the so-called Second Isaiah,"[71] there can be no doubt that the Babylonian military actions against Jerusalem and its population in 597 and 587 BCE had a deliberately debilitating impact on individuals and on institutions: "Disaster comes upon disaster, rumor follows rumor; they shall keep seeking a vision from the prophet; instruction shall perish from the priest, and counsel from the elders. The king shall mourn, the prince shall be wrapped in despair, and the hands of the people of the land will tremble" (Ezek 7:26-27a).[72] This was the heavy baggage of exile, which the prophet symbolically packs and takes up in Ezekiel 12. How many are the refugees and asylum seekers, undocumented economic migrants and other itinerants in our own century, who just might recognize in Ezekiel's baggage something of their own?

CONCLUSION

Edward Said writes,

> Exile is one of the saddest fates. In premodern times banishment was a particularly dreadful punishment since it not only meant years of aimless wandering away from family and familiar places, but also meant being a sort of permanent outcast, someone who never felt at home, and was always at odds with the environment, inconsolable about the past, bitter about the present and the future. . . . During the twentieth century, exile has been transformed . . . into a cruel punishment of whole communities and peoples, often the inadvertent result of impersonal forces such as war, famine and disease.[73]

By taking another look at Ezekiel 20 from a postcolonial perspective, this chapter has suggested that in some sense the river of deportees' tears that daily grows wider and deeper in our own day flows from as far upstream as the waters of Babylon in the sixth century BCE. Taking Ezekiel 20:32 as an expression of what Pérez-Firmat identified as destitution proves helpful in taking sides on the question of whether that verse describes defiance or despair. Reading the disputation speech in 20:33-44 as an expression of resistance, the call for a new Exodus, and a new settlement of the land of Israel acquires new significance as a minority discourse that rejects the mapping of metropolis and margins imposed on the Judeans by the Babylonian imperial ideology. Not everyone who was compelled to live under Babylon's eternal shadow found the shade comforting. For many it spelled the gloom of shattered hope. Is it any surprise that they sat and wept?

Finally, the praxeological turn, the question of the practical difference that reading makes. Recall Sugirtharajah's admonition to the would-be postcolonial biblical critic: "Postcolonial hermeneutics has to be a pragmatic engagement, an engagement in which praxis is not an extra option or a subsidiary enterprise taken on in the aftermath of judicious deconstruction and reconstruction of the texts."[74] In some sense, it is the present predicament of refugees, asylum seekers, and migrants that sent me back to Ezekiel 20

in the first place. If that is where I stay, then the work remains unfinished.[75]
If, on the other hand, this rereading of Ezekiel 20 returns us to the world in
front of the text with eyes and ears wide open to those in our own time who
shoulder an exile's baggage, and if the deportee prophet Ezekiel urges us to
seek and to enact deeds (and not just words) of resistance and hope, then
perhaps this sort of reading makes a difference.

7

"They Could Not Speak the Language of Judah": Rereading Nehemiah 13 between Brooklyn and Jerusalem[1]

READING NEHEMIAH IN BROOKLYN

Let me begin with a confession of sorts: I never read Ezra or Nehemiah in the seminary, and it is probably a good thing that I didn't and that my professors in biblical studies courses ignored this material altogether.[2] When I returned from Rome after seminary studies there, I was assigned to serve as parochial vicar at the Church of Our Lady of Loreto on Sackman Street, on the border between the Brownsville and East New York sections of Brooklyn. I had never heard of the place, and so just a few days after arriving back in New York I looked it up on the map and made my way there together with a classmate from La Crosse, Wisconsin, who was staying with my family for a few days. When my classmate and I arrived at the run-down rectory that stands beside this Italian Renaissance-style building and sat down with the pastor to make our acquaintances, the first words out of the pastor's mouth took the form of a question: he wanted to know what in the world I could possibly have done to deserve an assignment to that corner of the diocese.

As my classmate and I drove around the neighborhood later that afternoon, we continued to be haunted by the very same question. When I arrived at Our Lady of Loreto, which was founded to serve Italian immigrants of an earlier era, the church had become home to a mostly Hispanic (Puerto Rican and Dominican) and African American congregation, with notable exceptions that included three of the neighborhood's remaining Italian American matriarchs, Marie Disco, Margaret Giangone, and the now-centenarian Filomena ("Fannie") Di Napoli—who were everyone's honorary godmothers, grandmothers, and great-grandmothers. The first issue of the Roman Catholic Diocese of Brooklyn's weekly newspaper, *The Tablet* (April

4, 1908), carried a front-page story (with a photograph) about the dedication of the Church of Our Lady of Loreto.

Through whatever twist of chance or of providence—and possibly even a little of both—it was at Our Lady of Loreto that I got around to reading Ezra and Nehemiah for the first time and in ways that my seminary courses in biblical studies could never have taught me. Our Lady of Loreto was one of the founding members of East Brooklyn Churches (EBC),[3] an affiliate of Saul Alinsky's Industrial Areas Foundation (IAF). After getting its feet wet and its hands dirty in the hard work of community organizing during the late 1970s and early 1980s with small-scale and relatively easy victories such as food store cleanups and the installation of street signs, EBC took on the much more formidable task of building thousands of affordable single family, owner-occupied homes.[4]

Taking up the controversial idea of building developer and *New York Daily News* columnist I. D. Robbins that home ownership could generate community pride and stable neighborhoods in ways that high-rise rental housing could never achieve, this ecumenical organization launched a project that was dubbed the Nehemiah Plan on the basis of a sermon preached by the Reverend Johnny Ray Youngblood, the pastor of EBC member St. Paul's Community Baptist Church.[5] The words of Nehemiah became a rallying cry taken up even by the likes of New York's irascible mayor Ed Koch: "You see the trouble we are in, how Jerusalem lies in ruins with its gates burned. Come, let us rebuild the wall of Jerusalem, so that we may no longer suffer disgrace" (Neh 2:17). The response of the repatriated Jews of Yehud echoed across the centuries from Jerusalem to Brooklyn: "Then they said, 'Let us start building!' So they committed themselves to the common good" (Neh 2:18).

In *Commonwealth: A Return to Citizen Politics*, Harry Boyte quotes EBC lead organizer Michael Gecan, who explained that "The story connected our work to something real, not something bogus. . . . It got it out of the 'housing' field and the idea that you have to have a bureaucracy with 35 consultants to do anything. It made it a 'nonprogram,' something more than housing."[6] As EBC leader Celina Jamieson emphasized, "We are more than a Nehemiah Plan. We are about the central development of dignity and self-respect."[7]

Despite ongoing opposition and considerable foot dragging on the part of New York City government, several thousand Nehemiah homes were built in Brooklyn, and the project became a model for the rehabilitation of blighted urban areas across the United States.[8] As for EBC, it demonstrated what could happen when such unlikely partners as the Lutheran Church Missouri Synod, St. Paul's Community Baptist Church, and Roman Catholic parishes (like Our Lady of Loreto) founded by immigrants of earlier generations and now home to more recent arrivals, could come together to do something more than just read the Bible. Reading Nehemiah together in Brooklyn inspired the EBC's member congregations to do what was necessary to rebuild their community.

I never actually discovered what I might or might not have done that resulted in my being appointed as parochial vicar at Our Lady of Loreto fresh out of seminary. Even so, I did learn a great deal there about community organizing and about the politics of biblical interpretation from people like the Reverend Johnny Ray Youngblood, Mike Gecan, Stephan Roberson, Alice McCollum, Sister Immaculata Kennedy, Father John Powis, and Edgar Mendez, EBC leaders and IAF organizers who "committed themselves to the common good," knowing that the houses they helped build were only as strong as the community that organized, strategized, and mobilized to get them built.

On October 1, 1982, at the groundbreaking for the first Nehemiah homes, some time before I arrived in East New York, Reverend Youngblood addressed a gathering of some six thousand members from forty-two member churches and declared, "Contrary to popular opinion . . . we are not a 'grassroots' organization. . . . Grass roots grow in smooth soil. Grass roots are tender roots. Grass roots are fragile roots. Our roots are deep roots."[9]

REREADING NEHEMIAH: WALLS BUILT OF WORDS

It was not until many years later that I returned to reconsider Nehemiah, indirectly prompted to do so by a curious convergence of circumstances that got me to thinking about twenty-first-century walls and fences.[10] The first such prompting came by way of Samuel P. Huntington's article, "The Hispanic Challenge," excerpted from his book *Who Are We? The Challenges to America's National Identity*.[11] That article begins,

> The persistent inflow of Hispanic immigrants threatens to divide the United States into two peoples, two cultures, and two languages. Unlike past immigrant groups, Mexicans and other Latinos have not assimilated into mainstream U.S. culture, forming instead their own political and linguistic enclaves—from Los Angeles to Miami—and rejecting the Anglo-Protestant values that built the American dream. The United States ignores this challenge at its peril.[12]

Huntington's article concludes even more ominously:

> Continuation of this large immigration (without improved assimilation) could divide the United States into a country of two languages and two cultures. . . . A few stable, prosperous democracies—such as Canada and Belgium—fit this pattern. The transformation of the United States

into a country like these would not necessarily be the end of the world; it would, however, be the end of the America we have known for more than three centuries. Americans should not let that change happen unless they are convinced that this new nation would be a better one. Such a transformation would not only revolutionize the United States, but it would also have serious consequences for Hispanics, who will be in the United States but not of it. Sosa ends his book, *The Americano Dream*, with encouragement for aspiring Hispanic entrepreneurs. "The Americano dream?" he asks. "It exists, it is realistic, and it is there for all of us to share." Sosa is wrong. There is no Americano dream. There is only the American dream created by an Anglo-Protestant society. Mexican Americans will share in that dream and in that society only if they dream in English.[13]

Whether by free association or by some other caprice of intertextuality, reading the end of Huntington's anti-immigrant rant led me to reread the end of Nehemiah with different eyes, a text I found just as unsettling as Huntington's:

In those days also I saw Jews who had married women of Ashdod, Ammon, and Moab; and half of their children spoke the language of Ashdod, and they could not speak the language of Judah, but spoke the language of various peoples. And I contended with them and cursed them and beat some of them and pulled out their hair; and I made them take an oath in the name of God, saying, "You shall not give your daughters to their sons, or take their daughters for your sons or for yourselves. Did not King Solomon of Israel sin on account of such women? Among the many nations there was no king like him, and he was beloved by his God, and God made him king over all Israel; nevertheless, foreign women made even him to sin. Shall we then listen to you and do all this great evil and act treacherously against our God by marrying foreign women?" And one of the sons of Jehoiada, son of the high priest Eliashib, was the son-in-law of Sanballat the Horonite; I chased him away from me. Remember them, O my God, because they have defiled the priesthood, the covenant of the priests and the Levites. Thus I cleansed them from everything foreign, and I established the duties of the priests and Levites, each in his work; and I provided for the wood offering, at appointed times, and for the first fruits. Remember me, O my God, for good. (Neh 13:23-30)

These verses did *not* make it into Reverend Youngblood's sermon at St. Paul Community Baptist Church, the sermon that inspired EBC lead organizer Mike Gecan to dub the organization's housing initiative the

Nehemiah Plan.[14] This chapter is not the first time that the controversy over marriage with "foreign women" (*nashim nakriot*) comes to the surface in Ezra-Nehemiah, nor is it the first instance in Ezra-Nehemiah where tensions flare up between the returnees from exile and the inhabitants of the land. These tensions boil to the surface as early as Ezra 3, when Jeshua and his fellow priests and Zerubbabel and his kin "set out to build the altar of the God of Israel, to offer burnt offerings on it, as prescribed by the law of Moses the man of God" (Ezra 3:2). In the following verse we read, "Despite their fear of the peoples of the land, they replaced the altar on its foundations and offered holocausts to the LORD on it, both morning and evening (Ezra 3:3 NAB).[15] In Ezra 4:4 the lines are drawn between the "people of the land" (*am-ha'aretz*), whose opposition to the rebuilding of the temple by the returnees renders the "people of Judah" (*am-yehudah*) afraid to build.

The matter of exogamous marriage by the priests and Levites among the returnees is the focus of Ezra 9-10. There the Ezra memoir reports,

> The officials approached me and said, "The people of Israel, the priests, and the Levites have not separated themselves from the peoples of the lands with their abominations, from the Canaanites, the Hittites, the Perizzites, the Jebusites, the Ammonites, the Moabites, the Egyptians, and the Amorites. For they have taken some of their daughters as wives for themselves and for their sons. Thus the holy seed has mixed itself with the peoples of the lands, and in this faithlessness the officials and leaders have led the way." When I heard this, I tore my garment and my mantle, and pulled hair from my head and beard, and sat appalled. (Ezra 9:1-2)

The solution Ezra imposes on the priests and Levites requires them to "separate yourselves from the people of the land and from foreign wives" (Ezra 10:11), and the book ends with a listing of the names of those who sent away their "foreign wives" (Ezra 10:44). It would be more accurate to say, with H. G. M. Williamson and other commentators, that the narrative breaks off at the end of Ezra 10 without actually concluding.[16] On the unity of Ezra-Nehemiah, Williamson maintains "that there is good reason to approach Ezra and Nehemiah as two parts of a single work and that this work is to be regarded as complete as it stands."[17]

While an exploration of the question of whether Ezra-Nehemiah should be considered "complete as it stands" would be well beyond the scope of this study, the widely maintained position that affirms the original unity of Ezra-Nehemiah is presupposed here. Joseph Blenkinsopp offers a "reasonable guess" that the sudden ending of the Ezra narrative may indicate the failure of Ezra's mission (as a result of his opposition to exogamous marriage) and his recall by his Persian superiors "after a stay of no more than a year."[18]

In Nehemiah 13:1-3, the reading of "the book of Moses" builds walls of words that fix exclusionary boundaries even more effectively than walls of stone:

> On that day they read from the book of Moses in the hearing of the people; and in it was found written that no Ammonite or Moabite should ever enter the assembly of God, because they did not meet the Israelites with bread and water, but hired Balaam against them to curse them—yet our God turned the curse into a blessing. When the people heard the law, they separated from Israel all those of foreign descent.

This restriction (based on Deut 23:4-7 [MT], which recalls Num 22-24) provides Nehemiah with further ammunition against Tobiah, the Ammonite official who opposed the rebuilding project from the beginning (Neh 2:19), and against whom Nehemiah acts in 13:8, ejecting Tobiah's furnishings from the room in the temple that had been prepared for him by the priest Eliashib while Nehemiah himself was away from Jerusalem consulting with King Artaxerxes (Neh 13:4-9). The reference to Deuteronomy 23:4-7 provides Nehemiah with the legal basis for acting against his opponent. Blenkinsopp points out that the reading "from the book of Moses" is rather selective inasmuch as Nehemiah 13 makes no mention of the restriction against genitally mutilated males (Deut 23:1), against "those born of an illicit union" (Deut 23:2), or even of the less restrictive legislation regarding Edomites and Egyptians (Deut 23:7-8).[19]

We are introduced to Tobiah in Nehemiah 2:10, where, together with Sanballat the Horonite, he is said to oppose Nehemiah's mission "to seek the welfare of the people of Israel."[20] As soon as Nehemiah rallies the people, "Come, let us rebuild the wall of Jerusalem, so that we may no longer suffer disgrace" (Neh 2:17), an exhortation that follows his covert inspection of the wall by night (Neh 2:15-16), the project is said to meet with opposition from Sanballat the Horonite and Tobiah the Ammonite official (ha'ebed ha'ammoni) and Geshem the Arab, of whom Nehemiah says "They mocked and ridiculed us," and in response to whose opposition Nehemiah makes exclusive claims: "The God of heaven is the one who will give us success, and we his servants are going to start building; but you have no share or claim or historic right in Jerusalem" (Neh 2:20).[21]

While a number of studies have devoted attention to the matter of marriage with "foreign women" in Ezra and Nehemiah, far less attention has been devoted to the specific issue at stake in Nehemiah 13:23-24: Nehemiah's violent reaction to the returnees who married women of Ashdod, Ammon, and Moab, half of whose children "spoke the language of Ashdod, and they could not speak the language of Judah, but spoke the language of various peoples."[22] Clearly, the troublesome matter of intermarriage between

Yehudim and "women of Ashdod, Ammon, and Moab" has to do with much more than purity or with concern over land tenure and inheritance of real property. Here Nehemiah regards the inability of a significant number of the children of such "mixed" marriages to speak Yehudite to be a dangerous symptom of assimilation, underscoring the important links between language and group identity.

Disturbed that so many of the children of the *Yehudim* do not speak *Yehudit*, Nehemiah resorts to verbal and physical abuse: "I contended with them and cursed some of them and beat them and pulled out their hair" (Neh 13:25). Elsewhere in the Hebrew Bible, *Yehudit* is used to designate a language (2 Kgs 18:26, 28). During the Assyrian siege of Jerusalem, Hezekiah's officials beg the Rabshakeh, "Please speak to your servants in the Aramaic language (*Aramit*), for we understand it; do not speak to us in the language of Judah (*Yehudit*) within the hearing of the people who are on the wall," but the Rabshakeh ignores their plea and addresses the inhabitants of the besieged city in *Yehudit*.

The same term is used in the Isaian parallel (Isa 36:11, 13) and also in the Chronicler's account of the siege (2 Chron 32:18). As for the offending language in Nehemiah 13, "Ashdodite" (*Ashdodit*), Blenkinsopp notes, "There have been several guesses, all inconclusive, as to the language in question: a residue of the Philistine language—about which, unfortunately, we know next to nothing; an Aramaic dialect; perhaps even Phoenician, given the political and commercial Phoenician presence in the coastal area."[23] He thinks little of the suggestion by E. Ullendorf that *Ashdodit* "was simply a current designation for any unintelligible foreign language (as in our expression, 'It's all Greek to me')," inasmuch as this hypothesis "overlooks the actual issue, which is Jewish-Ashdodite marriages."[24] Indeed, as Blenkinsopp explains, "What was really at stake was not so much speaking a foreign language as the inability to speak Hebrew."[25]

For many commentators, at this point exegetical analysis of the issues at stake gives way to broad generalizations and unrestrained guesswork. Daniel L. Smith-Christopher observes that when dealing with the intermarriage issue in Ezra and Nehemiah, "contemporary commentators are frequently unsettled from typical 'scholarly reserve.'"[26] For example, Williamson suggests, "For a religion in which Scripture plays a central part, grasp of language is vital; one might compare the importance of Arabic for Islam. When religion and national culture are also integrally related, as they were for Judaism at this time, a knowledge of the community's language was indispensable; indeed, it was one of the factors that distinguished and sustained the community itself."[27]

With regard to the indication in Nehemiah 13:24 that *half* of the offspring of the mixed marriages spoke the language of Ashdod and could not speak *Yehudit*, Williamson finds this indication "curious" and wonders whether some fathers were "more conscientious about teaching their children their own language than others for whom the children's education was considered an entirely maternal concern? Or was it a question of age, a knowledge of Hebrew coming only as the children began to mix outside the immediate confines of the home?"[28] The text of Nehemiah offers us no information that would make it possible to resolve this question.

For his part Blenkinsopp opines, "In view of the dominant influence of the mother in the formative years, it is not surprising that many of the children spoke her language, though why the other half did not remains unexplained."[29] He adds, "Language has always been an important ingredient of national identity: whether Gaelic in Ireland or Welsh in Wales or, more to the point, Hebrew during the Bar Kokhba rebellion and in Israel during the modern period."[30] Even though Blenkinsopp does not linger very long over Nehemiah 13:24, his observation about the relationship between language and group identity deserves further attention. This is confirmed when we consider the six features that John Hutchinson and Anthony D. Smith identify as characteristics that establish the distinctiveness of ethnic groups:

1. a common proper name to identify the group;
2. a myth of common ancestry;
3. a shared history or shared memories of a common past, including heroes, events and their commemoration;
4. a common culture, embracing such things as customs, language, and religion;
5. a link with a homeland; and
6. a sense of communal solidarity.[31]

Reading Nehemiah 13:24 calls particular attention to the first and fourth characteristics, that is, to the proper name by which the group is distinguished (either prescriptively or diagnostically) from others, as well as the language that distinguishes the group. With regard to the first characteristic, a common proper name for the group, Ezra 4:4 identifies the returnees as "people of Judah" (*am-yehudah*); and this identification stands in marked contrast to the designation of their opponents in disparaging terms as "people of the land" (*am-ha'aretz*). This designation, as Gale Yee points out, was deployed as part of the strategy by which the immigrants established ideological distance between themselves and the members of the Judean population who had not been taken into exile.[32] In Nehemiah 13:23 the returnees are identified as *Yehudim*, and Nehemiah objects to their intermarriage with Ashdodite, Ammonite, and Moabite women.

With regard to language as a distinctive group characteristic, Nehemiah 13:14 describes the distinctive language of the *Yehudim* as *Yehudit*: the group is identified according to the language spoken by its members, and the language is identified as the language that is held in common by members of the group. On one level, it could be said that Nehemiah feared that the loss of the Judean language among the children of the Yehudites would lead to the dissipation of a distinctively Yehudite identity in the very next generation. Yet the vehemence of his response to the practice of intermarriage suggests that much more was at stake. As Yee demonstrates, neither the practice of intermarriage by the immigrant community nor Nehemiah's violent reaction against it is merely a matter of ethnic identity. She suggests that "One of the earliest economic issues faced by the immigrants was land tenure and gaining control of the principal means of production in Yehud from the natives."[33] Yee agrees with Mary Douglas, who explains that intermarriage was one of the strategies by which the immigrants acquired access to land: "marriage was the obvious way for the new arrivals to insert themselves into the farming economy."[34]

Reading this in the light of social exchange theory that attends to how agents weigh the costs and rewards that result from entering into particular relationships, Yee suggests that by intermarrying, "the immigrant political and cultic elites exchanged or parlayed their high status as imperial agents in order to gain access to the land as a means of production through noncoercive means. The natives exchanged their land to 'marry up' into the ranks of the returning elite, their ethnic kinsfolk who had good connections with the Persian authorities."[35] Thus, the practice of intermarriage by the immigrants should not be understood as a practice that had assimilation as its aim. Yee regards Nehemiah 13:23-30 as evidence that

> the *golah* community continued to intermarry for socioeconomic reasons, particularly into ethnically foreign families. For Nehemiah, such intermarriages meant the threat of foreign influence on Yehud's internal affairs during a time of economic depletion by the Persian Empire. Land tenure was also an issue. If women could inherit during the postexilic period, land could be transferred from the Jerusalem elite into ethnically foreign hands through marriages with foreign wives. Furthermore, since the temple was crucial to the economic affairs of Yehud, intermarriage with foreign women among the priestly class, in particular (Neh 13:28-29), could permit unwelcome or detrimental influence on these affairs from the outside.[36]

For Nehemiah, the Persian-appointed governor of Yehud, the problem of intermarriage was complicated by the fact that the children born of these marriages were learning the languages of their mothers. Discussing the intermarriage issue in Nehemiah 13 in the course of his analysis of the roles of Ezra and Nehemiah as governors of Yehud during the reign of Artaxerxes I (465-423 BCE), Jon L. Berquist notes,

The more specific problem is that the children of such marriages speak only the language of their mothers (Nehemiah 13:24); without a knowledge of Hebrew or Aramaic they would not be capable of assuming leadership positions within the community. Nehemiah then offers a comparison to Solomon's problems of dissipating alliances developed on the basis of intermarriage; thus Nehemiah indicates that the problems may involve foreign complicity within issues of colonial policy (Nehemiah 13:25-27).[37]

Dismissing the hypothesis put forward by many scholars that concern over ethnic purity lies at the heart of the intermarriage issue, Berquist suggests instead that the prohibition against intermarriage was intended to "solidify political control and economic security within the ruling stratum of Jerusalem society" and to guard against outside interference in the internal colonial affairs of Yehud.[38] Thus, for Nehemiah the fact that "half of their children spoke the language of Ashdod and could not speak the language of Judah" (Neh 13:24) is an alarming symptom of the deeper problem of the fast-moving erosion of the immigrant community as a distinctive group. The assimilation signified by the loss of the group's distinctive language among the children of the immigrants implied a loss of group cohesion and threatened "a further depletion of already scarce resources through dissipation into a widening social circle."[39] Nehemiah's violent reaction to the exogamous marriages of his fellow immigrants thus represents an act of anti-assimilationist resistance, an act that was as vehement as it was futile.

LANGUAGE AND THE POLITICS OF ETHNIC IDENTITY

"Losing a language is also losing part of one's self that is linked to one's identity and cultural heritage"[40]; and the emotional impact of the loss of a shared language across generations is captured vividly in the complaint of a thirty-two-year-old Cambodian woman who laments, "I have a niece living in East Boston who knows only English. I cannot talk to her because I don't speak English. . . . Those children act and talk like Americans. They eat American food like pizza and McDonald's . . . and they say to their parents, 'I don't want to live with you; I want to move in with a roommate.'"[41]

The intersections between language, ethnic identity, and colonization remain as complex for immigrants in the twenty-first century CE as they were during the fifth century BCE.[42] For Latin American immigrants to the United States and for their children, Nehemiah's outburst against the intermarrying immigrants and their Ashdodite-speaking children sounds frighteningly familiar, echoing in Samuel Huntington's nativist rhetoric: "There is no Americano dream. There is only the American dream created by an Anglo-Protestant society. Mexican Americans will share in that dream and in that society only if they dream in English."[43] This is nothing new. President Theodore Roosevelt insisted, "We have room for but one language here, and that is the English language, for we intend to see that the crucible turns our people out as Americans, and not as dwellers of a polyglot boarding house; and we have room for but one sole loyalty, and that is loyalty to the American people."[44] Roosevelt's remarks at the beginning of the twentieth century came to be reflected in the workings of U.S. colonial expansion, when the Spanish-American War resulted in the extension of U.S. sovereignty over Cuba and Puerto Rico. In 1920, the Department of War's Annual Report boasted, "The people of Porto Rico [sic] are American citizens. Perhaps the most important factor in their complete Americanization is the spreading of the English language. Diligent efforts along this line are being made and with very satisfactory progress."[45]

In their important study of the immigrant second generation in the United States, Alejandro Portes and Rubén G. Rumbaut explain,

> Immigrants arriving in a foreign land face a significant dilemma, one whose resolution lies at the very core of the process of acculturation. On the one hand, the languages that they bring are closely linked to their sense of self-worth and national pride. On the other hand, these languages clash with the imperatives of a new environment that dictate abandonment of their cultural baggage and learning a new means of communication. Language assimilation is demanded of foreigners not only for instrumental reasons but for symbolic ones as well. It signals their willingness to seek admission into the circles of their new country, leaving past loyalties behind. Precisely because a common language lies at the core of national identity, host societies oppose the rise of refractory groups that persist in the use of foreign tongues.[46]

With respect to language assimilation, Portes and Rumbaut point to research that supports the dominant scholarly view that the process typically takes three generations:

> Adult immigrants in the United States typically combine instrumental learning of English with efforts to maintain their culture and language. They also seek to pass this heritage to their children. . . . The instrumental acculturation of the first generation in the United States is followed by a second that speaks English in school and parental languages at home, often responding to remarks in those languages in English. Limited bilingualism leads, almost inevitably, to English becoming the home language in adulthood. By the third generation, any residual proficiency in the foreign language is lost since it is supported neither outside nor inside the home.[47]

Yet other research has begun to challenge this assumption, pointing especially to the persistence of Spanish among Latino/a children regardless of generation.[48] Research also shows that linguistic assimilation is significantly affected by intermarriage.[49] In one important study of mother-tongue shift to English, Gillian Stevens reports that "children of two foreign parents are most likely to learn a parent's non-English language; those with one foreign parent are less likely; and those with two native-born parents least likely."[50] Stevens reports that with almost half of the children in the study belonging to ethnically heterogamous backgrounds, "Few of these children learned a parent's non-English mother tongue," and Stevens therefore concludes that "non-English languages are disappearing through mother-tongue shift in large part because of ethnic intermarriage."[51] This recalls the situation described in Nehemiah 13, where Nehemiah complains that ethnic exogamy is resulting in mother-tongue shift among the children of Yehudites who have married Ashdodite, Ammonite, and Moabite women, so that half of their offspring "could not speak the language of Judah."

The complex and ongoing history of the U.S. colonization of Puerto Rico sheds important light on the tangled intertwinings of language, identity, and colonization. After Puerto Rico became a U.S. possession in 1898 in the wake of the U.S. war against Spain, the island's new colonial masters engaged in the ideological Americanization of the island, with policies that aimed at "fostering loyalty to the U.S. colonial project."[52] In 1907, Education Commissioner Martin G. Brumbaugh spelled it out in the following terms: "The first business of the American Republic, in its attempt to universalize its educational ideals in America, is to give these Spanish-speaking races the symbols of the English language in which to express the knowledge and culture which they already possess."[53] The "Americanization" of the Puerto Rican population went hand in hand with the disparagement of the language that had been spoken by the inhabitants of the island during its four centuries as a colony of Spain. The U.S. Commissioner of Education said of Puerto Ricans that they lack

> The same devotion to their native tongue or to any national ideal that animates the Frenchmen, for instance, in Canada or the Rhine provinces. . . . A majority of the people do not speak pure Spanish. Their language is a patois almost unintelligible to the natives of Barcelona and Madrid. It possesses no literature and little value as an intellectual medium. There is a bare possibility that it will be nearly as easy to educate these people out of their patois into English as it will be to educate them into the elegant tongue of Castile. Only from the very small intellectual minority in Puerto Rico, trained in Europe and imbued with European ideals of education and government, have we

to anticipate any active resistance to the introduction of the American school system and the English language.[54]

The English language was the medium, and "Americanization" was the unmistakable message. Puerto Rico's new colonial masters correctly recognized that it was the disempowered *criollo* elites that would mount the most vocal opposition to the use of English as the real and symbolic instrument for expressing the island's new status quo as a U.S. territory. In 1930, Victor Clark wrote,

> English is the chief source, practically the only source, of democratic ideas in Porto Rico. There may be little that they learn to remember, but the English school reader itself provides a body of ideas and concepts which are not to be had in any other way. It is also the only means which these people have of communication with and understanding of the country of which they are now a part.[55]

For the vast majority of the Puerto Rican population, mastery of English was positively associated with upward economic mobility, so that, according to a 1930 study published by the Brookings Institution,

> An opportunity to learn English, no matter how imperfectly and adequately, is one of the magnets that draws the children of the poorer classes to the public schools. To tens of thousands of disinherited in Puerto Rico, a knowledge of that language seems to promise—perhaps fallaciously—a better economic future. Popular willingness to make sacrifices for the schools is in some degree due to this pathetic faith.[56]

More than a century after Puerto Rico became a U.S. possession, the island's ambivalent colonial betwixt-and-betweenness in the economic and political spheres continues to surface in polemics over language. As Frances Negrón-Muntaner explains in a study of language and nationalism in Puerto Rico, "Although in the United States Puerto Ricans are legally 'first'-class citizens, they are often perceived as a racialized minority group and treated as such. On the other hand, in Puerto Rico Puerto Ricans are second-class citizens of the United States with little decision-making power, but islanders tend to think of themselves as an autonomous region and/or a separate country."[57] Bluntly declaring that "language nationalism is a farce," Negrón-Muntaner is duly critical of moves that sought to impose a Puerto Rican monolingual "essence," efforts that borrowed from the rhetoric of the "English only" movement in the United States to agitate for a linguistic nationalism that would establish Spanish as the wall of words that would enforce a cultural border between the island and the United States.[58]

In that vein, Nehemiah might well have found common cause across the centuries with Severo Colberg Ramírez, who insisted, "Vamos a ver quiénes son puertorriqueños 'de a verdad,' quiénes los son a medias y quiénes menosprecian el hecho de haber nacido aquí y haberse criado con el español como vernáculo" ("We will see who the 'real' Puerto Ricans are, who are only halfway, and who looks down on having been born here and being raised with Spanish as their native tongue").[59]

Negrón-Muntaner maintains that "Native command of Spanish does not signify or contain Puerto Ricanness."[60] Indeed, the English/Spanish binaries and the hard and fast linkages of language and ethnic identity collapse before the realities of transnationalism and globalization, conditions that nourish bilingualism and that result in such linguistic betwixts-and-betweens as Spanglish/*inglañol*.[61] What, then, of the identification of *Yehudim* with *Yehudit*? How might a Nuyorican Spanglish speaker reread Nehemiah 13? How might a twenty-first-century Brooklynite find words to lend to the Ashdodite-speaking offspring of ethnically mixed marriages whose own betwixt-and-betweenness in fifth century BCE Jerusalem led Nehemiah to curse their fathers? Afro-Puerto Rican poet Tato Laviera might help. In a poem entitled "my graduation speech," he confesses,

> I think in Spanish
> I write in English
> ....
> tengo las venas aculturadas
> escribo en Spanglish.[62]

In another poem, Laviera protests that he is neither assimil*ated* (English) nor asimil*ado* (Spanish), underscoring tensions between assimilation and resistance, between language and ethnic identity that resonate eloquently across the centuries between Brooklyn and Jerusalem, from the margins of the global metropolis to the colony at the fringes of the Persian Empire.[63] In a distinctively Puerto Rican idiom that attests to the linguistic *mestizaje/mulataje* that is itself the legacy of more than five centuries of colonization, he is, as the title of the poem itself proclaims, "asimilao,"

> assimilated? qué assimilated,
> brother, yo soy asimilao
> así mi la o sí es verdad
> tengo un lado asimilao
> ....
> but the sound LAO was too black
> for LATED, LAO could not be
> trans*lated*, assimilated,
> no, asimilao, melao,
> it became a black

spanish word but
we do have asimilados
perfumados and by the
last count even they
were becoming asimilao
how can it be analyzed
as american? así que se
chavaron
trataron
pero no
pudieron
con el AO
de la palabra
principal, dénles gracias a los prietos
que cambiaron asimilado al popular asimilao.[64]

8

The View from Northern Boulevard: Reading Matthew's Parable of the Day Laborers

I never heard Father George Nicholson preach about the parable of the day laborers (Matt 20:1-16), but I am convinced that George, the late pastor of St. John Vianney Parish in Flushing, New York, came to understand its meaning better than most people I know. Whatever he may or may not have learned about Matthew's parable during his courses in biblical studies in the seminary, he certainly understood it differently when he came face to face with the immigrant day laborers who gathered each morning along Northern Boulevard hoping for work to support themselves and their families.

Despite fairly vehement opposition from many of his own parishioners, he invited the immigrant laborers to gather in the church's parking lot and welcomed them into the parish center, which became a de facto hiring hall on weekday mornings. George really connected with these men, and his fluency in the language of respect more than made up for whatever was lacking in his heavily accented and halting Spanish. As time went on, the immigrant laborers organized themselves, doing what they could to support one another, to understand and protect their rights, and to guard against abuse by employers.

The daily struggle of immigrant workers across the United States and around the world calls us to revisit Matthew's parable of the day laborers, to reread it through the lens of their experience, to grapple with its meaning for us today, and with the challenges of its ongoing significance for various communities of interpreters.

CONVENTIONAL READINGS

The parable of the day laborer (Matt 20:1-16) is the first of three vineyard parables in Matthew's Gospel, and it is followed by the parable of the two

115

sons (21:28-32) and the parable of the tenant farmers (21:33-46). Two of these three parables are exclusive to Matthew, for only the parable of the tenant farmers has a parallel in Mark (Mark 12:1-12). Commentators on Matthew 20:1-16 have labored hard at distinguishing the sense of the parable in its literary setting in Matthew from the sense that it may have had as a parable of Jesus himself. In so doing, they often focus on its inclusion between Matthew 19:30 ("But many who are first will be last, and the last will be first" [NAB]) and Matthew 20:16 ("Thus, the last will be first, and the first will be last"). This Matthean frame suggests that in its redactional context, the parable has to do with status reversal, even though only the order in which the laborers are paid (v. 8) involves any sort of reversal, with the vineyard owner instructing his foreman to begin with the laborers who were last to be hired.[1]

Many commentators dismiss verse 16 as a Matthean addition, since, as Bernard Brandon Scott explains, "the parable does not furnish a good example of the last as first or the first as last."[2] Barbara E. Reid identifies the saying in verse 16 as a "floating proverb that is tagged on to various New Testament passages in diverse contexts," including Mark 10:31 and Luke 13:30 in addition to Matthew 19:30 and 20:16.[3] Scott points out that when the parable is considered apart from its setting in Matthew, "Most commentators see the accent of the original telling falling on the householder's graciousness, goodness, or generosity," but for Scott, "Such a reading involves curious interpretive gymnastics."[4]

In his classic study of the parables, Joachim Jeremias turns to Matthew 20:1-16 and asks,

> Why does the master of the house give the unusual order that all are to receive the same pay? Why especially does he allow the last to receive a full day's pay for only an hour's work? Is this a piece of purely arbitrary injustice? a caprice? a generous whim? Far from it! There is no question here of a limitless generosity, since all receive only an amount sufficient to sustain life, a bare subsistence wage. . . . Even if, in the case of the last labourers to be hired, it is their own fault that, in a time when the vineyard needs workers, they sit about in the market-place gossiping till late afternoon; even if their excuse that no one has hired them (v. 7) is an idle evasion . . . a cover for their typical oriental indifference, yet they touch the owner's heart. . . . It is because of his pity for their poverty that the owner allows them to be paid a full day's wages. In this case the parable does not depict an arbitrary action, but the behaviour of a large-hearted man who is compassionate and full of sympathy for the poor.[5]

For Daniel J. Harrington, Matthew 20:1-16 becomes "the parable of the good employer." Explaining that "The traditional title of the parable is 'the workers in the vineyard,'" Harrington maintains that "the laborers are really only foils for the central character who is the householder/master. Therefore some argue that a better title is 'the good employer' since he is the main character from start to finish."[6] The point? Harrington suggests that "the parable of the good employer defends Jesus' special concern for the marginal in Jewish society. . . . Just as it is possible to entitle Luke 15:11-32 the 'prodigal father,'" instead of the parable of the prodigal son, "so one can call Matthew 20:1-15 the 'prodigal employer.'"[7]

In their *Social Science Commentary on the Synoptic Gospels*, Bruce J. Malina and Richard Rohrbaugh present Matthew 20:1-16 as "God as Generous Patron." They explain that "day laborers were economically among the poorest persons in the society. They were usually landless peasants who had lost their ancestral lands and drifted into cities and villages looking for work. Moreover, loss of land usually meant loss of family and the supporting network that implied. Survival for such people was often a bitter struggle."[8] Like most other commentators, Malina and Rohrbaugh read the parable theologically, assuming that the vineyard owner is a stand-in for God and explaining that correspondence in the light of the dynamics of patron–client relations in the first-century Mediterranean world. While their reading illustrates the severity of the struggle for survival that day laborers faced, Malina and Rohrbaugh foreground the behavior of the owner of the vineyard, who behaves "like a typical Mediterranean patron."[9]

In another effort to apply the insights of social scientific interpretation to the parable, John H. Elliott translates Matthew 20:16b as, "Is your eye evil because I am good?" explaining the protests of the early arrivals among the laborers at the wages given the latecomers as an instance of evil-eyed envy. In the end, though, Elliott's conclusion does not stray far from the theological conclusion of his fellow commentators: "This parable, as initially told by Jesus, was a story illustrating the unlimited favor of God and condemning Evil Eyed envy and invidious comparisons as incompatible with social life governed by the rule of God. God, represented by the householder and the *kyrios* (20:8), the parable affirms, is good in both his fidelity to his commitments and his generosity."[10]

In his 1988 study of the parable, Puerto Rican Lutheran theologian José David Rodríguez refers to Matthew 20:1-16 "in the tradition of Jeremias," as "the parable of the Affirmative Action Employer," explaining,

When I first thought about giving a different title to this story, I considered "The Equal Opportunity Employer." But after a careful study of its content, I concluded that this would be a mistake. The parable does not provide us with a description of someone who is willing to give equal opportunity to people provided they show the same number of credentials, the same curriculum vitae, or the same experience. The story describes an employer whose criteria go beyond merit to focus on need.[11]

Reading the parable through the lens of the Reformation principle of justification by grace through faith, Rodríguez declares, "All that God gives is a product of grace. We cannot earn what God gives us; we cannot deserve it; what God gives is given out of the goodness of God's heart; what God gives us is not pay, but a gift; not a reward, but a product of love."[12] What distinguishes Rodríguez's reading in an important and helpful way from those of many other commentators is the ethical implication that he draws from the parable. Addressing his fellow Lutherans, he insists that "in the Christian church seniority does not necessarily translate into privilege," urging a welcoming attitude toward members of ethnic groups who are more recent arrivals in the United States and insisting, "We confess that God is an Affirmative Action Employer, and we believe that such a confession ought to become incarnate also in our own employment practices and attitudes towards the poor."[13] For Rodríguez, Matthew's parable of the Affirmative Action Employer is a powerful and convincing narrative metaphor for the preferential option for the poor.

RESISTING CONVENTIONAL READINGS

In his provocative book *Parables as Subversive Speech: Jesus as Pedagogue of the Oppressed*, William R. Herzog II offers a reading of the parables that resists the conventional understanding of these narratives simply as "primers of ethics and theology."[14] He asks, "What if the parables of Jesus were neither theological nor moral stories but political and economic ones? What if the concern of the parables was not the reign of God but the reigning systems of oppression that dominated Palestine in the time of Jesus?"[15]

While I would argue that there is no hard and fast distinction between the realm of theological ethics and the realm of politics and economics (for, in fact, this is the intersection where Catholic social teaching provides guidance), it is startling to note that Herzog's chapter on Matthew 20:1-16 is entitled "Blaming the Victims of Oppression." Here, Herzog concludes that when the original parable was picked up by Matthew, the vineyard came to be understood—in the light of Isaiah 5:1-7—as a metaphor for Israel or the church, and the householder (described in Matthew 20:8 as "the lord of the vineyard") as a metaphor for God, assigning allegorical correspondences that end up dulling the sharp edges of the parable and the dire predicament it depicts. Herzog complains that the identification of the vineyard owner as God by many ancient and modern readers of the parable leads them to "simply pass over the man. So strong is the assumption that he is a God figure that he merits little attention."[16]

The details of the characterization of the vineyard owner warrant further attention. For example, "To reinforce the extent of the householder's holdings, Jesus portrays him as making numerous trips to the agora to hire additional day laborers. His imminent harvest is so great that even he cannot calculate accurately the amount of help needed."[17] Herzog adds,

> The successive trips to the agora serve another purpose by reinforcing the unilateral power of the landowner. On his first trip, he apparently bargains with the day laborers, although this bargaining is more like a "take it or leave it" proposition. If he can go to the agora an hour before sundown and still find workers there, those workers have no bargaining power. . . . Far from being generous, then, the householder is taking advantage of an unemployed work force to meet his harvesting needs by offering them work without a wage agreement.[18]

Commentators who fail to question the "generosity" of the vineyard owner pass over details of the parable that call attention to his elite socioeconomic status and the enormous distance between his privileged condition and the miserable state of the day laborers because they take it for granted that he represents God. Herzog observes, "If the owner of the vineyard has been invisible in commentary on this parable, the day laborers have not. They have been the object of every conceivable calumny."[19] Jeremias, for example, dismisses their reply to the vineyard owner's question in verse 7 ("Why do you stand here idle all day?") as "a cover for typical oriental indifference."[20] In fact, the answer they give is simple and straightforward: "Because no one has hired us." The grumbling against the landowner by those who worked the longest is taken as unjustified envy at the good fortune of others and not as a legitimate complaint at the way in which their work has been significantly undervalued.

ANOTHER LOOK AT THE PARABLE

A late-model black Lexus pulls up and is quickly surrounded by several men. Raising his index finger, the driver indicates that the job requires just one. The worker who reaches the car first is motioned in; the transaction takes less than a minute.

Where he will go, what kind of work he will do, how much—or if—he will get paid, the worker knows not. For the day laborer, as well as the employer, uncertainty is part of the underground labor market. Usually Spanish-speaking and marked by well-worn, often paint-splattered clothes, the men who work as day laborers can be found outside home-improvement stores, small convenience stores and on busy street corners. . . .

At a site in Anaheim, workers exchange stories like troops showing off battle scars. . . . Speaking in Spanish, nearly all recount sad, scary or just plain strange dealings with employers. Daniel Tomas said he and another man were hired by a woman to help the family move. When she discovered that her purse was missing, the woman's husband returned to the site and took the workers to a police station. They were soon released, Tomas says, for a lack of proof. "They blame you for anything . . . something missing, we're blamed," says Tomas.

A worker from Guerrero, Mexico, recounted the time he received $160 for seven full days of work. "The owner didn't like the way the work was done," says Faustino Molina, 35, who was hired by a subcontractor. "The guy says, 'If I lose, so do you'," said Molina, who was paid by check. "And checks always bounce or the accounts end up being closed," chimes in Tomas.[21]

This report from the *Los Angeles Times* is no parable, no morality tale. It is a snapshot of the day-in, day-out struggle for survival by tens of thousands of twenty-first-century day laborers across the United States. According to the January 2006 National Day Labor Study, "On any given day, approximately 117,600 workers are either looking for day-labor jobs or working as day laborers."[22] Who are these day laborers? According to the study,

> The day-labor workforce in the United States is predominantly immigrant and Latino. Most day laborers were born in Mexico (59 percent) and Central America (28 percent), but the third-largest group (7 percent) was born in the United States. Two-fifths (40 percent) of day laborers have lived in the United States for more than 5 years. Three-quarters (75 percent) of the day-labor force are undocumented migrants. About 11 percent of the undocumented day-labor workforce has a pending application for adjustment of their immigration status.[23]

They find work—when they can—as construction laborers, gardeners, landscapers, painters, roofers, house cleaners, carpenters, drywall installers, farm workers, dishwashers, car washers, and cooks. What challenges do they face? According to the authors of the study,

- Day laborers regularly suffer employer abuse. Almost half of all day laborers experienced at least one instance of wage theft in the two months prior to being surveyed. In addition, 44 percent were denied food/water or breaks while on the job.
- Workplace injuries are common. One in five day laborers has suffered a work-related injury, and more than half of those who were injured in the past year did not receive medical care. More than two-thirds of injured day laborers have lost time from work.
- Merchants and police often unfairly target day laborers while they seek work. Almost one-fifth (19 percent) of all day laborers have been

subjected to insults by merchants, and 15 percent have been refused services by local businesses. Day laborers also report being insulted (16 percent), arrested (9 percent), and cited (11 percent) by police while they search for employment.[24]

For George Nicholson and the immigrant laborers in the parking lot at St. John Vianney, much of what commentators have written about Matthew 20:1-16 runs against the grain of lessons they learned the hard way. Each and every day, this parable replays itself in real life for immigrant laborers across the United States. The website of the anti-immigrant organization deceptively named "Federation for American Immigration Reform (FAIR)" claims,

> The proliferation of day laborer hiring sites has paralleled the explosion of the illegal alien problem in the United States. What was once largely a problem confined to large city sweatshops and seasonal crop agriculture has expanded enormously as illegal aliens have spread across the country into the meat processing industry, construction, assembly-line work, services such as landscaping, and all sorts of casual day labor jobs.[25]

In words that are less subtle and no less insulting than Jeremias's characterization of the last-hired day laborers in the parable as a matter of "typical oriental indifference," the Federation for American Immigration Reform alleges, "In some areas, these informal hiring sites have caused traffic disturbances, and the lack of sanitary facilities has often led to public urination. Nearby established businesses have often complained to the police that the gatherings drive away their clients. Other common complaints include public drunkenness and harassment of pedestrians."[26]

SEEING THE FACE OF CHRIST IN THE IMMIGRANT LABORER?

For immigrant laborers who regularly face abuse from their employers, the words of the vineyard owner to his foreman in verse 8 of the parable represent a familiar tactic: "Summon the laborers and give them their pay, beginning with the last and ending with the first." By instructing his foreman to start with the most recently hired and to end with those who had labored in the vineyard all day, the vineyard owner is teaching his employees a lesson. Yet the lesson is not about his generosity or his magnanimity but about his own power, about their dependence on him, and about the insignificance of their own toil. This is not a matter of gifts or grace but of a fair day's wage for a fair day's work: "These last ones worked only one hour, and you have made them equal to us, who bore the day's burden and the heat" (v. 12).

When the workers complain, the vineyard owner deploys yet another altogether familiar strategy: he singles out one of their number and takes him to task in front of the others. Herzog explains, "'Friend' (*hetaire*) is not a friendly term. It is condescending and subtly reinforces their different social stations, yet it feigns courtesy. If he were addressing a social equal, he would have used *phile*."[27] Making an example of this laborer, the vineyard owner dismisses him: "Take what is yours and go." As Herzog observes, "The spokesperson has been banned, shunned, blackballed, or blacklisted; he will not likely find work in that neighborhood again."[28]

For the rest, the unspoken message is unmistakable: what happened to him could just as well have happened to any of them. Behind the vineyard owner's rhetorical question, "Am I not free to do as I wish with my own money?" may well lurk a capricious and impulsive conscience. Today's immigrant laborers know altogether too well that their employers do as they wish with their money. How hard it is to recognize the face of a gracious and generous God in this figure of the vineyard owner!

If, instead, like George Nicholson, we recognize the face of Christ in the faces of today's immigrant day laborers, then what lessons does Matthew's vexing parable hold for us now? As for the last being first and the first being last, today's immigrant laborers know more than enough about being last. Perhaps another text from Matthew can help:

> Then the righteous will answer him and say, "Lord, when did we see you hungry and feed you, or thirsty and give you drink? When did we see you a stranger and welcome you, or naked and clothe you? When did we see you ill or in prison, and visit you?" And the king will say to them in reply, "Amen, I say to you, whatever you did for one of these least brothers of mine, you did for me." (Matt 25:37-40)

9

The Bible and the Exegesis of Empire: Reading Christopher Columbus's *El libro de las profecías*

BEGINNING WITH THE APOCALYPSE

From its place at the edge of the New Testament canon, the Revelation of John provokes both fascination and frustration in equal measure among interpreters both sympathetic and otherwise. I have suggested that

[b]oth in Latin America and elsewhere, the liberationist optic reads the Apocalypse as a hopeful book, an empowering utopian manifesto that redefines the innocent suffering to which the faithful are subjected as a participation in the paradoxical victory of Christ as the slaughtered Lamb. The book is read as an unflinching prophetic proclamation of justice that speaks the truth to power no matter the cost, and as a divine declaration that the violent designs of the powers "of this world" will result in their own undoing.[1]

What gets lost in the mix more often than not is that apocalyptic literature and its interpreters are deeply implicated in the beginnings of the American colonial predicament, its postcolonial dénouement, and its byproducts in globalization and in neocolonial formations.[2] Taking a long-range view, the roots of twenty-first-century migrations can be traced back more than five hundred years to a journey that sought its rationale in millenarian terms by appealing to the book of Revelation as predictive prophecy. In 1892, Pope Leo XIII (otherwise much celebrated as the author of *Rerum novarum*, the 1891 encyclical at the beginning of modern Catholic social teaching) celebrated the Columbus Quadricentennial in the following words:

Now that four centuries have sped since a Ligurian first, under God's guidance, touched shores unknown beyond the Atlantic, the whole world is eager to celebrate the memory of the event, and glorify its author. Nor could a worthier reason be found where through zeal should be kindled. For the exploit is in itself the highest and grandest which any age has ever seen accomplished by man; and he who achieved it, for the greatness of his mind and heart, can be compared to but few in the history of humanity. By his toil another world emerged from the unsearched bosom of the ocean: hundreds of thousands of mortals have, from a state of blindness, been raised to the common level of the human race, reclaimed from savagery to gentleness and humanity; and, greatest of all, by the acquisition of those blessings of which Jesus Christ is the author, they have been recalled from destruction to eternal life.[3]

What a difference a century made. In 1990, anticipating the Columbus Quincentennial of 1992, the Governing Board of the National Council of Churches of Christ in the U.S.A. adopted a quite dissimilar tone in its resolution entitled, "A Faithful Response to the 500th Anniversary of the Arrival of Christopher Columbus":

In 1992, celebrations of the 500th anniversary of the arrival of Christopher Columbus in the "New World" will be held. For the descendants of the survivors of the subsequent invasion, genocide, slavery, "ecocide," and exploitation of the wealth of the land, a celebration is not an appropriate observation of this anniversary. . . . The Church, with few exceptions, accompanied and legitimized this conquest and exploitation. Theological justifications for destroying native religious beliefs while forcing conversion to European forms of Christianity demanded a submission from the newly converted that facilitated their total conquest and exploitation. . . . Therefore, it is appropriate for the church to reflect on its role in that historical tragedy and, in pursuing a healing process, to move forward in our witness for justice and peace.[4]

While there is surely no reason to reopen the Pandora's box of controversy over the Columbus Quincentennial, even at a safe distance,[5] it may be salutary to recall both the non-innocence and the non-neutrality of biblical interpretation and scholarship past *and* present.[6] It has often been said that the *conquistadores* arrived in the Americas with the sword in one hand and the Bible in the other. Much attention has been devoted, and rightly, to how the colonizers wielded the sword, yet comparatively little energy has been invested in considering the ways in which the Bible was understood and employed in the colonial undertaking. The Bible furnished the substance of colonial evangelization efforts in the sermons and catechetical materials directed to the colonized by the colonizers. At the same time, the Bible played a crucial role among the colonizers themselves as they sought to frame their enterprise in terms of a worldview shaped in large measure by their understanding of the Bible.

Several important studies address the religious dimension of the conquest of the Americas, yet scholars of religion have devoted relatively little attention to this period in the history of biblical interpretation or to the place of the Bible in shaping the Spanish colonial enterprise in the Americas. Centuries later, that undertaking continues to have repercussions for twenty-first-century geopolitical challenges, including the pressing reality of human migration.

Among the earliest and most fascinating witnesses to the influence of the Bible in the Iberian colonial project is a manuscript of eighty-four folios, dated between September 13, 1501, and March 23, 1502, and now preserved in the *Biblioteca Columbina* in Seville. It begins, "This is the beginning of the book or collection of *auctoritates*, sayings, opinions, and prophecies concerning the need to recover the holy city and Mount Zion, and the discovery and conversion of the islands of the Indies and of all peoples and nations, for Ferdinand and Isabella, our Spanish rulers."[7]

This manuscript, more commonly known as *El libro de las profecías* (*LP*), the *Book of Prophecies*, was compiled by Christopher Columbus himself, in collaboration with Gaspar Gorricio, a Carthusian monk of Italian origin, who belonged to the monastery of Santa María de las Cuevas in Seville. The manuscript begins with Gorricio's transcription of the September 13, 1501 letter in which Columbus explained the project and asked for his assistance:

Reverend and very devoted father: When I came here [*to Granada*], I began to collect in a book excerpts from authoritative sources that seemed to me to refer to Jerusalem; I planned to review them later and to arrange them appropriately. Then I became involved in my other activities and did not have time to proceed with my work; nor do I now. And so I am sending the book to you so that you can look at it. Perhaps your soul will motivate you to continue the project and our Lord will guide you to genuine *auctoritates*. The search for texts should be continued in the Bible and the *Commentary*[8] is often useful and should be used for clarification.[9] (*LP* §001)

Gorricio also includes his March 23, 1502, reply to Columbus in the manuscript, explaining, "My lord, you will see in my handwriting the few things that I have added and inserted. I submit everything to the approval of your intelligence and your prudent judgment" (*LP* §002). The contributions of Gorricio are somewhat more substantial than his modesty suggests, and these are identified by scholars of the manuscript by Gorricio's distinctive handwriting.[10] The manuscript proper is a collection of biblical texts, ancient and medieval commentaries, fragments of Spanish poetry, and occasional comments by Columbus himself.[11] Its intended addressees, as the *incipit* indicates, were Ferdinand and Isabella, before whom Columbus hoped that the *Book of Prophecies* would justify his imperiled project, for the work took shape after Columbus's far-from-glorious return from his third voyage (May 1498-October 1500).[12]

The letter of Columbus to Gorricio suggests that, in its extant form, the *Book of Prophecies* represents only a draft that Columbus intended to revise. He writes, "I began to collect in a book excerpts from authoritative sources that seemed to me to refer to Jerusalem; I planned to review them later and to arrange them appropriately" (*LP* §001).[13] Some have gone so far as to suggest, based on this letter, that Columbus intended to incorporate the material in the *Book of Prophecies* into a poem ("para después tornarlas a rrever e las poner en rrima").[14] Whatever the intended genre of the projected revision might have been, there is no evidence that the *Book of Prophecies* was ever actually sent to the king and queen or that the manuscript was ever revised or further redacted or edited.[15]

The *Book of Prophecies* has received very mixed reviews among Columbus scholars and biographers. For example, in 1866 Henri Harisse described it as "a deplorable lucubration which we hope will never be published."[16] In fact, it was not until 1892, in the full fervor of the Columbus Quadricentennial, that a modern edition of the *Book of Prophecies* appeared.[17] In 1906, Filson Young complained, "Good heavens! In what a dark and sordid stupor is our Christopher now sunk—a veritable slough and quag of stupor out of which, if he does not manage to flounder himself, no human hand can pull him."[18] As late as 1985, biographer Gianni Granzotto suggested that the *Book of Prophecies* is evidence that Columbus had, with his advancing years,

> drifted farther and farther away from reality. . . . In his mild delirium he came to believe that he had been chosen by God for his exploits. . . . He also projected these convictions—or delusions—into the future. He started compiling a Book of Prophecies, collecting passages from the Bible in which he found some connection to his discoveries and designs. If he had once been able to fulfill biblical prophecy by shattering the ocean's barriers, who was to say that new exploits, foreseen by the scriptures, were not within his grasp.[19]

More measured assessments of the *Book of Prophecies* have also appeared in recent decades from the pens of historians and others who rightly regard it as a document that offers valuable insights into Columbus and his times.[20] At the same time, the *Book of Prophecies* has received very little attention from biblical scholars or from historians of biblical interpretation.[21] The essay by Hector Avalos, "Columbus as Biblical Exegete: A Study of the *Libro de las profecías*," is an especially noteworthy exception to that rule.[22]

The approach I employ in this chapter works at the intersection of two convergent methodological currents. The first of these is the turn to the reader—not the intratextual implied reader of formalist literary criticism but the real reader, the "flesh and blood reader, historically and culturally conditioned, with a field of vision fundamentally informed and circumscribed by such a social location."[23] I will consider Columbus as just such a reader and interpreter of the Bible, addressing the ways in which his field of vision was both informed and circumscribed by the particulars of his social location.

The second methodological current is the influence of postcolonial theory on biblical studies, which R. S. Sugirtharajah explains is a matter of "scrutinizing and exposing colonial domination and power as these are embodied in biblical texts and in interpretations."[24] Sugirtharajah cites Sanjay Seth, Leela Gandhi, and Michael Dutton, who suggest that the term postcolonialism is "undeniably and necessarily vague, a gesture rather than a demarcation, [and] points not towards a new knowledge, but rather towards an examination and critique of knowledges."[25] An analogous eclecticism characterizes postcolonialist biblical criticism, which takes on as one of its tasks the interrogation of "both colonial and metropolitan interpretations. The aim here is to draw attention to the inescapable effects of colonization and colonial ideologies on interpretative works such as commentarial writings, and on historical and administrative record which helped to (re) inscribe colonial ideologies and consolidate the colonial presence."[26]

The *Book of Prophecies* offers a valuable opportunity to attend specifically to this task, for it represents the first efforts to bring the Bible to bear on the nascent European colonial enterprise. While Columbus's first voyage (1492-1493) could be construed as a modestly equipped voyage of discovery, a modest expedition of three ships and a crew estimated at between 90 and 120, the second voyage (1493-1496) already represented a significant investment in a process of colonization, with its seventeen ships carrying 1,200 crew and colonists.

COLUMBUS AND HIS BIBLE

Because Columbus was neither a cleric nor an academic, a study of the *Book of Prophecies* gives us some idea of how the Bible and late medieval biblical scholarship were appropriated by one especially well-read layman.[27] The Latin Vulgate was the version of the Bible used by Columbus and his collaborators in the *Book of Prophecies*, perhaps in an edition that also included the *Postilla litteralis* of Nicholas of Lyra.[28] The importance of the Bible for Columbus and his project becomes clear in the letter to the Spanish sovereigns that is included in the *Book of Prophecies*. There he explains that "I have studied all kinds of texts: cosmography, histories, chronicles, philosophy, and other disciplines. Through these writings, the hand of Our

Lord opened my mind to the possibility of sailing to the Indies and gave me the will to attempt the voyage. With this burning ambition I came to your highnesses" (*LP* §011).[29]

As for the reception his project received, he confesses, "Everyone who heard about my enterprise rejected it with laughter and ridicule" (*LP* §011).[30]

It was from the Bible and not from other writings, Columbus suggests, that his illumination came, and it was that illumination that ultimately gained his project a favorable hearing from the king and queen:

> Neither all the sciences I mentioned previously nor citations drawn from them were of any help to me. Only Your Highnesses had faith and perseverance. Who could doubt that this flash of understanding was the work of the Holy Spirit, as well my own? The Holy Spirit illuminated by his holy and sacred Scripture, encouraging me in a very strong and clear voice from the forty-four books of the Old Testament, the four evangelists, and twenty-three epistles from the blessed apostles, urging me to proceed. (*LP* §011)[31]

He further insists:

> I am not relying on my lifetime of navigation and the discussions I have had with people from many lands and religions, or on the many disciplines and texts that I spoke of previously. I base what I say only on holy and sacred Scripture, and on the prophetic statements of certain holy persons who through divine revelation have spoken on the subject. (*LP* § 011)[32]

Columbus willingly confessed his unlettered state as a layman: "Perhaps Your Highnesses and all the others who know me and to whom this letter may be shown will criticize me, publicly or privately, as an uneducated man, an uninformed sailor, an ordinary person, etc." (*LP* §011).[33]

Defending himself against this anticipated critique, he identified himself with the innocents mentioned in Matthew 11:25, "Oh, Lord, how many things you have kept secret from the wise and have made known to the innocent,"[34] and in Matthew 21:15-16, "As our Lord entered Jerusalem, the children sang, 'Hosanna, son of David!' In order to test him, the scribes asked him if he had heard what they were saying and he answered that he had, saying, 'Don't you know that truth comes from the mouths of innocent children?'"[35] Despite these protestations, it is quite clear that Columbus read the Bible through lenses supplied by late medieval biblical interpretation.

For Columbus, the canon within the canon of the Bible takes shape around the eschatological urgency of his enterprise: "Holy Scripture attests in the Old Testament, through the mouths of the prophets, and in the New Testament through our redeemer Jesus Christ, that this world will end. The signs of when this must happen are described by Matthew and Mark and Luke, and the prophets frequently predicted the event" (*LP* §011).[36]

Relying on the calculations of Pierre d'Ailly, Columbus was convinced that "only 155 remain of the 7,000 years in which, according to the authorities cited above, the world must come to an end. Our redeemer said that before the consummation of this world all that had been written by the prophets would have to be fulfilled" (*LP* §011).[37]

To this Columbus adds a clue to his own hermeneutical strategy as a reader of the prophets: "The prophets wrote about the future as if it were the past and about the past as if it were yet to happen, and similarly with the present. Sometimes they spoke figuratively, other times more realistically, and on occasion quite literally. One says more or less than another or expresses it in a better way" (*LP* §011).[38]

If the prophets are at the heart of Columbus's canon within the canon, Isaiah is at the core of the innermost canon. With the exception of the Psalms, Isaiah is the biblical book to which the *Book of Prophecies* refers most, with more than forty citations of various portions of the book.[39] Columbus tells the Spanish sovereigns that "Isaiah is the prophet who is most highly praised by St. Jerome and St. Augustine and the other teachers and is appreciated and greatly revered by all. Concerning Isaiah, they say that he was not just a prophet, but also an evangelist; he put all his efforts into describing the future and calling all people to our holy Catholic faith" (*LP* §011)[40].

In a similar vein, in a letter to Doña Juana de la Torre, the nurse of Prince Juan, Columbus explained,

> I came to serve this King and Queen with profound affection, and I have rendered service never before seen or spoken of. God made me the messenger of the new heaven and the new earth of which he spoke through Saint John in the Apocalypse, after having spoken of it through Isaiah, and he showed me to that location. There was disbelief in everyone, and spiritual intelligence gave to the Queen my Lady its inspiration and great power and made her the beneficiary of everything.[41]

Some of the quotations from Isaiah in the *Book of Prophecies* are quite extensive, while others are briefer citations grouped under the heading of "The following things have been written about the islands of the sea in sacred Scripture" (*LP* §248).[42] Of Columbus's presentation of his enterprise as a mission informed by Isaiah and the Apocalypse, Djelal Kadir observes,

> Isaiah's prophecy of "new heavens and a new earth" (65:17) is a source Columbus cites repeatedly. We find it in his letter to Doña Juana de la Torre and in the preamble letter to his book of prophecies. In both instances he joins John the Divine to Isaiah as prophets of his

own mission and New World enterprise. The connection he forges
between those prophetic voices and his project is clearly typological
and figurative and his procedure is in keeping with the hermeneutic
procedures of the medieval tradition. We have an idea of how licit such
connections are, and how pervasive the ideological force authorizing
them, from the fact that Father Bartolomé de Las Casas, commenting
on Columbus's invocation of Isaiah in his letter on the third voyage,
states simply that since Isaiah was a prophet he could well have been
prophesying the discovery of the New World (*Historia* Bk. 1, chap.
127). Columbus was clearly laboring under the aegis of perfectly licit
and canonically legitimate criteria.[43]

It is curious, though, given the apocalyptic urgency of Columbus's
argument, that the *Book of Prophecies* cites the Apocalypse of John only
three times, referring to Revelation 1:9; 6:14, and 16:20 in a list of biblical
texts "about the islands of the sea" (*LP* §§272-74).

While, in its present form, the *Book of Prophecies* appears to be a
somewhat haphazard collection of materials drawn from many sources, the
exegetical principles that shape the materials and the comments by Columbus
clearly reflect mainstream late medieval practices of biblical interpretation.
Several additions to the manuscript by Gorricio reinforce this. After the
letter from Columbus to Gorricio and Gorricio's reply, and after Gorricio's
superscription, we find, first, a quotation on the fourfold interpretation of
Scripture taken "From the *Summa angelica*, under the rubric 'exposition,'"
that is, the 1499 *Summa angelica de casibus conscientiae* of Angelus de
Clavasio (*LP* §004).[44]

This is reinforced by a quotation of the well-known trope on the fourfold
interpretation of Scripture attributed to Jean Gerson, "Littera gesta docet,
quid credas allegoria, moralis quid agas, quo tendas allegoria" (The literal
teaches the facts; allegory, what you should believe; the moral, that which
you do; the anagogical where you are going) (*LP* §005).[45] The equally familiar
illustration of the fourfold meaning of Scripture from the 1482 *Rationali
divinorum officiorum* follows:

> The fourfold interpretation of Holy Scripture is clearly implicit in the
> word Jerusalem. In a historical sense, it is the earthly city to which
> pilgrims travel. Allegorically, it indicates the church in the world.
> Tropologically, Jerusalem is the soul of every believer. Anagogically,
> the word means the Heavenly Jerusalem, the celestial fatherland and
> kingdom. (*LP* §006)[46]

This evidence confirms the judgment of Avalos that "Columbus was
conservative in his exegetical principles, following earlier medieval exegetical

traditions without much deviation."[47] Particular attention is given in the *Book of Prophecies* to the hermeneutics of the prophets, beginning with the observation, "In Sacred Scripture one tense is often used in place of another; for example, the past tense instead of the future, etc." (*LP* §008).[48] As Avalos explains,

> This was an ancient and pervasive exegetical principle that allowed Columbus to claim as prophecies many texts that, judging by the original grammar and context, otherwise refer to past events. Thus, in a section devoted to passages concerning "The Future" (*De futuro*), one finds many passages dealing with places (e.g., Tarshish) involved in events that occurred in the days of the Old Testament (e.g., 1 Kings 10:21-22; Jonah 1:3). However, those past events are viewed as prophecies that oblige Columbus to seek lost biblical lands.[49]

Later, also in Gorricio's hand, the *Book of Prophecies* includes a lengthy quotation from Isidore's *Etymologiae* on the seven different kinds of prophecy:

> There are seven kinds of prophecy. The first is The first is ecstasy, a transport of the mind; for example, when Peter, in a state of mental confusion, saw the vessel containing various animals being lowered from heaven [Acts 14:10-11]. The second kind is a vision, exemplified by the words of Isaiah, "I saw the Lord seated on a lofty throne" [Isa 6:1]. The third is a dream; for example, Jacob, sleeping, saw a ladder leading to heaven [Gen 28:12]. The fourth kind of prophecy occurs in a cloud, for example, when God spoke to Moses and to Job after his misfortune [see Exod 19:16-24; Job 38-40]. The fifth is a voice from heaven, like the one that spoke to Abraham saying, "Do not lay a hand on that boy" [Gen 22:11-12], and to Saul on the highway, "Saul, Saul, why do you persecute me?" [Acts 9:4]. The sixth kind is received through a parable; for example, Solomon in Proverbs and Balaam when he was commissioned by Balak [see Num 22-24]. The seventh kind of prophecy is permeation by the Holy Spirit, experienced by nearly all the prophets. (*LP* §079)[50]

Immediately afterwards we find a further quotation of Isidore, distinguishing three kinds of visions:

> Others have said that there are three kinds of vision. The first is received by means of the eyes of the body; etc. Another is received through the mind when we form mental images of those things that the body experiences; etc. The third kind of vision involves neither physical

sensation nor any part of the mind in which images of physical things are conceived, but comes through an intuitive understanding of truth, and so forth, in the same selection. (*LP* §080)

On the basis of Columbus's own claims to divine illumination and inspiration, it is hard to avoid the impression that this quotation serves both to provide an appropriate hermeneutical framework for the interpretation of the texts marshaled in the *Book of Prophecies* and *also* to validate the role of Columbus himself both as an interpreter of biblical prophecy *and* as the chosen instrument of its fulfillment through his journeys. As he claimed in his letter to Doña Juana, "God made me the messenger of the new heaven and the new earth of which he spoke through Saint John in the Apocalypse, after having spoken of it through Isaiah, and he showed me to that location."[51] Columbus read and announced the fulfillment of Scripture *by traveling*.

COLUMBUS AS EXEGETE OF EMPIRE

John Leddy Phelan writes, "The discovery and conquest of America was the last crusade."[52] Leonard I. Sweet adds, "If Columbus is to be taken at his word, he needs to be understood as a chiliastic crusader."[53] The *Capitulaciones de Santa Fé*, the charter granted to Columbus by Ferdinand and Isabella on April 17, 1492, was drafted at Santa Fe de la Vega, in the military camp from which the sovereigns mounted their assault against Muslim Granada, where the curtain fell on the final episode of the *reconquista* on January 2, 1492. March 30, 1492, saw the promulgation of the edict that expelled from Spain all Jews who refused Christian baptism, and that edict was enforced beginning on July 31, 1492. By ironic coincidence, Columbus sailed from Palos on his first voyage only three days later. In the journal of that first voyage, he wrote,

> Your Highnesses, as Catholic Christians, and princes who love and promote the Christian faith, and are enemies of the doctrine of Mahomet, and of all idolatry and heresy, determined to send me, Christopher Columbus, to the above-mentioned countries of India, to see the said princes, people and territories, and to learn their disposition, and the proper method of converting them to our holy faith; and furthermore, directed that I should not proceed by land to the East, as is customary, but by a westerly route, in which direction we have hitherto no evidence that anyone has gone. So, after having expelled the Jews from your dominions, your Highnesses, in the same month of January, ordered me to proceed, with sufficient armament, to the said region of India, and for that purpose granted me great

favors, ennobled me that thenceforth I might call myself Don, and be High Admiral of the Sea, and perpetual Viceroy and Governor in all the lands and continents which I might discover and acquire.[54]

The agenda Columbus undertook was nothing less that the completion of a totalizing imperial design, scripted in specifically and exclusively Christian terms. With competing Jewish and Muslim discourses forcibly eliminated from the Iberian Peninsula by the expulsion of Jews and Muslims, and with Christian hegemony solidly established there, the imperial project turned toward expansion of that hegemony in a colonial enterprise that was conceived from the outset as a matter of discovery *and conquest*.[55] Commmenting on the *Capitulaciones de Santa Fe*, Kadir points to a certain irony in the privileges conferred on Columbus:

The Catholic monarchs granted Columbus, in exchange for "discovering and conquering" islands and mainlands in the Ocean sea, the privileges of their realms' Admiralty and the viceroyalty and governorship of territories to be discovered and conquered. Clearly, then, the would-be New World already has a governor even before its discovery and conquest outside of the charter that engendered it. What their Highnesses capitulate to Columbus is not merely a patent for exploratory activity, or even for a mercantile and exploitive venture, but a charter for the founding of an empire.[56]

Constructed as an exegesis of incipient empire, the *Book of Prophecies* maps the enterprise of discovery and conquest in deliberately biblical terms along the axes of time and space. Along the axis of time, Columbus works within the framework of an urgently millennialist eschatology, while, along the axis of space, Columbus maps his project according to an explicitly biblical cosmology. For the former, the influence of Joachim of Fiore looms especially large, while for the latter it was the work of Pierre d'Ailly that had the greatest impact. While this is not the place to embark on an extended consideration of the influence of Joachim of Fiore, we cannot proceed without acknowledging the profound and pervasive influence of Joachimism on Spain generally and on Columbus in particular.[57]

As Kadir notes,

[U]ltimately the eschatological scaffolding that sustains the edifice of explanation and self-sanction for the Old World's enterprise in the New is constructed with the lapidary and scriptural elements of Europe's prophetic tradition and Judeo-Christian mythology. And this is why the most significant manual that guides Columbus in his obsessive project is the spectral and majestic *Imago Mundi* of the Cardinal Pierre D'Ailly. Columbus's personal copy contains 898 marginal notations in the Admiral's hand, a relatively preponderant referential base when we consider that the total number of postils Columbus made in all his books amount to 2,125. . . . Pierre D'Ailly epitomizes that enchanted blend of Medieval mythos and scientific ethos that, eventually, would naturalize and appropriate the New World and, in doing so, legitimize its own enterprise *ad maiorem Dei gloriam*.[58]

While he operated within the framework of known and accepted principles of biblical interpretation, to be sure, by charting his voyages of discovery and conquest according to the coordinates of biblical maps, Columbus was in fact employing the Bible in a radically new way. It furnished both the ideology of conquest and the rationale for his millennialist and messianic designs.[59] Thus, the *Book of Prophecies* functions, to borrow an expression from Michel de Certeau, as an instance of "writing that conquers."[60] Columbus's voyages of discovery and conquest were framed in eschatological terms as the fulfillment of biblical prophecy and as necessary undertakings at the end of the ages to hasten the millennium. Along the axis of space, Columbus's voyages of discovery and conquest served to confirm and to claim for Catholic Spain the "islands of the sea" that were already presumed to exist on the basis of their mention in the Bible.[61]

PROVISIONAL CONCLUSIONS

Postcolonial theorists are among their own harshest critics. Marxist critic Terry Eagleton, who would not consider himself a postcolonial theorist despite his sympathy for the emancipatory agenda(s) advanced by postcolonial theorists, quips, "There must surely be in existence a secret handbook for aspiring postcolonial theorists, whose second rule reads: 'Begin your essay by calling into question the whole notion of postcolonialism' (The first rule reads: 'Be as obscurantist as you can decently get away with without your stuff going absolutely unread')."[62] The quibbling goes on at frustrating lengths, extending to such weighty matters as whether to hyphenate, viz., "post-colonial," or not to hyphenate, viz., "postcolonial."[63]

Eagleton's critique of "postcolonialism" takes a more serious turn when he suggests that "'Postcolonialism,' like postmodernism in general, is among other things a brand of culturalism, which inflates the significance of cultural factors in human affairs. This is a vice to which literary intellectuals are especially prone."[64] One might add that biblical scholars are by no means immune from the same tendency.

Here Arif Dirlik adds a strong materialist critique,

Methodologically, one of the interesting byproducts of postcolonial criticism seems to be that there is little significant difference between the world and its representations in fiction. . . . Contrary to the promise of a "new historicism," that wished to historicize literature, historical thinking over the last decade has been converted into a subfield of literature, with emphasis shifting from questions of evidence to questions of narrativization and representation, with consequences that undermine epistemologies in both literature and history.[65]

While these cautions urge against collapsing the world into textual projections and representations, postcolonial literary criticism does serve to underscore the entanglements of texts and other cultural products in their larger sociopolitical contexts of empire, of the mapping and remapping of metropolis and margins. Postcolonial *biblical* interpretation, for its part, foregrounds the place of Christian discourses in the construction and legitimation of Western colonial-imperial expansion in Africa, Asia, and the Americas.[66] To that end, it mobilizes an eclectic collection of tools and methods, to the extent that it appears "undeniably and necessarily vague, a gesture rather than a demarcation, [and] points not towards a new knowledge, but rather towards an examination and critique of knowledges."[67]

By opening Christopher Columbus's *El libro de las profecías* in this chapter, I have engaged in just this sort of thing, taking advantage of the unusual opportunity that book provides to examine the biblical "charts" of the Spanish colonization of the Americas at the very earliest stages of that process.[68] Columbus's manuscript may not itself have exerted any immediately measurable effect either on the admiral's royal patrons or on other participants in the political and religious conquest of the Americas. Even so, it yields much valuable testimony to the foundational (and abiding) implication of the Bible (as visionary charter and as the vehicle of a sometimes violent evangelism) in the construction of the Spanish empire, its colonial legacy in the Americas, and the echoes of that history into the present day.

Epilogue

Reading the New Normal

According to the International Organization for Migration (IOM),

Over the next few decades, international migration is likely to transform in scale, reach and complexity, due to growing demographic disparities, the effects of environmental change, new global political and economic dynamics, technological revolutions and social networks. These transformations will be associated with increasing opportunities—from economic growth and poverty reduction, to social and cultural innovation. However, they will also exacerbate existing problems and generate new challenges—from irregular migration, to protecting the human rights of migrants. Most States in the world (and not just in the developing world) lack the capacity to effectively manage the international mobility of persons today, not to mention respond to new dynamics.[1]

Looking ahead at migration trends, the IOM observes,

There are far more international migrants in the world today than ever previously recorded—214 million according to UN DESA [United Nations Department of Economic and Social Concerns] (2009)—and their number has increased rapidly over the last few decades, up from 191 million in 2005. If the migrant population continues to increase at the same pace as the last 20 years, the stock of international migrants worldwide by 2050 could be as high as 405 million. At the same time, internal migrants account for 740 million migrants (UNDP, 2009) [United Nations Development Programme] bringing the total number of migrants to just under 1 billion worldwide today.[2]

Far from being a temporary condition that affects only a few nations and only a small number of people, migration of various sorts—including immigrants, refugees, internally displaced persons, temporary workers, as well as victims of human trafficking—is a permanent reality on an enormous scale. With just under a billion migrants in a global population estimated by the U.S. Census Bureau at nearly seven billion, one in seven of the world's population is a migrant.[3] This reality is the new normal, and it is further complicated by the fact that, as IOM observes, "International migration involves a wider diversity of ethnic and cultural groups than ever before. Significantly more women are migrating today on their own or as heads of households; the number of people living and working abroad with irregular status continues to rise; and there has been a significant growth in temporary and circular migration."[4]

Facing the phenomenon of migration head on, as a matter of the new normal and not as a temporary exception to business as usual, constitutes an urgent imperative for those who embrace the challenge with which the Second Vatican Council's Constitution on the Church in the Modern World begins: "The joys and the hopes, the griefs and the anxieties of the men [and women] of this age, especially those who are poor or in any way afflicted, these are the joys and hopes, the griefs and anxieties of the followers of Christ. Indeed, nothing genuinely human fails to raise an echo in their hearts" (*Gaudium et Spes* 1).

It is encouraging to see that biblical scholars and theologians have begun to attend to this task in vigorous ways, so that it can no longer be said that little has been written about migration from a theological perspective.[5] This book is a modest effort to bring biblical studies and theology into constructive conversation about people on the move, taking on the global by reading texts that speak of migration as a permanent part of human experience, ever ancient and ever new, inscribed in all its complexity in the foundational narratives of the Christian tradition.

My conviction that all theology is local does not imply that it functions merely within the limited community of those who share the same vernacular. The fact that I read the Bible and write about it from where I stand at the intersection of multiple belongings—as the New York-born son of parents who were people on the move, as a Roman Catholic, as a Latino, as someone involved in higher education and in the life of the local church—should not mean that what I say necessarily gets lost in translation in intercontextual conversations with others who are differently located. Biblical scholarship and theology, which are necessarily contextual even when practitioners do not explicitly acknowledge their situatedness, are also necessarily intercontextual if they are to be successful at all in sharing knowledge, if catholicity (and Catholicity) mean anything at all. This book is not just for Latinos/as; nor is it only (or even mainly) for other biblical scholars or theologians and by no means is it written only for my fellow New Yorkers.[6] As a contribution to sociopolitically engaged biblical scholarship, it participates in an ongoing consideration of people on the move that is still in the early stages of coming to terms with the new normal of the twenty-first century.

In that vein, I should underscore what I have deliberately tried *not* to do in this book, leaving aside the inevitable errors of omission. First, I have very deliberately avoided an approach that would presume to offer a comprehensive overview of what the Bible has to say about people on the move as though the Bible speaks with a single voice. To have done so would have failed to do justice both to the rich variety of voices that speak—sometimes in complex harmonies and sometimes with harsh dissonances—through the many pages of the book of books that is the Bible. Such an approach would also do injustice to the flesh-and-blood readers of the Bible in all the diversity of their contexts and reading strategies.

I have instead read around the edges of the canon, focusing specifically on a selection of texts that are not often invoked by sociopolitically engaged biblical scholars, theologians, or pastoral agents as they seek to shape individual consciences and to influence public policy on behalf of people on the move. For example, in chapter 4, I chose to read the Genesis 12:10-20 narrative of Abram and Sarai's seeking relief from famine in Egypt rather than the Genesis 17 account of their hospitality toward the three mysterious visitors. By offering readings of texts from across the biblical canon that speak in very different ways about a range of people on the move, I have suggested that no single biblical text can be said to constitute the canon within the canon for productive conversation with and about people on the move in the world in front of the text.[7]

For biblical scholars, theologians, and pastoral agents alike, doing justice to the whole range of ways in which people on the move are represented in biblical texts is more than a matter of responsible reading and accurate exegesis. Given our responsibility for building bridges of words where some have built walls of words, employing reading strategies that are respectful of the complexities of the world behind the text opens the door to a similar respect for the many diverse constituencies with whom we read these highly nuanced narratives. That is the case whether or not we are reading with those who share the conviction that there is, as M. Daniel Carroll R. suggests, "a divine viewpoint on immigration."[8]

It has also been my very deliberate intention to avoid the implication that there ought to be—or even that there can be—a *single* theology of migration. In calling for bridge-building between biblical scholars and theologians in our shared commitment to the process of *teología de conjunto* that goes hand in hand with *pastoral de conjunto*, I would insist that all theology is *local* theology. To imagine otherwise and to assume that there can or should be a *single* theological approach to the complexities of people on the move does disservice to the catholicity of the theological task as an ecclesial task, inasmuch as unity does not call for uniformity.[9] Thus, for example, a theology of immigration that focuses exclusively on hospitality falls short if it obscures the power differential between the ones who are extending hospitality and those who are its intended beneficiaries.[10] The language of "welcoming the stranger" pure and simple runs the risk of perpetuating the otherness of the "stranger" who is the object of a hospitality that is assumed to be temporary, since the veiled hope is that the "stranger" will either move on or assimilate. A narrow focus on an ethic of hospitality assumes, perhaps only unintentionally, that the phenomenon of people on the move is temporary and ultimately inconsequential in its impact on the global status quo.

If migration is the new normal, then biblical scholars and theologians have much work to do, working not only with each other but *en conjunto* with scholars, activists, community leaders, and government officials as we give serious attention to the many millions of people on the move, their families, their stories, and their sighs, without simplifying or romanticizing, without stereotyping or proof-texting. By listening attentively, by reading responsibly, and by acting justly, we are called to imagine into being a world of solidarity in justice. In that world, barriers of brick and barbed wire no longer keep people apart; the walls of xenophobic words that make people strangers to each other come crumbling down, and the differences between us lead not to intolerance and distrust but to graced growth in shared understanding that makes for authentic human flourishing.

Notes

1. See Jean-Pierre Ruiz, *Ezekiel in the Apocalypse: The Transformation of Prophetic Language in Revelation 16, 17-19, 10.* European University Studies 23:376 (Frankfurt am Main: Peter Lang, 1989).

2. Arturo Bañuelas became pastor of St. Pius X parish in El Paso, profiled in Paul Wilkes's book *Excellent Catholic Parishes: The Guide to Best Places and Practices* (Mahwah, NJ: Paulist Press, 2001), 19-38. He was also the founder of the Tepeyac Institute, the El Paso diocese's highly successful ministry formation center, and was among the co-founders of the Academy of Catholic Hispanic Theologians of the United States (ACHTUS). The year 1995 saw the publication of an anthology he edited, which presented essays by fourteen first-generation Latino/a theologians, *Mestizo Christianity: Theology from the Latino Perspective* (Maryknoll, NY: Orbis Books, 1995; reprt. Eugene, OR: Wipf & Stock, 2004).

3. Arturo Bañuelas, "The Lies Are Killing Us: The Need for Immigration Reform," *U.S. Catholic* (December 2010), 34-36. Internet edition (October 25, 2010), www.uscatholic.org/culture/social-justice/2010/10/lies-are-killing-us-need-immigration-reform?page=0,0.

4. Bañuelas, "The Lies Are Killing Us."

5. Academy of Catholic Hispanic Theologians of the United States, "Statement on Just, Comprehensive, and Humane Immigration Reform," June 7, 2006, www.achtus.org/ImmigrationReform.html.

6. Academy of Catholic Hispanic Theologians of the United States, "Statement Supporting the Passage of the DREAM Act," April 12, 2009, www.achtus.org/ACHTUSNEWS.html. For further information, see the DREAM Act portal: www.dreamact.info/. Carmen Nanko-Fernández writes, "In the United States we have currently created the conditions for a permanent invisible but plain-in-sight underclass of young people with little hope. Optimistic about the so-called American dream, they learn, after they have followed what they thought were the rules, that their true identity precludes them from further dreaming. These alternately documented—by now Spanglish speaking—kids discover, usually in their teens, that they cannot move on because, unlike their younger brothers or sisters, they were not born legally in the United States. With limited options and the fear of returning to *las tierras* they

do not know, these kids live and work in the shadows" (*Theologizing en Espanglish: Context, Continuity, and Ministry* [Maryknoll, NY: Orbis Books, 2010], 27).

7. Bañuelas, "The Lies Are Killing Us."

8. Ibid.

9. Catholic News Agency, "Archbishop Gomez Reminds Catholic Business Leaders Christ was an Immigrant," www.catholicnewsagency.com/news/arch bishop-gomez-reminds-catholic-business-leaders-christ-was-an-immigrant/. Many of the comments posted on the Catholic News Agency website reflect the sort of resistance to Archbishop Gómez's stance, underscoring the importance of his observation that, "Right now in this country, there are a lot of people—a lot of good people—who are saying things they know they should never be saying about immigrants. . . . Their anger and frustration is understandable. But their rhetoric and many of their political responses are not worthy of the Gospel."

10. "UNHCR starts work on new camp for internally displaced in Côte d'Ivoire," February 16, 2011, www.unhcr.org/4d5be1819.html.

11. Gemma Tulud Cruz, *An Intercultural Theology of Migration: Pilgrims in the Wilderness.* Studies in Systematic Theology 5 (Leiden: Brill, 2010). Also see Gemma Tulud Cruz, "Between Identity and Security: Theological Implications of Migration in the Context of Globalization," *Theological Studies* 69 (1998): 357-75. Latino/a biblical scholars are not alone in dealing with the Bible and people on the move. See, for example, van Thanh Nguyen, "Asia in Motion: A Biblical Reflection on Migration," *Asia Christian Review* 4, no. 2 (Winter 2010): 18-31.

12. Carmen Nanko-Fernández, "A Hybrid God in Motion: Theological Implications of Migrations, A Latin@ Perspective," unpublished paper presented at the 2010 Spring Institute for Lived Theology, "Theology, Migration, and the Borderlands," at the University of San Diego, April 27, 2010. An audio version of the paper is available at www.livedtheology.org/silt2010.html. See Fumitaka Matsuoka and Eleazar Fernandez, eds., *Realizing the America of Our Hearts: Theological Voices of Asian Americans* (St. Louis: Chalice Press, 2003).

13. Alex García-Rivera writes, "More often than not, the 'Big Story' account of reality turns out not to be so much a universal tale of human being, but merely a skewed or specialized story, an insider's story that makes sense only to those who tell it. Such a complaint is more than a call for clarity or a recall of technical language. More is at stake. A 'Big Story' as a true and universal account of human reality, affects all members of society." There are also "little stories . . . told by assembly line workers and university professors alike," and it is these "little stories," García-Rivera suggests, that "may be the antidote for the contemporary malaise affecting our society's specialists—the twin complaints of lack of meaning and irrelevance" (Alex García-Rivera, *St. Martín de Porres: The "Little Stories" and the Semiotics of Culture* [Maryknoll, NY: Orbis Books, 1995], 1-2, 5).

14. On "othercide," see Nanko-Fernández, *Theologizing en Espanglish*, 68-70. Here Nanko-Fernández adopts the term defined by Ilan Stavans as "the elimination of people or attributes different to us or ours" (in Ilan Stavans, *Spanglish: The Making of a New American Language* [New York: Rayo HarperCollins, 1993], 185).

15. See Aquiles Ernesto Martínez, Old Testament Legislation and Foreigners: An Alternative Majority Group Response," *Journal of Hispanic/Latino Theology* (January 23, 2011), www.latinotheology.org/2011/old-testament-foreigners.

16. United States Conference of Catholic Bishops and Conferencia del Episcopado Mexicano, *Strangers No Longer: Together on the Journey of Hope* (January 22, 2003), nos. 22-27, www.usccb.org/mrs/stranger.shtml#4.

17. United States Conference of Catholic Bishops and Conferencia del Episcopado Mexicano, *Strangers No Longer*, no. 26.

18. M. Daniel Carroll R., *Christians at the Border: Immigration, the Church, and the Bible* (Grand Rapids, MI: Baker Academic, 2008), 19.

19. Ibid., 20.

20. Ibid., 23.

21. On "little stories," see note 13 above.

22. Fernando F. Segovia, "Toward a Hermeneutics of the Diaspora: A Hermeneutics of Otherness and Engagement," in *Reading from This Place*, volume 1: *Social Location and Biblical Interpretation in the United States*, ed. Fernando F. Segovia and Mary Ann Tolbert (Minneapolis: Fortress Press, 1995), 72.

23. Ibid., 67.

24. Ibid.

25. On Ricoeur's notions of the "world behind the text" and the "world in front of the text," see the concise explanation provided by Walter Brueggeman, *Theology of the Old Testament: Testimony, Dispute, Advocacy* (Minneapolis: Fortress Press, 2005), 57-58.

26. Nanko-Fernández, "A Hybrid God in Motion."

27. Daniel G. Groody, "Jesus and the Undocumented Immigrant: A Spiritual Geography of a Crucified People," *Theological Studies* 70 (2009): 302.

1. GOOD FENCES AND GOOD NEIGHBORS?

1. An earlier version of this chapter was presented at the 2003 Annual Convention of the Catholic Theological Society of America. A subsequent revision of that presentation was published in the *Journal of Hispanic/Latino Theology* (www.latinotheology.org), May 29, 2007. In an article entitled "Galilean Journey Revisited: Mestizaje, Anti-Judaism, and the Dynamics of Exclusion" (*Theological Studies* 70, no. 2 [June 2009]: 377-400), Michael E. Lee makes reference to this essay in an effort to deflect the critique of Elizondo articulated here. I stand by that critique and find Lee's defense of *Galilean Journey* unconvincing.

2. Krister Stendahl, "Biblical Theology, Contemporary," in *Interpreter's Dictionary of the Bible*, ed. Keith Crim (Nashville: Abingdon Press, 1962), 1:418-32.

3. Bernard J. F. Lonergan, *Method in Theology* (New York: Seabury, 1972), 168. Here Lonergan acknowledges his debt to Albert Descamps, "Réflexions sur la méthode en théologie biblique," *Sacra Pagina* (Paris: Gabalda; Gembloux: Duculot, 1959), 1:142f. In 1973, Bishop Descamps, former rector of the Catholic University of Leuven, was appointed secretary of the reorganized Pontifical Biblical Commission.

4. Lonergan, *Method in Theology*, 171.

5. Ibid., 172.

6. Gerald O'Collins and Daniel Kendall, *The Bible for Theology: Ten Principles for the Theological Use of Scripture* (New York: Paulist Press, 1997), 1.

7. Ibid., 6.

8. Ibid., 6-7.

9. Ibid., 25.

10. George A. Kelly, *The New Biblical Theorists: Raymond E. Brown and Beyond* (Ann Arbor, MI: Servant Books, 1983).

11. See the spirited defense of the Catholic appropriation of the historical-critical approach mounted by Joseph Fitzmyer, "Historical Criticism: Its Role in Biblical Interpretation and Church Life," *Theological Studies* 50 (1989): 249-52.

12. "Biblical Interpretation in Crisis: On the Question of the Foundations and Approaches of Exegesis Today," in *Biblical Interpretation in Crisis: The Ratzinger Conference on Bible and Church (Encounter Series)*, ed. Richard John Neuhaus (Grand Rapids, MI: Eerdmans, 1989), 1.

13. Pontifical Biblical Commission, *The Interpretation of the Bible in the Church* (Vatican City: Editrice Vaticana, 1993).

14. Ibid.

15. Stephen E. Fowl, "Introduction," in *The Theological Interpretation of Scripture: Classical and Contemporary Readings*, ed. Stephen E. Fowl (Cambridge, MA: Blackwell, 1997), xiii-xiv. Also see Fowl, *Engaging Scripture: A Model for Theological Interpretation* (Malden, MA: Blackwell, 1998), especially 1-31.

16. Stephen E. Fowl, "Introduction," in *The Theological Interpretation of Scripture*, xv. At times, biblical scholars *qua* practitioners of historical-critical approaches have taken great pains to insist that they are engaged in strictly historical and not theological research. For example, in volume 3 of his massive study *A Marginal Jew*, John P. Meier reminds his readers, tongue-in-cheek, of what his *historical* investigation of the "historical Jesus" involves: "To illustrate what a *historical* as distinct from a *theological* investigation of Jesus must involve, I have proposed the fantasy of the 'unpapal conclave': a Catholic, a Protestant, a Jew, and an agnostic—all honest historians cognizant of 1st-century religious movements—are locked up in the bowels of the Harvard Divinity School library, put on a Spartan diet, and not allowed to emerge until they have hammered out a consensus document on Jesus of Nazareth" (*A Marginal Jew*, volume 3: *Companions and Competitors*, Anchor Bible Reference Library [New York: Doubleday, 2001], 9). Despite the enormous erudition and critical acumen Meier displays in this exceptionally valuable study, and despite the explicit modesty of his own goals, the project's blind spot is its lack of historiographical-hermeneutical sophistication, its uncomplicated embrace of history as the narrative of "how things really happened."

17. Fernando F. Segovia writes, "In terms of theory and methodology, the historical paradigm was remarkably inbred, and thoroughly hegemonic. The theoretical discussion, such as it was, consisted mostly of an in-house affair conducted within certain well-established parameters: acquaintance with the various stages of historical criticism and a reading of previous exegesis on the area of research in question. Dialogue with other critical models and disciplines was largely nonexistent" ("'And They Began to Speak in Other Tongues': Competing Modes of Discourse in Contemporary Biblical Criticism," in *Reading from This Place*, volume 1: *Social Location and Biblical Interpretation in the United States*, ed. Fernando F. Segovia and Mary Ann Tolbert (Minneapolis: Fortress Press, 1995), 13. Also see William H. Myers, "The Hermeneutical Dilemma of the African-American Biblical Student," in *Stony the Road We Trod: African American Biblical Interpretation*, ed.

Cain Hope Felder (Minneapolis: Fortress Press, 1991), 40-56; Elisabeth Schüssler Fiorenza, *Rhetoric and Ethic: The Politics of Biblical Studies* (Minneapolis: Fortress Press, 1999); Kwok Pui Lan, *Discovering the Bible in the Non-Biblical World* (Maryknoll, NY: Orbis Books, 1995); R. S. Sugirtharajah, *The Bible and the Third World: Precolonial, Colonial, and Postcolonial Encounters* (Cambridge: Cambridge University Press, 2001).

18. Among Latino/a biblical scholars and theologians, Fernando F. Segovia's proposal for what he calls intercultural criticism is especially promising. See Fernando F. Segovia, *Decolonizing Biblical Studies: A View from the Margins* (Maryknoll, NY: Orbis Books, 2000); Jean-Pierre Ruiz, "Reading across Canons: U.S. Hispanic Reflections on Globalization and the Senses of Scripture," *Journal of Hispanic/Latino Theology* 10, no. 4 (May 2003): 22-44.

19. See the review of Latino/a biblical interpretation by Fernando F. Segovia, "Toward Intercultural Criticism: A Reading Strategy from the Diaspora," in *Reading from This Place*, volume 2: *Social Location and Biblical Interpretation in Global Perspective*, ed. Fernando F. Segovia and Mary Ann Tolbert (Minneapolis: Fortress Press, 1995), 303-30. Also see Justo L. González, *Santa Biblia: The Bible through Hispanic Eyes* (Nashville: Abingdon, 1996); Miguel A. De La Torre, *Reading the Bible from the Margins* (Maryknoll, NY: Orbis Books, 2002); Jean-Pierre Ruiz, "Beginning to Read the Bible in Spanish: An Initial Assessment," *Journal of Hispanic/Latino Theology* 1, no. 2 (February 1994): 28-50; idem, "Tell the Next Generation: Racial and Ethnic Minority Scholars and the Future of Biblical Studies," *Journal of the American Academy of Religion* 69 (2001): 649-71. On the project sponsored by the University of San Diego's Center for the Study of Latino/a Catholicism to reconfigure systematic theology *latinamente*, see Orlando O. Espín and Miguel H. Díaz, eds., *From the Heart of Our People: Latino/a Explorations in Systematic Theology* (Maryknoll, NY: Orbis Books, 1999), including the essay by Jean-Pierre Ruiz, "The Bible and U.S. Hispanic American Theological Discourse: Lessons from a Non-Innocent History" (100-120). Also see Francisco García-Treto, "Reading the Hyphens: An Emerging Biblical Hermeneutics for Latino/Hispanic U.S. Protestants," in *Protestantes/Protestants: Hispanic Christianity within Mainline Traditions*, ed. David Maldonado, Jr. (Nashville: Abingdon, 1999), 160-73.

20. Revised and expanded edition (Maryknoll, NY: Orbis, 2000). See the discussion of Elizondo's work from a different angle by Benjamin Valentín, "Nuevos Odres para el Vino: A Critical Contribution to Latino/a Theological Construction," *Journal of Hispanic/Latino Theology* 5, no. 4 (May 1998): 30-47.

21. Roberto S. Goizueta, *Caminemos con Jesús: Toward a Hispanic/Latino Theology of Accompaniment* (Maryknoll, NY: Orbis Books, 1995), 188.

22. Virgilio P. Elizondo, *Galilean Journey: The Mexican-American Promise* (Maryknoll, NY: Orbis Books, 2000), 51-54, as cited in Goizueta, *Caminemos con Jesús*, 188.

23. Goizueta, *Caminemos con Jesús*, 188.

24. Roberto S. Goizueta, "A Christology for a Global Church," in *Beyond Borders: Writings of Virgilio Elizondo and Friends,* ed. Timothy Matovina (Maryknoll, NY: Orbis Books, 2000), 150. Recent years have indeed witnessed a flurry of important scholarship about Galilee from the pens of biblical scholars and archaeologists. See, for example, Richard A. Horsley, *Galilee: History, Politics, People* (Valley Forge,

PA: Trinity Press International, 1995); idem, *Archaeology, History and Society in Galilee: The Social Context of Jesus and the Rabbis* (Valley Forge, PA: Trinity Press International, 1996); Eric M. Meyers, ed., *Galilee through the Centuries: Confluence of Cultures*, Duke Judaic Studies Series 1: Second International Conference on Galilee in Antiquity (Winona Lake, IN: Eisenbrauns, 1999); Jonathan L. Reed, *Archaeology and the Galilean Jesus: A Re-Examination of the Evidence* (Harrisburg, PA: Trinity Press International, 2000); Marianne Sawicki, *Crossing Galilee: Architectures of Contact in the Occupied Land of Jesus* (Harrisburg, PA: Trinity Press International, 2000). Far from supporting Goizueta's rather expansive claim, the complexity of this body of research itself recommends modesty with respect to affirmations about the first-century economic, political, religious and social context of Jesus, and even greater modesty in bridging the distance between the first and the twenty-first centuries of our era.

25. Miguel H. Díaz, *On Being Human: U.S. Hispanic and Rahnerian Perspectives* (Maryknoll, NY: Orbis Books, 2001), 28.

26. Elizondo, *Galilean Journey*, 53, as cited in Díaz, *On Being Human*, 28.

27. Díaz, *On Being Human*, 29.

28. Elizondo, *Galilean Journey*, xvii.

29. Ibid., xvii-xviii.

30. Ibid., 48.

31. Mary C. Boys, *Has God Only One Blessing? Judaism as a Source of Christian Self Understanding* (New York: Paulist Press, 2000), 314 n. 19. Boys is very clear about her own positive view of the goals of liberation theologies, but she is equally clear about the shortcomings of the portrayal of Jews and Judaism in the work of some liberationists: "I am sympathetic to liberation theologies and indebted to its practitioners for their rereading of the tradition, commitment to the poor and minorities, and critique of Western, white, middle-class Christianity. I take exception, however, to the caricature of Judaism that has too often accompanied liberation theologies since their inception. Consequently, many people drawn to liberation theology because of their own commitments to the poor have unwittingly reinforced the teaching of contempt. Ironically—and therefore, perhaps most insidiously—this anti-Judaism has even infected liberation theologies in areas where there are few Jews, such as Asia" (*Has God Only One Blessing?* 13).

32. Elizondo, *Galilean Journey*, 51-52.

33. Ibid., 69.

34. Ibid., 51.

35. Ibid., 71.

36. Ibid., 111.

37. Shawn Kelley, *Racializing Jesus: Race, Ideology and the Formation of Modern Biblical Scholarship* (London: Routledge, 2002). Also see Susannah Heschel, "When Jesus Was an Aryan: The Protestant Church and Antisemitic Propaganda," in *Betrayal: German Churches and the Holocaust*, ed. Robert P. Ericksen and Susannah Heschel (Minneapolis: Fortress Press, 1999), 68-89; as well as Susannah Heschel, *Abraham Geiger and the Jewish Jesus* (Chicago: University of Chicago Press, 1998).

38. Heschel, "When Jesus Was an Aryan," 78-79.

39. Ibid., 78.

40. Pontifical Biblical Commission, *The Interpretation of the Bible in the Church.*

41. This must be the case if, in the words of *Dei Verbum*, Scripture is to be understood as the soul of theology (*Dei Verbum* 24). See Joseph A. Fitzmyer, *Scripture: The Soul of Theology* (New York: Paulist Press, 1994).

42. For Segovia, the hermeneutics of otherness and engagement suggests that "First, the text is to be regarded as a socially and culturally conditioned other. The question of access is crucial. Rather than positing any type of direct or immediate entrance into the text, the hermeneutics of otherness and engagement argues for distantiation from it as a working desideratum, emphasizing thereby the historical and cultural remoteness of the text. . . . Second, the reader is also to be regarded as socially and culturally conditioned, as an other to both text and other readers. The question of critical honesty is crucial. Rather than seeking after impartiality or objectivity, presuming to universality, and claiming to read like anyone or everyone, the hermeneutics of otherness and engagement argues for a self-conscious exposition and analysis of the reader's strategy for reading, the rhetorical foundations behind this strategy, and the social location underlying such a strategy" ("Toward a Hermeneutics of the Diaspora: A Hermeneutics of Otherness and Engagement," in *Reading from This Place*, 1: 68-69). A judicious exercise of the hermeneutics of otherness and engagement might well serve to prevent the sort of precipitous efforts to affirm the linear correspondence of first-century texts with twenty-first century contexts that is characteristic of some Latin American liberationist readers and some of their Latino/a heirs.

43. On Scripture and sacrament, see Sandra M. Schneiders, *The Revelatory Text: Interpreting the New Testament as Sacred Scripture*, 2nd ed. (Collegeville, MN: Liturgical Press, 1999).

2. THE BIBLE AND LIBERATION

1. Third General Conference of the Latin American Episcopate, convened at Puebla, Mexico, January 1979, *Final Documents: Evangelization in Latin America's Present and Future*, # 12, as cited in *Puebla and Beyond*, ed. John Eagleson and Philip Scharper (Maryknoll, NY: Orbis Books, 1979), 125-26.

2. Pope John Paul II, "Communion, Participation, Evangelization," 6.9, in *Origins* 10, no. 9 (July 31, 1980): 135, as cited in Carmen Nanko-Fernández, *Theologizing en Espanglish: Context, Community, and Ministry* (Maryknoll, NY: Orbis Books, 2010), 121.

3. Second General Conference of Latin American Bishops, *The Church in the Present-Day Transformation of Latin America in the Light of the Council*, 2nd ed. (Washington, DC: USCC Division for Latin America, 1973), 188.

4. Ibid., 191-92.

5. Gustavo Gutiérrez, "Toward a Theology of Liberation," in *Liberation Theology: A Documentary History*, ed. Alfred T. Hennelly (Maryknoll, NY: Orbis Books, 1990), 72-73.

6. Carlos Mesters, "'Listening to What the Spirit Is Saying to the Churches': Popular Interpretation of the Bible in Brazil," in *The Bible and Its Readers*, ed. Wim Beuken, Sean Freyne, and Anton Weiler, *Concilium* 1991, no. 1 (London: SCM Press; Philadelphia: Trinity Press International, 1991), 102.

7. Ibid., 103.

8. Ibid.

9. Carlos Mesters, "The Use of the Bible in Christian Communities of the Common People," in *Liberation Theology: A Documentary History*, ed. Alfred T. Hennelly (Maryknoll, NY: Orbis Books, 1990), 25.

10. Paulo Fernando Carneiro de Andrade, "Reading the Bible in the Base Ecclesial Communities of Latin America: The Meaning of Social Context," in *Reading from This Place*, volume 2: *Social Location and Biblical Interpretation in Global Perspective*, ed. Fernando F. Segovia and Mary Ann Tolbert (Minneapolis: Fortress Press, 1995), 242.

11. Mesters, "'Listening to What the Spirit Is Saying,'" 101.

12. Mesters, "The Use of the Bible," 23.

13. Elsa Tamez, "Women's Rereading of the Bible," in *Voices from the Margin: Interpreting the Bible in the Third World*, ed. R. S. Sugirtharajah, 2nd ed. (London: SPCK; Maryknoll, NY: Orbis Books, 1995), 55.

14. Pablo Richard, "Indigenous Biblical Hermeneutics: God's Revelation in Native Religions and the Bible (after 500 Years of Domination)," in *Text and Experience: Towards a Cultural Exegesis of the Bible*, ed. Daniel Smith-Christopher (Sheffield, UK: Sheffield Academic Press, 1995), 271.

15. Pablo Richard, "The Hermeneutics of Liberation: A Hermeneutics of the Spirit," in *Reading from This Place*, volume 2: *Social Location and Biblical Interpretation in Global Perspective*, ed. Fernando F. Segovia and Mary Ann Tolbert (Minneapolis: Fortress Press, 1995), 273.

16. Richard, "The Hermeneutics of Liberation," 275. With respect to the enforced hegemony of European and North American historical critical reading strategies in the academy and in the marketplace, consider the opening lines of Georg Strecker's *The Sermon on the Mount: An Exegetical Commentary* (Nashville: Abingdon, 1988): "'No proper exegesis of the Sermon on the Mount can ignore the results of more than two hundred years of historical critical research into the New Testament.' It rules out at the outset the right of a reader or an interpreter to use any other means to understand the text, and those who do not practice these methods are seen as outside the circle. The implication here is that the Western academy sets the ground rules for interpretation and defines what tools shall be used, and these are paraded as universally applicable in opening up the text" (as cited by R. S. Sugirtharajah, "Afterword: Cultures, Texts, and Margins: A Hermeneutical Odyssey," in *Voices from the Margin*, 460).

17. Justin S. Ukpong, "Reading the Bible in a Global Village: Issues and Challenges from African Readings," in Justin S. Ukpong et al., *Reading the Bible in the Global Village: Cape Town* (Atlanta: Society of Biblical Literature, 2002), 22.

18. Gerald O. West, *The Academy of the Poor: Towards a Dialogical Reading of the Bible*, Interventions 2 (Sheffield, UK: Sheffield Academic Press, 1999), 14.

19. Ibid., 37.

20. Ibid.

21. Ukpong, "Reading the Bible in a Global Village," 23. On "reading with," see Gayatri Chakravorty Spivak, "Can the Subaltern Speak? In *Marxism and the Interpretation of Culture*, ed. Cary Nelson and Lawrence Grossberg (Urbana: University of Illinois Press, 1988), 277-313.

22. Ukpong, "Reading the Bible in a Global Village," 23-24.

23. Ibid., 23-24.

24. R. S. Sugirtharajah, *The Bible and the Third World: Precolonial, Colonial, and Postcolonial Encounters* (Cambridge: Cambridge University Press, 2001), 241.

25. Nanko-Fernández, *Theologizing en Espanglish*, 132.

26. Ibid., 132.

27. Sugirtharajah, *The Bible and the Third World*, 260.

28. Ibid., 260.

29. Mesters, "'Listening to What the Spirit Is Saying,'" 101.

30. Nancy Cardoso Pereira, "Changing Seasons: About the Bible and Other Sacred Texts in America," in *Feminist Interpretation of the Bible and the Hermeneutics of Liberation*, ed. Silvia Schroer and Sophie Bietenhard (Sheffield, UK: Sheffield Academic Press, 2003), 51.

31. Ibid., 52. Also see Ivone Gebara, "What Scriptures Are Sacred Authority? Ambiguities of the Bible in the Lives of Latin American Women," in *Women's Sacred Scriptures*, ed. Kwok Pui-Lan and Elisabeth Schüssler Fiorenza, *Concilium* 1998, no. 3 (London: SCM; Maryknoll, NY: Orbis Books, 1998), 7-19. Gebara takes particular issue with Pablo Richard, "who seems to insist," she suggests, "on the fact that communal reading of the Bible in Latin America takes on the 'cultural, generic, and ecological dimension of the People of God.' Furthermore, he states, the interpretation made by the basic communities is carried out 'in the tradition of the churches and under the leadership of the church authorities'" [citing Richard, "Hermeneutica de la liberación: teoría para una lectura de la Biblia," *Pasos* 5 (1995): 37-43]. This statement does not correspond either to my experience or to that of many colleagues. Are we now still under the same hierarchical system of ideological control?"

32. Cardoso Pereira, "Changing Seasons," 53.

33. Gustavo Gutiérrez, *We Drink from Our Own Wells: The Spiritual Journey of a People*, trans. Matthew J. O'Connell (Maryknoll, NY: Orbis Books, 1984).

34. So it can be said, as Elsa Tamez does, that women's lives are sacred texts ("Women's Lives as Sacred Text," in *Women's Sacred Scriptures*, 57-64).

3. LATINO/A BIBLICAL STUDIES AS PUBLIC THEOLOGY

1. Julia Preston, "Immigrants' Speedy Trials after Raid Become Issue," *New York Times*, August 9, 2008, www.nytimes.com/2008/08/09/us/09immig.html.

2. "Statement of Most Reverend John C. Wester on the First Anniversary of the Postville, Iowa, Work Site Enforcement Action May 12, 2009," United States Conference of Catholic Bishops Office of Media Relations, www.usccb.org/comm/archives/2009/09-102.shtml. Emphasis mine.

3. See Colbert Nation, April 9, 2009, www.colbertnation.com/the-colbert-report-videos/224128/april-09-2009/bart-ehrman. Ehrman also appeared on The Colbert Report on June 20, 2006, to market an earlier book, *Misquoting Jesus: The Story Behind Who Changed the Bible and Why* (New York: Harper One, 2007). See Colbert Nation, June 20, 2006, www.colbertnation.com/the-colbert-report-videos/70912/june-20-2006/bart-ehrman.

4. Steve Paulson, "Gospel according to Judas," Salon.com, April 2, 2007, www.salon.com/books/feature/2007/04/02/elaine_pagels/print.html.

5. Ehrman, *Jesus Interrupted*, 1.

6. Vincent Wimbush, "In Search of a Usable Past: Reorienting Biblical Studies," in *Toward a New Heaven and a New Earth: Essays in Honor of Elisabeth Schüssler Fiorenza*, ed. Fernando F. Segovia (Maryknoll, NY: Orbis Books, 2003), 180. Wimbush's critique of academic biblical studies for its deployment of "a dizzying number of sophisticated methods and approaches" echoes an earlier critique of the discipline from another quarter, namely, Joseph Ratzinger's 1988 Erasmus Lecture at St. Peter's Lutheran Church in New York, in which Ratzinger traced the trajectory of biblical studies as an academic discipline as one in which "the picture became more and more confused. The various theories increased and multiplied and separated one from the others, and became a veritable fence which blocked access to the Bible for all the uninitiated" (Joseph Ratzinger, "Biblical Interpretation in Crisis: the Foundations and Approaches of Exegesis Today," in *Biblical Interpretation in Crisis: The Ratzinger Conference on Bible and Church*, ed. Richard John Neuhaus [Grand Rapids: Eerdmans, 1989], 2). Curiously enough, Wimbush and Ratzinger converge both in their description of the symptoms of the crisis (the practical irrelevance of academic biblical studies) and in their etiology (the narrow focus on texts to the exclusion of attention to the communities that are the matrices for meaning-making *with* texts).

7. Wimbush, "In Search of a Usable Past," 181. Is the negative outcome of such "fetishization of texts" an unintended consequence of the Reformation tenet *sola Scriptura*? On this, in relation to a Latino/a theology of revelation, see Jean-Pierre Ruiz, "The Word Became Flesh and the Flesh Becomes Word: Notes toward a U.S. Latino/a Theology of Revelation," in *Building Bridges, Doing Justice: Constructing a Latino/a Ecumenical Theology*, ed. Orlando O. Espín (Maryknoll, NY: Orbis Books, 2009), 47-68, as well as the companion piece written *en conjunto*, albeit asynchronously, by Efraín Agosto, "*Sola Scriptura* and Latino/a Protestant Hermeneutics: An Exploration," in *Building Bridges, Doing Justice*, 69-87. It is heartening to read Agosto's conclusion that in "Latino/a theology, both Protestant and Catholic, we are not too far from a Latino/a theology of biblical revelation" (73).

8. Wimbush, "In Search of a Usable Past," 181. Wimbush draws on the important work of Wilfred Cantwell Smith, especially Smith's *What Is Scripture? A Comparative Approach* (Philadelphia: Fortress Press, 1993). Smith writes, "No plant is 'objectively a weed; the term designates any plan that grows uncultivated in a situation where it is unwanted by human beings. No person is a husband in and of himself; he is a husband in correlation with another person, in this case a wife. No one is a king except in relation to a certain society and a form of government; no building is a temple except in relation to a given community of persons. Fundamental, we suggest, to a new understanding of scripture is the recognition that no text is a scripture in itself and as such. People—a given community—make a text into scripture, or keep it scripture: by treating it in a certain way. I suggest: *scripture is a human activity*—the quality of being scripture is not an attribute of texts. It is a characteristic of the attitude of persons—groups of persons—to what outsiders perceive as texts. It denotes a relation between a people and a text" (Smith,

What Is Scripture? 18). Smith adds an important consideration: "Even those who regard one particular scripture as God-given, or as transcendentally absolute, must recognize that without a human response to it, without a community reception and preservation of it, it is otiose" *(What Is Scripture?* 21).

9. Wimbush, "In Search of a Usable Past," 185.

10. Elisabeth Schüssler Fiorenza, *The Power of the Word: Scripture and the Rhetoric of Empire* (Minneapolis: Fortress Press, 2007). With regard to G*d, the*logy, and "the*logical," Schüssler Fiorenza explains, "In order to indicate the brokenness and inadequacy of human language to name the Divine, I have switched in my book, *Jesus, Miriam's Child, Sophia's Prophet: Critical Issues in Feminist Christology* (New York: Continuum, 1994), from the orthodox Jewish writing of G-d, which I had opted in *But She Said* and *Discipleship of Equals*, to the spelling of G*d with an asterisk, which seeks to avoid the conservative malestream association which the writing of G-d has for Jewish feminists. Since the*logy means 'speaking about G*d' or 'G*d-talk,' I write it in the same way" *(The Power of the Word,* 1 n. 6).

11. See, for example, D. Michael Lindsay, *Faith in the Halls of Power: How Evangelicals Joined the American Elite* (New York: Oxford University Press, 2007). Also see Helen Kennedy, "George Bush Got Memos from Rumsfeld That Used Scripture to Push Iraq War," *New York Daily News,* May 18, 2009, www.nydailynews. com/news/us_world/2009/05/18/2009-05-18_rummys_memos_suggest_a_crusade_ after_all_used_scripture_to_prod_w_in_iraq_war.html. See the cover sheets of Rumsfeld's Worldwide Intelligence Updates, featuring wartime images accompanied by biblical verses, at www.nydailynews.com/news/politics/galleries/intel_it_on_the_ mountain_rumsfelds_bush_briefings/intel_it_on_the_mountain_rumsfelds_bush_ briefings.html#ph0.

12. Schüssler Fiorenza, *The Power of the Word,* 24. She cites Nancy Fraser, "Mapping the Feminist Imagination: From Redistribution to Recognition to Representation," *Constellations* 12, no. 3 (2005): 295-307; quoting from 303.

13. Schüssler Fiorenza, *The Power of the Word,* 10.

14. Ibid., 10. With regard to her transliteration of *ekklēsia*, Schüssler Fiorenza explains that while "*ekklēsia* (Gk. 'assembly') is usually translated as a religious term, 'church,' but is primarily a political term of ancient democracy" *(The Power of the Word,* 9 n. 32).

15. John H. Collins, *The Bible after Babel: Historical Criticism in a Postmodern Age* (Grand Rapid: Eerdmans, 2005), 83.

16. Ibid., 53-74. Others mentioned in the footnotes of the same chapter include Gerald O. West, Itumeleng J. Mosala, Desmond Tutu, Robert Allen Warrior, and R. S. Sugirtharajah. "For a good history of the movement," that is, liberation theology, Collins recommends David Tombs, *Latin American Liberation Theology* (Leiden: Brill, 2002) (Collins, *The Bible after Babel,* 53 n. 1). Tombs is no stranger to readers of Latino/a theology: see his "The Legacy of Ignacio Ellacuria for Liberation Theology in a 'Post-Marxist' Age," *Journal of Hispanic/Latino Theology* 8, no. 1 (August 2000): 38-53; also his "Honor, Shame, Conquest: Male Identity, Sexual Violence, and the Body Politic," *Journal of Hispanic/Latino Theology* 9, no. 4 (May 2002): 21-40.

17. Let it not be said that Latino/a biblical scholars have focused exclusively on the New Testament. The work of Cuban-American Presbyterian Hebrew Bible scholar Francisco O. García-Treto deserves recognition. See, for example, García-

Treto's "A Reader-Response Approach to Prophetic Conflict: The Case of Amos 7.10-17," in *The New Literary Criticism and the Hebrew Bible*, ed. J. Cheryl Exum and David J. A. Clines (Sheffield, UK: JSOT Press, 1993), 114-24; idem, "The Lesson of the Gibeonites: A proposal for Dialogic Attention as a Strategy for Reading the Bible," in *Hispanic/Latino Theology: Challenge and Promise*, ed. Ada María Isasi-Díaz and Fernando F. Segovia (Minneapolis: Fortress Press, 1996), 73-85; idem, "Mixed Messages: Encountering Mestizaje in the Old Testament," *Princeton Seminary Bulletin* 22 (2001): 150-71. Guatemalan-American M. Daniel Carroll R. is another important Latino voice in the study of the Hebrew Bible.

18. See Fernando F. Segovia, "My Personal Voice: The Making of a Postcolonial Critic," in Segovia's *Decolonizing Biblical Studies: A View from the Margins* (Maryknoll, NY: Orbis Books, 2000), 146-56.

19. Ibid., 152-53.

20. See Carmen M. Nanko-Fernández, "¡Cuidado! The Church Who Cares and Pastoral Hostility," *New Theology Review* 19, no. 1 (February 2006): 24-33. See the revised version of that essay in Carmen Nanko-Fernández, *Theologizing en Espanglish: Context, Community and Ministry* (Maryknoll, NY: Orbis Books, 2010), 77-86.

21. Fernando F. Segovia, "Toward Latino/a American Biblical Criticism: Latin(o/a)ness as Problematic," in *They Were All Together in One Place? Toward Minority Biblical Criticism*, ed. Randall C. Bailey, Tat-siong Benny Liew, and Fernando F. Segovia, Semeia Studies 57 (Atlanta: Society of Biblical Literature, 2009), 200-201.

22. What Segovia said in his ACHTUS presidential address still rings true. See his "Theological Education and Scholarship as Struggle: The Life of Racial/Ethnic Minorities in the Profession," *Journal of Hispanic/Latino Theology* 2, no. 2 (1994): 5-25. Segovia observes, "It is, after all, dominant critics who control the centers of learning and the professional organizations; who set the ethos, the driving values and goals, of all such venues; who stand guard over admission into the ranks of students and faculty or into the corps of leaders and officers; who pass judgment regarding ability and worth in the case of evaluation and promotion or of exposure and responsibilities, who shape the contents, modes, and means of knowledge transmission in teaching and learning or of knowledge dissemination in presentations and publications; and who exercise close vigilance, directly and indirectly, over matters of recommendation and employment or recognition and advancement" ("Toward Latino/a American Biblical Criticism," 194 n. 1). It is refreshing to see, and energizing to have been associated (in some small measure) with the work of David A. Sánchez, whose revised Union Theological Seminary dissertation has been published as *From Patmos to the Barrio: Subverting Imperial Myths* (Minneapolis: Fortress Press, 2008).

23. Segovia, "Toward Latino/a American Biblical Criticism," 201.

24. Ibid., 222.

25. Ignacio Ellacuría, "The Task of a Christian University," in *Companions of Jesus: The Jesuit Martyrs of El Salvador*, ed. Jon Sobrino (Maryknoll, NY: Orbis Books, 1990), 149, as cited in María Pilar Aquino, "The Dynamics of Globalization and the University: Toward a Radical Democratic-Emancipatory Transformation," in *Toward a New Heaven and a New Earth: Essays in Honor of Elisabeth Schüssler*

Fiorenza, ed. Fernando F. Segovia (Maryknoll, NY: Orbis Books, 2003), 395. On the political role of the university, see also Ignacio Ellacuría, *Escritos universitarios* (San Salvador: UCA Editores, 1999), 94-95. As the martyrdom of Ellacuría and his companions shows, such an understanding of the political dimension of the university does not go unnoticed by the powers that be.

26. Edited by Randall C. Bailey, Tat-siong Benny Liew, and Fernando F. Segovia; Semeia Studies 57 (Atlanta: Society of Biblical Literature, 2009). The Latino/a participants were biblical scholars Francisco O. Garcia Trento, Jean-Pierre Ruiz, and Fernando Segovia, together with constructive theologian Mayra Rivera. The African American participants were Cheryl B. Anderson, Randall C. Bailey, and Gay L. Byron, together with Christian education scholar Evelyn Parker. The Asian American participants were Jae Won Lee, Tat-siong Benny Liew, and Gale A. Yee, together with Asian American studies scholar James Kyung-Jin Lee.

27. Randall C. Bailey, Tat-siong Benny Liew, and Fernando F. Segovia, "Toward Minority Biblical Criticism: Framework, Contours, Dynamics," in *They Were All Together in One Place?* 5. The editors likewise note that alliance building among minoritized racial-ethnic groups is "much more than a defensive reaction to the dominant society's divide-and-conquer strategy and history . . . alliance work may (1) challenge and change the agonistic ethos that seems to govern interracial-interethnic interaction in the U.S. and (2) defy a carefully contained 'multiculturalism' that is reduced to 'an image of living-apart-together'" ("Toward Minority Biblical Criticism," 13; citing Ien Ang, *On Not Speaking Chinese: Living between Asia and the West* [New York: Routledge, 2001], 14).

28. Aquino, "The Dynamics of Globalization and the University," 395-96.

29. With respect to "reading with" as an interpretive strategy, see Jean-Pierre Ruiz, "Abram and Sarai Cross the Border: Reading Genesis 12:10-20 with People on the Move," in *Border Crossings: Cross-Cultural Hermeneutics*, ed. D. N. Premnath (Maryknoll, NY: Orbis Books, 2007), 15-34.

30. M. Daniel Carroll R., *Christians at the Border: Immigration, the Church, and the Bible* (Grand Rapids, MI: Baker Academic, 2008).

31. See, for example, M. Daniel Carroll R., "The Prophetic Text and the Literature of Dissent in Latin America: Amos, García Márquez and Cabrera Infante Dismantle Militarism," *Biblical Interpretation* 4, no. 1 (1996): 76-100; idem, *Amos—The Prophet and His Oracles: Research on the Book of Amos* (Louisville, KY: Westminster John Knox, 2002).

32. Carroll R., *Christians at the Border*, 19-20.

33. Ibid., 132. Carmen Nanko-Fernández writes, "Labeling human beings as illegals and/or aliens desensitizes individuals and communities to our shared humanity that is grounded in our being created in the divine image. Humans are not illegal, actions are; and migration is a human right with responsibilities not a criminal act" ("Beyond Hospitality: Implications of Im/migration for Teología y Pastoral de Conjunto," *Perspectivas* [Fall 2006]: 57; and see the revised version of this essay in Nanko-Fernández, *Theologizing en Espanglish*, 110-19 [citation on 115]).

34. Carroll R., *Christians at the Border*, 131-32.

35. Ibid., 132.

36. Ibid., 20. It may even be that this disclaimer heightens his credibility among some sectors of the evangelical community, suspicious as some are about

developments in biblical scholarship that appear to undermine the authority of the Bible.

37. Carroll R., *Christians at the Border*, 121-23.

38. Gilberto Ruiz, "A Migrant Being at Work: John's Christology of Migration and Its Implications," *Journal of Hispanic/Latino Theology* (January 23, 2011), www.latinotheology.org/2011/migrant-worker-migration.

39. It is also heartening to see in the developing work of Gilberto Ruiz the continuing friendship of U.S. Latino/a biblical scholars with the Johannine literature, a curious phenomenon I noted in "The Word Became Flesh and the Flesh Becomes Word," 48.

40. Gilberto Ruiz, "A Migrant Being at Work."

41. Ibid.

42. See Nanko-Fernández, "Beyond Hospitality," 57.

43. Carroll R., *Christians at the Border*, 123, 125.

44. Gilberto Ruiz, "A Migrant Being at Work."

45. See, for example, Leticia Guardiola-Saenz, "Borderless Women and Borderless Texts: A Cultural Reading of Matthew 15:21-28," *Semeia* 78 (1997): 69-81; Hisako Kinukawa, *Women and Jesus in Mark: A Japanese Feminist Perspective* (Maryknoll, NY: Orbis Books, 1994), 51-65; Kwok Pui-lan, *Discovering the Bible in the Non-Biblical World* (Maryknoll, NY: Orbis Books, 1995), 71-83; Gail R. O'Day, "Surprised by Faith: Jesus and the Canaanite Woman," *Listening: A Journal of Religion and Culture* 24 (Fall 1989): 290-301; Jim Perkinson, "A Canaanitic Word in the Logos of Christ; or The Difference the Syrophoenician Woman Makes to Jesus," *Semeia* 75 (1996): 61-85; Petr Pokorný, "From a Puppy to the Child: Some Problems of Contemporary Biblical Exegesis Demonstrated from Mark 7.24-30/Matt 15.21-8," *New Testament Studies* 41 (1995): 321-37; Nancy Proctor, "Anti Luz's Matthew: The Dog Woman and the Dialectic," *Journal of Higher Criticism* 10, no. 1 (2003), 110-20; Ranjanini Wickramaratne Rebera, "The Syrophoenician Woman: A South Asian Feminist Perspective," in *A Feminist Companion to Mark*, ed. Amy-Jill Levine, with Marianne Blickenstaff (Cleveland, OH: Pilgrim Press, 2001), 101-10; Elisabeth Schüssler Fiorenza, *But She Said: Feminist Practices of Biblical Interpretation* (Boston: Beacon, 1992), 11-13, 96-100; Gerd Theissen, *The Gospels in Context: Social and Political History in the Synoptic Tradition*, trans. Linda M. Maloney (Edinburgh: T & T Clark, 2002), 61-80; Elaine M. Wainwright, "A Voice from the Margin: Reading Matthew 15:21-28 in an Australian Feminist Key," in *Reading from This Place*, volume 2: *Social Location and Biblical Interpretation in Global Perspective*, ed. Fernando F. Segovia and Mary Ann Tolbert (Minneapolis: Fortress Press, 1995), 132-53. Also see Sean Freyne, "The Galilean Jesus and a Contemporary Christology," *Theological Studies* 70, no. 2 (June 2009): 292-93.

46. In *A Feminist Companion to Mark*, ed. Amy-Jill Levine, with Marianne Blickenstaff (Cleveland, OH: Pilgrim Press, 2001), 79-100.

47. Sharon H. Ringe, "A Gentile Woman's Story," in *Feminist Interpretation of the Bible*, ed. Letty M. Russell (Philadelphia: Westminster, 1985), 65-72.

48. Ringe, "A Gentile Woman's Story, Revisited," 99.

49. Ibid., 79.

50. Ibid., 80-81.

51. Ibid., 84-85.

52. Ibid., 81.

53. Ibid., 86.

54. Ibid.

55. Theissen, *The Gospels in Context*, 70. The New Revised Standard Version renders *Hellēnis* as "Gentile," transposing Mark's ethnic marker into religious terms to identify the woman as a non-Jew. The Biblia de América makes the same sort of move, rendering *Hellénis* as "*pagana*." The Versión Reina-Valera (Revision de 1960) correctly renders *Hellénis* as "*griega*." The New American Bible does likewise, translating *Hellēnis* as "Greek." Theissen explains, "Certainly knowledge of Greek had also penetrated the lower classes: otherwise the Greek inscriptions in Palestine forbidding grave-robbing would make no sense. But an ordinary woman with little knowledge of Greek would no more be described as a 'Helene' than a German with average English skills would be called an 'Anglophile'" (*The Gospels in Context*, 71).

56. Ibid., 74.

57. Ibid., 75.

58. Ibid.

59. Ringe, "A Gentile Woman's Story, Revisited," 87.

60. Ibid., 90.

61. Ibid.

62. Ibid., 92. That does seem to be the direction in which Matthew 15 reshapes the Markan narrative. First, Matthew identifies the woman not as a Greek Syrophoenician, but as a Canaanite, a designation that appears only once in the Gospels, and that transposes the socioeconomic and interethnic tension of the Markan pericope into the sphere of specifically *religious* difference between Jews and non-News. Second, Matthew's version gives the woman more speaking lines, including an opening that is explicitly christological: "Have mercy on me, Lord, Son of David" (Matt 15:22). Third, in Matthew's version, Jesus' first words are spoken to his disciples, and these underscore Matthew's redactional focus on the beginnings of a mission to the Gentiles: "I was sent only to the lost sheep of the house of Israel" (Matt 15:24). Finally, where the Markan Jesus grants the woman's request because her words have won the day (Mark 7:29), for Matthew's Jesus it is the woman's faith that leads him to fulfill her request (Matt 15:28). For further discussion on theism, see Ringe, "A Gentile Woman's Story, Revisited," 98.

63. See note 45 above.

64. Kinukawa, *Women and Jesus in Mark*, 62-64; Ringe, "A Gentile Woman's Story, Revisited," 40.

65. Guardiola-Saenz, "Borderless Women and Borderless Texts," 69-81; Ringe, "A Gentile Woman's Story, Revisited," 95.

66. Kwok, *Discovering the Bible*, 82; Ringe, "A Gentile Woman's Story, Revisited," 96.

67. Ringe, "A Gentile Woman's Story, Revisited," 97. Ringe asks, "Should I as a woman celebrate the picture of this woman's loyalty to her beloved daughter, and the woman's wit and quick tongue that change Jesus' mind? I do. Or should I read it with lament and even rage at the picture of the treatment she receives at the hand— or more accurately the mouth—of the one I confess as Emmanuel? I do that, too. And I am left perplexed" (99).

68. *Pace* Allan Figueroa Deck, who suggests, "The gospel teaching on God's

universal love which echoes the tradition on love of strangers, aliens and sojourners on the land shows itself in several places. One may point to the parable of the Good Samaritan in which the one who shows the neighborly quality of mercy is the outsider, a reviled one at that, not the priest nor the Levite. It is seen also in the Syro-Phoenician woman who sought a cure for her daughter (Mk 7:24-30) and the Roman centurion whom Jesus praises for his faith even though he is an outsider and, even worse, one identified with the oppressors themselves (Mt 8:15-13)" ("Christian Perspectives on Migration: Retelling the Story," unpublished paper presented at the 2009 Academy of Catholic Hispanic Theologians of the United States Colloquium and General Meeting, Chicago 2009). From the standpoint of postcolonial theory and empire studies, much more could be written about the encounter with Jesus and the centurion in Matthew 5:8-13 than is possible here. Even more could be said about the Lukan version (Luke 7:1-10), in which the complexities of the patron–client, dominance–subordination, relationships between imperial occupying forces and those under their control are underscored by the appeal of the Jewish elders on the centurion's behalf: "He is worthy of having you do this for him, for he loves our people, and it is he who built our synagogue for us" (Luke 7:4-5). Whatever the centurion's personal motivations may have been for this act of patronage, it is a military tactic repeated again and again over the centuries to "build strong relationships" with occupied populations. Quite unlike the situation in Mark 7:24-30, and aside from the centurion's reputation as a benefactor to the Jewish community at Capernaum, Jesus is hardly in a position to turn down the centurion's request. That is clear from Luke 7:8, where the centurion spells out for Jesus what he and other residents of occupied territory already knew very well: "I also am a man set under authority, with soldiers under me; and I say to one, 'Go,' and he goes, and to another, 'Come,' and he comes, and to my slave, 'Do this,' and the slave does it." Despite the niceties of the centurion's rhetoric, what he asks of Jesus is more than just a request. Furthermore, the relationship between the one who requests the healing in Mark 7 is also much different from the situation in Luke 7: The Syrophoenician woman asks Jesus to heal her *daughter*, whereas the centurion asks Jesus to heal a slave whom the centurion regards as a valuable commodity (Luke 7:2). It seems that neither in Mark 7 nor in Luke 7 do Jesus' actions have much at all to do with love.

69. So Joel Marcus, *Mark 1–8: A New Translation with Introduction and Commentary*, Anchor Bible 27 (New York: Doubleday, 1999), 466. Marcus makes reference to the study in which C. Focant asks why "anyone would create or shape a story in such a way that the point of view voiced by Jesus ended up being refuted" (Marcus, *Mark 1–8*, 466; referring to C. Focant, "Mc 7, 24-31 par. Mt 15, 21-29. Critique des sources et/ou étude narrative," in *The Synoptic Gospels: Source Criticism and the New Literary Criticism*, ed. C. Focant [Leuven: Leuven University Press, 1993], 39-79).

70. Stanley E. Porter, "Jesus and the Use of Greek in Galilee," in *Studying the Historical Jesus: Evaluations of the State of Current Research*, ed. Bruce Chilton and Craig A. Evans (Leiden: Brill, 1994), 149-50.

71. For further discussion of this, see Jean-Pierre Ruiz, "'They Could Not Speak the Language of Judah': Rereading Nehemiah 13 between Brooklyn and Jerusalem," in *They Were All Together in One Place?* 79-95, especially 89-93.

72. See Theissen, *The Gospels in Context*, 69.

73. On the othering-as-romanticization of the Canaanite woman in the Matthean parallel to Mark 7:24, 30, see Guardiola-Saenz, "Borderless Women and Borderless Texts," 75-76. Guardiola-Saenz writes, "In my social-historical condition of dispossessed neighbor, born and bred in the borderlands of the U.S. empire, I am certainly determined to take the bread from the table and not wait until the crumbs fall from it. I am convinced that it is only at the level of the table—as equals—and not under the table—as inferiors—that a constructive dialogue and a fair reconstitution of the world can be achieved" (69).

74. Ruiz, "Abram and Sarai Cross the Border," 22.

75. James Carroll, "Silent Reading in Public Life," *Boston Globe*, February 12, 2007, www.boston.com/news/globe/editorial_opinion/oped/articles/2007/02/12/silent _reading_in_public_life/.

76. "Cum legebat, oculi ducebantur per paginas et cor intellectum rimabatur, vox autem et lingua quiescebant. Saepe cum adessemus (non enim vetabatur quisquam ingredi aut ei venientem nuntiari mos erat), sic eum legentem vidimus tacite et aliter numquam, sedentesque in diuturno silentio (quis enim tam intento esse oneri auderet?)" (J. J. O'Donnell, ed., *The Confessions of Saint Augustine* 6.3.3, www.stoa.org/hippo/text6.html).

77. Segovia, "Toward Latino/a American Biblical Criticism," 222.

78. Schüssler Fiorenza, *The Power of the Word*, 10. Because the reading practices we have discussed call upon us to read across borders, our concern for people on the move cannot be limited to those who immigrate to the United States mainly from Latin America. Our attention and advocacy must extend to the many hundreds of millions of refugees, asylum-seekers, internally displaced persons, stateless persons, guest workers, economic migrants around the world.

79. This underscores the importance of such coalition building as bears first-fruits in *They Were All Together in One Place?*

80. Ringe, "A Gentile Woman's Story, Revisited," 90.

4. ABRAM AND SARAI CROSS THE BORDER

1. R. S. Sugirtharajah, "A Postcolonial Exploration of Collusion and Construction in Biblical Interpretation," in *The Postcolonial Bible*, ed. R. S. Sugirtharajah; The Bible and Postcolonialism 1 (Sheffield, UK: Sheffield Academic Press, 1998), 113. Sugirtharajah explains, "A postcolonial critic's role is not simply limited to textual dealings or literary concerns. Postcolonial hermeneutics has to be a pragmatic engagement, an engagement in which praxis is not an extra option or a subsidiary enterprise taken in the aftermath of judicious deconstruction and reconstruction of the texts. Rather, this praxeological involvement is there from the outset of the hermeneutical process, informing and contesting the whole procedure. If we neglect this, we may become ridiculous figures like the Lavatrie Alltheorie portrayed in Rukun Advani's novel *Beethoven among the Cows*. In the longest chapter of the book, entitled 'S/he, or A Postmodern Chapter on Gender and Identity,' Lavatrie Alltheorie is described as a 'Post-modern theoretician, boa deconstructor, discourse analyst, post-structural critic, feminist historian of subalternity, colonialism and

gender.' A diasporic Indian academic, she offers courses to packed audiences of white students on 'the semiology of Deconstruction and the Deconstruction of semiology.' The danger is that we will be seen as deliberately using catchphrases and buzzwords as a form of posture and power play. As Arun Mukherjee says, it is not enough to fight the colonizer with the 'textual weapons of irony and parody.' If we do so, we may, like Lavatrie Alltheorie, become renowned for 'specialization in Complete Bunkum'" (11).

2. On "reading with" as a hermeneutical stance, see Fernando F. Segovia, "Reading across: Intercultural Criticism and Textual Posture," in *Interpreting Beyond Borders*, ed. Fernando F. Segovia; The Bible and Postcolonialism 3 (Sheffield, UK: Sheffield Academic Press, 2000), 68-72, a presentation and analysis of the work of Gerald West.

3. Hereinafter *Erga migrantes*. Available on the Internet at www.vatican. va/roman_curia/pontifical_councils/migrants/documents/rc_pc_migrants_ doc_20040514_erga-migrantes-caritas-christi_en.html#The%20challenge%20 of%20human%20mobility.

4. See Aelred Cody, O.S.B., "'Little Historical Creed' or "Little Historical Anamnesis,'" *Catholic Biblical Quarterly* 68 (2006): 1-10.

5. United States Conference of Catholic Bishops and Conferencia del Episcopado Mexicano, *Strangers No Longer: Together on the Journey of Hope. A Pastoral Letter Concerning Migration from the Catholic Bishops of Mexico and the United States* (Washington, DC: United States Conference of Catholic Bishops, 2003), available at www.usccb.org/mrs/stranger.shtml.

6. *Strangers No Longer*, nos. 24 and 25. The citation "Gn 37:45" is incorrect (There is no verse 45 in Genesis 37!). The citation should probably read Genesis 37-45, the chapters that contain the Joseph story.

7. The *New York Times* reports that as Georgia governor Sonny Perdue signed into law the Georgia Security and Immigration Compliance Act, a harsh anti-immigrant measure, "The crowd waved American flags and cheered as State Representative Melvin Everson, a black Republican in the House, denounced illegal immigration as a cancer. 'The last time I checked,' Mr. Everson said, 'America was the land of English, not Spanish'" (*New York Times*, April 18, 2006. A16).

8. Gerald Kicanas, Thomas Olmsted, Donald Pelotte, and William Skurla, "You Welcomed Me: Migration Pastoral Letter," *Origins* 35, no. 29 (January 5, 2006): 477-83. In reflecting on the biblical foundations of the church's response to the situation of people on the move, the Arizona bishops draw on the November 15, 2000, statement of the U.S. Catholic bishops, *Welcoming the Stranger among Us: Unity in Diversity*, available at www.usccb.org/mrs/unity.shtml#church.

9. See Joe Feuerherd, "Bishops United on Immigration," *National Catholic Reporter*, April 21, 2006. The October 18, 2005, "Interfaith Statement in Support of Comprehensive Immigration Reform," with more than a hundred Jewish, Christian, and Muslim signatories, likewise urged Congress to "enact comprehensive immigration reform legislation that establishes a safe and humane immigration system consistent with our values. Our diverse faith traditions teach us to welcome our brothers and sisters with love and compassion." The document cites Leviticus 19 as a biblical foundation for such a faith-based stance and is available at www. ctcatholic.org/documents/InterfaithStatement.pdf.

10. The *New York Times*, March 3, 2006. A22. Cardinal Mahony himself contributed an op ed piece to the *New York Times* in which he explained his opposition to HR 4437 and his call for just and comprehensive immigration reform. See Roger Mahony, "Called by God to Help," *New York Times*, March 22, 2006, A25.

11. George Neumayr, "Cardinal Sin," *National Review Online* (April 12, 2006), www.nationalreview.com/comment/neumayr200604120719.asp.

12. Glenn Thrush, "LI Congressman Takes a Controversial Stance," *Newsday*, April 2, 2006, www.bishopaccountability.org/news2006/03_04/2006_04_02_Thrush_LiCongressman.htm.

13. Thrush, "LI Congressman Takes a Controversial Stance," *Newsday*, April 2, 2006.

14. See United States Conference of Catholic Bishops, *Welcoming the Stranger among Us*, available at www.usccb.org/mrs/unity.shtml. In his March 25, 2006, radio address, President George Bush himself referred to the United States as "a nation of immigrants" and a "nation of laws" (usinfo.org/wf-archive/2006/060327/epf104.htm). In a speech delivered at a March 27, 2006, naturalization ceremony, President Bush boasted: "Our immigrant heritage has enriched America's history. It continues to shape our society. Each generation of immigrants brings a renewal to our national character and adds vitality to our culture" (www.uscis.gov/files/nativedocuments/USCISToday_April_06.pdf).

15. These statistics are reported on the Hispanic Affairs web page of the United States Conference of Catholic Bishops, and they represent the results of pre-2000 surveys. It is entirely likely that these numbers have increased considerably since these data were collected (United States Conference of Catholic Bishops, Hispanic Affairs, "Demographics / Statistics," www.usccb.org/hispanicaffairs/demo.shtml#4).

16. For an insightful analysis of "they"/"us" language vis-à-vis church documents regarding the preferential option for the poor, see Carmen M. Nanko, "Justice Crosses the Border: The Preferential Option for the Poor in the United States," in *A Reader in Latina Feminist Theology: Religion and Justice*, ed. María Pilar Aquino, Daisy Machado, and Jeanette Rodriguez (Austin: University of Texas Press, 2002), 177-203, esp. 186-87. Also see Carmen M. Nanko-Fernández, "We Are Not Your Diversity, We Are the Church! Ecclesiological Reflections from the Marginalized Many," *Perspectivas: Hispanic Theological Initiative Occasional Papers 10* (Fall 2006): 81-117, with a revised version also available in Carmen Nanko-Fernández, *Theologizing en Espanglish: Context, Community and Ministry* (Maryknoll, NY: Orbis Books, 2010), 1-20.

17. Dianne Bergant, "Ruth: The Migrant Who Saved the People," in *Migration, Religious Experience, and Globalization*, ed. Gioacchino Campese and Pietro Cialella (New York: Center for Migration Studies, 2003), 51.

18. Francisco O. García-Treto, "El Señor guarda a los emigrantes," *Apuntes* 1, no. 4 (Winter 1981): 4, as translated by and cited in Justo L. González, *Santa Biblia: The Bible through Hispanic Eyes* (Nashville: Abingdon, 1996), 94. With regard to xenophobic attitudes in the Bible itself, see Francisco O. García-Treto, "The Lesson of the Gibeonites: A Proposal for Dialogic Attention as a Strategy for Reading the Bible," in *Hispanic / Latino Theology: Challenge and Promise*, ed. Ada María Isasi-Díaz and Fernando F. Segovia (Minneapolis: Fortress Press, 1996), 73-85.

19. González, *Santa Biblia*, 94.

20. García-Treto, "El Señor guarda a los emigrantes," 6-7, as translated and cited in González, *Santa Biblia*, 94. On Leviticus 25:23, see Jacob Milgrom, *Leviticus 23-27: A New Translation with Introduction and Commentary*, Anchor Bible 3B (New York: Doubleday, 2001), 2183-91.

21. A variety of other texts might yield equally provocative readings. The book of Ruth, for example, is a text that vividly illustrates the tensions between identity and assimilation, and the difficult and painful decisions that face people on the move. See Laura Donaldson's re-reading of the book of Ruth as a Cherokee woman: "The Sign of Orpah: Reading Ruth through Native Eyes," in *Vernacular Hermeneutics*, ed. R. S. Sugirtharajah; The Bible and Postcolonialism 2 (Sheffield, UK: Sheffield Academic Press, 1999), 20-36.

22. See Luis R. Rivera Rodríguez, "Immigration and the Bible: Comments by a Diasporic Theologian," in *Perspectivas*, 23-36. Also see Harold V. Bennett, *Injustice Made Legal: Deuteronomic Law and the Plight of Widows, Strangers, and Orphans in Ancient Israel* (Grand Rapids: Eerdmans, 2002); Christiana van Houten, *The Alien in Israelite Law* (Sheffield, UK: JSOT Press, 1991).

23. Robert Alter, *The Art of Biblical Narrative* (New York: Basic Books, 1981), 49.

24. Susan Niditch, "Genesis," in *The Women's Bible Commentary*, ed. Carol A. Newsom and Sharon H. Ringe (Louisville, KY: Westminster/John Knox Press, 1992), 18.

25. Ibid., 18. Niditch provides a clear and concise sketch of the narrative nuances of the three different versions of the tale.

26. Gordon Wenham, *Genesis 1-15*, Word Biblical Commentary 1 (Waco, TX: Word Books, 1987), 286. Wenham identifies C (vv. 14-16) as "Fulfillment of Abram's fears." I suggest instead that the ruse works, inasmuch as verse 16 tells us that for Sarai's sake Pharaoh dealt well with Abram, just as in verse 13 Abram expressed his hope that it would.

27. Ibid., 287-88.

28. Claus Westermann, *Genesis 12-36: A Commentary*, trans. John J. Scullion (Minneapolis: Augsburg Fortress Press, 1985), 164.

29. Niditch, "Genesis," 18-19.

30. Nahum M. Sarna, *The JPS Torah Commentary: Genesis* (Philadelphia: Jewish Publication Society, 1989), 94.

31. Niditch, "Genesis," 18. Wenham notes that in verse 15, "was taken" is an expression that "properly denotes the formal taking of a woman as a wife . . . it can be used more loosely to describe all aspects of marriage" (*Genesis 1-15*, 289).

32. Sarna, *The JPS Torah Commentary*, 94-95.

33. Thus, for example, Wenham reports the suggestion by E. A. Speiser that we find in this story "an allusion to a Hurrian custom whereby a man could take a woman to be both wife and sister at the same time," and Wenham likewise observes that Speiser's hypothesis "is rejected by more recent writers (Wenham, *Genesis 1-15*, 288; also see Westermann, *Genesis 12-36*, 164).

34. Gloria Anzaldúa, *Borderlands/La Frontera: The New Mestiza*, 2nd ed. (San Francisco: Aunt Lute Books, 1999), 34-35.

35. See Joseph Nevins, *Operation Gatekeeper: The Rise of the "Illegal Alien"*

and the Making of the U.S.-Mexico Boundary (New York: Routledge, 2002).

36. United States Government Accountability Office, *Illegal Immigration: Border-Crossing Deaths Have Doubled since 1995; Border Patrol's Efforts to Prevent Deaths Have Not Been Fully Evaluated* (Washington, DC: United States Government Accountability Office, 2006), 3, 13.

37. R. S. Sugirtharajah, "A Postcolonial Exploration," 113.

5. SYMBOLISM ON THE STREET

1. Justo L. González, *Santa Biblia: The Bible through Hispanic Eyes* (Nashville: Abingdon, 1996), 91.

2. Fernando F. Segovia, "In the World but Not of It: Exile as a Locus for a Theology of the Diaspora," in Ada María Isasi-Díaz, ed., *Hispanic/Latino Theology: Challenge and Promise* (Minneapolis: Fortress Press, 1996), 91.

3. It was in Jaime Carrero's poem "*Jet Neorriqueño*/Neo-Rican Jetliner," first published in 1965, that this term first found its way into literary print. The poem is available in *The Puerto Ricans: A Documentary History*, ed. Kal Wagenheim and Olga Jiménez de Wagenheim (Princeton, NJ: Markus Wiener, 1994), 276-81.

4. Alberto Sandoval Sánchez, "Puerto Rican Identity Up in the Air: Air Migration, Its Cultural Representations and Me 'Cruzando el Charco,'" in *Puerto Rican Jam: Rethinking Colonialism and Nationalism*, ed. Frances Negrón Muntaner and Ramón Grosfoguel (Minneapolis: University of Minnesota Press, 1997), 189-90.

5. As I read Ezekiel from my hyphenated place, I am encouraged to discover that I am not alone in doing so. Francisco García-Treto considers Ezekiel 4:9-15, another of Ezekiel's symbolic actions, together with two other texts (Gen 4:13-14 and 18:22-33), three narratives that present characters (Cain, Abraham, and Ezekiel) who are "all, in one way or another, and for a variety of reasons, exiles. . . . When we remember that the writers and redactors of the Hebrew Bible were themselves products of a culture massively influenced by exile, we can understand the special appropriateness of the hermeneutical stance of contemporary [exiles of one sort or another] for interpreting the texts that they penned and the characters they depicted" ("Crossing the Line: Three Scenes of Divine-Human Engagement in the Hebrew Bible," in *Teaching the Bible: The Discourses and Politics of Biblical Pedagogy*, ed. Fernando F. Segovia and Mary Ann Tolbert [Maryknoll, NY: Orbis Books, 1998], 106).

6. Walter Brueggemann, *Hopeful Imagination: Prophetic Voices in Exile* (Philadelphia: Fortress Press, 1986), 51.

7. Moses Maimonides, *The Guide for the Perplexed*, 2d ed. rev., trans. M. Friedländer (New York: Dover, 1956) 2, 46 (p. 246). Maimonides' concern, "God forbid that God would make his prophets appear an object of ridicule and sport in the eyes of the ignorant, and order them to perform foolish acts," addresses the taunt found in *b. Sanhedrin* 39a, "A heretic said to R. Abbahu, 'Your God is a joker; first he commands to lie on the left side, then on the right side,'" a taunt that reflects perplexity over Ezekiel 4:4-8.

8. Peter C. Craigie, *Ezekiel*, Daily Study Bible (Edinburgh: Saint Andrew's Press, 1983), 83.

9. Craigie, *Ezekiel*, 85.

10. See Ronald M. Hals, *Ezekiel*. Forms of the Old Testament Literature 19 (Grand Rapids, MI: Eerdmans, 1989), 74-80, 354-55. The standard treatment of the genre is Georg Fohrer, *Die symbolische Handlungen der Propheten*, 2d ed. (Zurich: Zwingli, 1968). With respect to the literary structure of what he calls the "narratives of sign-actions," Walther Zimmerli suggests that the form underwent evolution from a simpler form "in which a) an explanation of the circumstances is followed by b) an account of the action followed by c) the interpretation" to a later stage in which "the explanation (a) is replaced as it happens by the divine command. . . . This leads to a type of narrative in which the carrying out of the action is no longer narrated, but everything is swallowed up in Yahweh's command" (*Ezekiel 1*, trans. Ronald E. Clements [Hermeneia; Philadelphia: Fortress, 1979], 156).

11. J. Lindblom, *Prophecy in Ancient Israel* (Philadelphia: Fortress Press, 1962), 172.

12. Bernhard Lang, "Street Theater, Raising the Dead and the Zoroastrian Connection in Ezekiel's Prophecy," in *Ezekiel and His Book: Textual and Literary Criticism and Their Interrelation*, ed. J. Lust (Leuven: Leuven University Press, 1986), 298-316.

13. Lang, "Street Theater," 300, 302.

14. See Fernando F. Segovia and Mary Ann Tolbert, eds., *Reading from This Place*, volume 1: *Social Location and Biblical Interpretation in the United States* (Minneapolis: Fortress Press, 1995), and idem, *Reading from This Place*, volume 2: *Social Location and Biblical Interpretation in Global Perspective* (Minneapolis: Fortress Press, 1995).

15. Segovia, "In the World but Not of It," 210.

16. Lang, "Street Theater," 303.

17. Ibid., 304.

18. Ibid., 305.

19. Ibid.

20. Ibid., 302.

21. Cited in ibid., 302.

22. Ibid.

23. Jan Cohen-Cruz, "Introduction," in Jan Cohen-Cruz, ed., *Radical Street Performance: An International Anthology* (London: Routledge, 1998), 5.

24. Examples of performance as witness included in the anthology edited by Cohen-Cruz include Steven Durlans, "Witness: The Guerrilla Theater of Greenpeace," *Radical Street Performance* (67-73); Diana Taylor, "Making a Spectacle: The Mothers of the Plaza de Mayo" (74-85); and Marguerite Walker's study of Las Comadres, a women's group on the U.S.–Mexico border, "Border *Boda* or Divorce *Fronterizo?*" (86-89). Examples of performance as integration include a treatment of the die-ins staged in the 1980s to protest a NATO decision to base cruise missiles at Greenham in South Wales ("Taking Direct Action," 160-63).

25. Moshe Greenberg, *Ezekiel 1-20*, Anchor Bible 22 (Garden City, NY: Doubleday, 1983), 220.

26. Ellen F. Davis, *Swallowing the Scroll: Textuality and the Dynamics of Prophecy in Ezekiel's Prophecy*, Bible and Literature Series 21 (Sheffield, UK: Almond Press, 1989), 68.

27. Davis, *Swallowing the Scroll*, 71.

28. Ibid., 37.

29. Ibid., 39.

30. In her study "You Are What You Eat: Ezekiel and the Scroll" (*Journal of Biblical Literature* 117 [1998]: 201-27), Margaret S. Odell suggests (unconvincingly, at least for me) that Ezekiel 3:16-5:17, with the symbolic acts presented there, constitutes an extension of the call narrative in which the symbolic acts constitute a series of ritual enactments that prepare Ezekiel to assume his prophetic role.

31. With respect to the continuum between orality (and, by extension, the sorts of nonverbal performance presented in the symbolic actions) and literacy, the studies of Susan Niditch and Raymond F. Person, Jr., reinforce this suggestion by arguing that "ancient Israelite scribes were not mere copyists but were also performers"(Raymond F. Person, Jr., "The Ancient Israelite Scribe as Performer," *Journal of Biblical Literature* 117 [1998]: 602). See Susan Niditch, *Oral World and Written Word: Ancient Israelite Literature* (Louisville, KY: Westminster/John Knox, 1996).

32. Richard Schechner, "Drama, Script, Theatre and Performance," in *Essays on Performance Theory 1970-1976* (New York: Drama Book Specialists, 1977), 39.

33. *Ezekiel 1-20*, 219. For his part, David J. Halperin suggests a psychoanalytic approach in *Seeking Ezekiel: Text and Psychology* (University Park: Pennsylvania State University Press, 1993), 227-31, an approach that represents yet another permutation among the many unsatisfying efforts to resolve perceived inconsistencies in Ezekiel at the psychological (and sometimes psychopathological) level.

34. Zimmerli, *Ezekiel 1*, 267.

35. The multiple displacements that occurred as the tradition of the text grew through time also deserve another look from a contextual standpoint. As Ezekiel 12:1-16 now stands, the tension between people and prince is inescapable. In effect, the displacement of attention from what was to befall the inhabitants of Jerusalem to what has become of the king raises questions about the relative visibility of the powerful and the powerless in history. Ironically enough, in a text that is about seeing Ezekiel's performance, it is the blinded king who becomes more and more visible to readers. The fate of one man, horrible though it may have been, relegates the fate of many men, women, and children who went into exile into the literary exile of anonymity at the periphery of the text.

36. Greenberg, *Ezekiel 1-20*, 220.

37. See Davis, *Swallowing the Scroll*, 63.

38. Zimmerli, *Ezekiel 1*, 156, 268.

39. Louis Ramlot, in *Supplément au Dictionnaire de la Bible* (Paris: Cerf, 1972), 8:973, as cited in Lang, "Street Theater," 307.

40. Lang, "Street Theater," 305.

41. *Jeremiah's and Ezekiel's Sign Acts: Rhetorical Nonverbal Communication* (Sheffield, UK: Sheffield Academic Press, 1999).

42. Davis, *Swallowing the Scroll*, 61.

6. AN EXILE'S BAGGAGE

1. Edward Said, "The Mind of Winter: Reflections on Life in Exile," *Harpers* (September 1983), 50, as cited in Daniel L. Smith-Christopher, *A Biblical Theology of Exile*, Overtures in Biblical Theology (Minneapolis: Fortress Press, 2002), 21.

2. Ada María Isasi-Díaz, "'By the Rivers of Babylon': Exile as a Way of Life," in *Reading from This Place,* volume 1: *Social Location and Biblical Location in the United States*, ed. Fernando F. Segovia and Mary Ann Tolbert (Minneapolis: Fortress Press, 1995), 149.

3. United Nations High Commissioner for Refugees, *2009 Global Trends: Refugees, Asylum-seekers, Returnees, Internally Displaced and Stateless Persons* (Geneva: United Nations High Commissioner for Refugees, 2010), available at www.unhcr.org/4c11f0be9.html.

4. Fernando F. Segovia, "Toward a Hermeneutics of the Diaspora: A Hermeneutics of Otherness and Engagement," in *Reading from This Place,* volume 1: *Social Location and Biblical Interpretation in the United States*, ed. Fernando F. Segovia and Mary Ann Tolbert (Minneapolis: Fortress Press, 1995), 68-69.

5. Lisa H. Malkki, "National Geographic: The Rooting of Peoples and the Territorializing of National Identity among Scholars and Refugees," in *Culture, Power, and Place: Explorations in Critical Anthropology*, ed. A. Gupta and J. Ferguson (Durham, NC: Duke University Press, 1997), 52.

6. Daniel L. Smith-Christopher, "Ezekiel on Fanon's Couch: A Postcolonialist Dialogue with David Halperin's *Seeking Ezekiel*," in *Peace and Justice Shall Embrace: Power and Theopolitics in the Bible. Essays in Honor of Millard Lind*, ed. Ted Grimsrud and Loren L. Johns (Telford, PA: Pandora Press; Scottdale, PA: Herald Press, 1999), 110-11.

7. Segovia, "Toward a Hermeneutics of the Diaspora," 68.

8. Ibid., 69.

9. For a convenient introduction to postcolonialism, see Leela Gandhi, *Postcolonial Theory: A Critical Introduction* (New York: Columbia University Press, 1998); Ania Loomba, *Colonialism/Postcolonialism* (London: Routledge, 1998).

10. Arif Dirlik, *The Postcolonial Aura: Third World Criticism in the Age of Global Capitalism* (Boulder, CO: Westview Press, 1997), ix.

11. Bill Ashcroft, Gareth Griffiths, and Helen Tiffin, *The Empire Writes Back: Theory and Practice in Postcolonial Literatures* (London: Routledge, 1989).

12. Dirlik, *The Postcolonial Aura*, 8.

13. R. S. Sugirtharajah, "Biblical Studies after the Empire: From a Colonial to a Postcolonial Mode of Interpretation," in *The Postcolonial Bible*, ed. R. S. Sugirtharajah; The Bible and Postcolonialism 1 (Sheffield, UK: Sheffield Academic Press, 1998), 16. Also see R. S. Sugirtharajah, *The Bible and the Third World: Precolonial, Colonial and Postcolonial Encounters* (Cambridge: Cambridge University Press, 2001). Also see Laura E. Donaldson, ed., "Postcolonialism and Scriptural Reading," *Semeia* 75 (1996): 1-240.

14. Fernando F. Segovia, "Interpreting beyond Borders: Postcolonial Studies and Diasporic Studies in Biblical Criticism," in *Interpreting beyond Borders*, ed. Fernando F. Segovia; The Bible and Postcolonialism 3 (Sheffield, UK: Sheffield Academic Press, 2000), 11-12.

15. Stephen D. Moore, "Postcolonialism," in *Handbook of Postmodern Biblical Interpretation*, ed. A. K. M. Adam (St. Louis: Chalice Press, 2000), 188.

16. Russell Jacoby, "Marginal Returns: The Trouble with Post-Colonial Theory," *Lingua Franca* 5, no. 6 (September/October 1995): 30.

17. Terry Eagleton, "Postcolonialism and 'Postcolonialism,'" *Interventions* 1, no. 1 (1998): 24. Eagleton rightly critiques the sort of postcolonialism that is "a brand of culturalism, which inflates the significance of cultural factors in human affairs. This is a vice to which literary intellectuals are especially prone. It would, to be sure, be comforting for them if what was at stake between the north and south of the globe really was in the first place questions of value, signification and history, identity, cultural practice, rather than arms, trade agreements, military alliances, drug trafficking and the like. 'Poscolonialism' has been on the whole rather stronger on identity than on the International Monetary Fund, more fascinated by marginality than by margins" (Eagleton, "Postcolonialism and 'Postcolonialism,'" 26). Also see Eagleton, "In the Gaudy Supermarket," *London Review of Books* 21:10 (May 13, 1999), available at www.lrb.co.uk/v21/n10/eagl01_.html. This is Eagleton's review of postcolonial theorist Gayatri Chakravorty Spivak's *A Critique of Post-Colonial Reason: Toward a History of the Vanishing Present* (Cambridge, MA: Harvard University Press, 1999).

18. Sugirtharajah, "A Postcolonial Exploration of Collusion and Construction in Biblical Interpretation," in *The Postcolonial Bible*, ed. R. S. Sugirtharajah; The Bible and Postcolonialism 1 (Sheffield, UK: Sheffield Academic Press, 1998), 113.

19. Sugirtharajah, *The Bible and the Third World*, 258. In a similar vein, Moore explains that "postcolonialism is not *a* method of interpretation (any more than is feminist criticism, say) so much as a critical sensibility attuned to a specific range of interrelated textual and historical phenomena" (Moore, "Postcolonialism," 183).

20. Sugirtharajah, *The Bible and the Third World*, 250-57.

21. Justo L. Gonález, *Santa Biblia: The Bible through Hispanic Eyes* (Nashville: Abingdon, 1996), 92.

22. Francisco García-Treto, "Hyphenating Joseph: A View of Genesis 39-41 from the Cuban Diaspora," in *Interpreting beyond Borders*, ed. Fernando F. Segovia; The Bible and Postcolonialism 3 (Sheffield, UK: Sheffield Academic Press, 2000), 134-45; Gustavo Pérez Firmat, *Life on the Hyphen: The Cuban-American Way* (Austin: University of Texas Press, 1994). García-Treto also acknowledges his debt to the work of Cuban-American anthropologist Ruth Behar, *The Vulnerable Observer: Anthropology that Breaks Your Heart* (Boston: Beacon Press, 1996).

23. Pérez Firmat, *Life on the Hyphen*, 7, as cited in García-Treto, "Hyphenating Joseph," 137.

24. Avivah Gottlieb Zornberg, *Genesis: The Beginning of Desire* (Philadelphia: Jewish Publication Society, 1995), 274, as cited in García-Treto, "Hyphenating Joseph," 137.

25. Pérez Firmat, *Life on the Hyphen*, 10, as cited in García-Treto, "Hyphenating Joseph," 139.

26. García-Treto, "Hyphenating Joseph," 139.

27. Ibid., 139.

28. Ibid., 140.

29. I distinguish the world behind the text, the world of the text, and the world before (or in front of) the text following Sandra M. Schneiders, *The Revelatory Text:*

Interpreting the New Testament as Sacred Scripture (San Francisco: Harper, 1991), 97-179.

30. García-Treto, "Hyphenating Joseph," 145.

31. Albert Memmi, "The Impossible Life of Frantz Fanon," *The Massachusetts Review* 14, no. 1 (Winter 1973): 39, as cited in Loomba, *Colonialism/Postcolonialism*, 143. See David Macey, *Frantz Fanon: A Biography* (New York: Picador, 2001); *Fanon: A Critical Reader*, ed. Lewis R. Gordon, T. Denean Sharpley-Whiting, and Renee T. White (London: Blackwell, 1996).

32. Frantz Fanon, *Peau noire, masques blancs* (Paris: Seuil, 1952), English translation: *Black Skin, White Masks*, trans. Charles L. Markmann (New York: Grove, 1967). See Hussein Abdilahi Bulhan, *Frantz Fanon and the Psychology of Oppression* (New York: Plenum, 1985).

33. Frantz Fanon, *L'an V de la révolution algérienne* (Paris: Maspero, 1959), English translation: *A Dying Colonialism*, trans. Haakon Chevalier (New York: Grove, 1965); idem, *Les damnés de la terre* (Paris: Maspero, 1961), English translation: *The Wretched of the Earth*, trans. Constance Farrington (New York: Grove, 1963); David Macey, *Frantz Fanon: A Biography* (New York: Picador, 2001).

34. Smith-Christopher, "Ezekiel on Fanon's Couch," 141.

35. David J. Halperin, *Seeking Ezekiel: Text and Psychology* (University Park: Pennsylvania State University Press, 1993). Halperin's study is, in some sense, a reprise of Edwin C. Broome's article "Ezekiel's Abnormal Personality," *Journal of Biblical Literature* 65 (1946): 277-92.

36. Smith-Christopher, "Ezekiel on Fanon's Couch," 134-35.

37. Ibid., 144.

38. Ibid., 134.

39. Ibid., 142.

40. Both in this study and elsewhere, Smith-Christopher expresses strong skepticism toward "recent trends to discount the importance of the Exile and to minimize its impact" (ibid., 112 n. 9; 114-15). He makes reference to *Leading Captivity Captive: "The Exile" as History and Ideology*, ed. Lester L. Grabbe (Sheffield, UK: Sheffield Academic Press, 1998). Also see Daniel L. Smith, *The Religion of the Landless: The Social Context of the Babylonian Exile* (Bloomington, IN: Meyer Stone, 1989); Daniel L. Smith-Christopher, "Reassessing the Historical and Sociological Impact of the Babylonian Exile (597/587-539 BCE)," in *Exile: Old Testament, Jewish, and Christian Conceptions*, ed. James M. Scott (Leiden: Brill, 1997), 7-36; idem, *A Biblical Theology of Exile*, Overtures to Biblical Theology (Minneapolis: Fortress Press, 2002). In the editor's foreword to Smith-Christopher's *A Biblical Theology of Exile*, Walter Brueggemann writes, "There is now a powerful skeptical opinion among some scholars, especially in Britain, concerning the deep characterization of exile reported in the Old Testament text. That opinion suggests that exile is largely an ideological construct designed to advance the influence and legacy of one segment of emerging Judaism" (*A Biblical Theology of Exile*, vii).

41. Homi K. Bhabha, *The Location of Culture* (New York: Routledge, 1994), 5, as cited in Smith-Christopher, "Ezekiel on Fanon's Couch," 110.

42. Making himself very clear, Smith-Christopher writes: "In this work I am not exclusively focused on the exilic events of the ancient Judeans. I argue that ancient Israelite responses to exile and diaspora, as reflected in the biblical texts, can provide the building blocks for rethinking the role of the Hebrew Bible in informing the

modern Christian theological enterprise. . . . I no longer have much interest in, or patience with, attempting to hide the theological agenda that partially motivates my interest in the subject of the Babylonian exile and the Hebrew textual and religious responses" (*A Biblical Theology of Exile*, 6-7).

43. See Jean-Pierre Ruiz, "Exile, History and Hope: A Hispanic Reading of Ezekiel 20," *The Bible Today* (March 1997): 106-13, and also Jean-Pierre Ruiz, "Among the Exiles by the River Chebar: A U.S. Hispanic American Reading of Prophetic Cosmology in Ezekiel 1:1-3," *Journal of Hispanic/Latino Theology* 6, no. 2 (November 1998): 43-67.

44. Frantz Fanon, "On National Culture," in *The Wretched of the Earth*, 170, reprinted in *Colonial Discourse and Postcolonial Theory: A Reader*, ed. Patrick Williams and Laura Chrisman (New York: Columbia University Press, 1994), 37.

45. Daniel I. Block, *The Book of Ezekiel Chapters 1-14*, New International Commentary on the Old Testament (Grand Rapids, MI: Eerdmans, 1997), 5-6. The standard work on Assyrian policies and practices of deportation is Bustenay Oded, *Mass Deportations and Deportees in the Neo-Assyrian Empire* (Wiesbaden: L. Reichert, 1979).

46. Martin Noth, *The History of Israel*, 2nd ed. (London: Adam & Charles Black, 1960), 296.

47. Bustenay Oded, "Judah and the Exile," in *Israelite and Judean History* (Philadelphia: Westminster, 1977), 483. See the critique of this position in Smith-Christopher, *A Biblical Theology of Exile*, 65-73.

48. Bustenay Oded, "Observations on the Israelite/Judean Exiles in Mesopotamia during the Eight-Sixth Centuries B.C.E.," in *Immigration and Emigration within the Ancient Near East. Festschrift E. Lipiński*, ed. K. Van Lerberghe and A. Schoors; Orientalia Lovaniensia Analecta 65 (Leuven: Peeters, 1995), 209.

49. Hans M. Barstad, *The Myth of the Empty Land: A Study in the History and Archaeology of Judah during the "Exilic" Period*, Symbolae Osloenses Fasc. Supp. 28 (Oslo: Scandinavian University Press, 1996), 63-65.

50. Pérez Firmat, *Life on the Hyphen*, 10.

51. Moshe Greenberg, *Ezekiel 1-20: A New Translation with Introduction and Commentary*, Anchor Bible 22 (Garden City, NY: Doubleday, 1983), 362.

52. Ibid., 371.

53. Walther Zimmerli, *Ezekiel 1: A Commentary on the Book of the Prophet Ezekiel 1-24*, trans. Ronald E. Clements; Hermeneia (Philadelphia: Fortress Press, 1979), 414. Ronald E. Clements sides with Zimmerli (*Ezekiel*, Word Biblical Commentary [Louisville, KY: Westminster John Knox Press, 1996], 91).

54. Ibid., 414.

55. Ibid., 402.

56. Leslie C. Allen, *Ezekiel 20-48*, Word Biblical Commentary 29 (Dallas, TX: Word, 1990), 3.

57. Adrian Graffy, *A Prophet Confronts His People: The Disputation Speech in the Prophets*, Analecta Biblica 104 (Rome: Pontifical Biblical Institute, 1984), 66. Risa Levitt Kohn notes, "The idolatrous practice of worshiping 'wood and stone' appears predominantly in Deuteronomic passages that foretell Israel's future exile. . . . The people are thus portrayed as worshiping in this manner in foreign nations. The expression also describes the idolatrous practices witnessed by Israel in Egypt

(Deut. 29.17)" (Risa Levitt Kohn, *A New Heart and a New Soul: Ezekiel, the Exile and the Torah* [London: Sheffield Academic Press, 2002], 92). Also see J. Pons, "Le vocabulaire d'Ez 20. Le prophète s'oppose à la vision deutéronomiste de l'histoire," in *Ezekiel and His Book: Textual and Literary Criticism and Their Interrelation*, ed. J. Lust (Leuven: Peeters, 1986), 227-28. Eichrodt, who deletes "serving wood and stone" as an instance of deuteronomic editing, suggests that Ezekiel 20:32 announces the plans of the elders of Judah to establish a cultic center to YHWH in Babylon (Walther Eichrodt, *Der Prophet Hesekiel* [Göttingen: Vandenhoeck & Ruprecht, 1968], 181).

58. Graffy, *A Prophet Confronts His People*, 65.

59. Ibid., 66-67.

60. Ibid., 66.

61. Greenberg, *Ezekiel 1-20*, 372.

62. Zimmerli, *Ezekiel 1*, 416.

63. David Stephen Vanderhooft, *The Neo-Babylonian Empire and Babylon in the Latter Prophets*, Harvard Semitic Manuscripts 59 (Atlanta, GA: Scholars Press, 1999), 42.

64. Ibid., 43.

65. See Kalinda Rose Stevenson, *The Vision of Transformation: The Territorial Rhetoric of Ezekiel 40-48*, Society of Biblical Literature Dissertation Series 154 (Atlanta, GA: Scholars Press, 1996).

66. Graffy, *A Prophet Confronts His People*, 65.

67. On the dates in Ezekiel, see K. S. Freedy and D. B. Redford, "The Dates in Ezekiel in Relation to Biblical, Babylonian and Egyptian Sources," *Journal of the America Oriental Society* 90 (1970): 462-85; Henry McKeating, *Ezekiel* (Sheffield, UK: Sheffield Academic Press, 1993), 62-72.

68. Segovia, "In the World but Not of It: Exile as a Locus for a Theology of the Diaspora," in Ada María Isasi-Díaz, ed., *Hispanic/Latino Theology: Challenge and Promise* (Minneapolis: Fortress Press, 1996), 210.

69. Ian M Duguid, *Ezekiel and the Leaders of Israel*, Vetus Testamentum Supplements 56 (Leiden: Brill, 1994), 117-18.

70. On the question of identity and the mechanisms of ethnicity in the context of exile, see Smith, *The Religion of the Landless*, 58-63. Also see Fredrik Barth, *Ethnic Groups and Boundaries: The Social Organization of Cultural Difference* (Oslo: Universitetsforlaget, 1969).

71. Oded, "Judah and the Exile," 484.

72. On the impact of exile on Ezekiel as a priest-become-prophet, see Andrew Mein, "Ezekiel as a Priest in Exile," in *The Elusive Prophet: The Prophet as a Historical Person, Literary Character, and Anonymous Artist*, ed. Johannes C. De Moor (Leiden: Brill, 2001), 199-213.

73. Edward Said, *Representations of the Intellectual* (New York: Random House Vintage Books, 1996), 47.

74. Sugirtharajah, "A Postcolonial Exploration of Collusion and Construction in Biblical Interpretation," 113.

75. I am much persuaded by the proposal for an ethics of interpretation articulated by Elisabeth Schüssler Fiorenza in *Rhetoric and Ethic: The Politics of Biblical Studies* (Minneapolis: Fortress Press, 1999).

7. "THEY COULD NOT SPEAK THE LANGUAGE OF JUDAH"

1. I owe special thanks to my St. John's University graduate research assistants Louis Maione and Richard Omolade for the time and energy they contributed to my research for this chapter.

2. The neglect of Nehemiah in the seminary classroom might be justified in view of the fact that this book does not have a high profile in the liturgy. Appearing only rarely in the Roman Catholic *Lectionary for Mass*, it is used only once in the three-year Sunday lectionary cycle: Nehemiah 8:2-4a, 5-6, 8-10 is the first reading for the Third Sunday in Ordinary Time in Cycle C.

3. When a synagogue became a member in 1988, East Brooklyn Churches became East Brooklyn Congregations, retaining EBC as its acronym.

4. Harry Boyte, *Commonwealth: A Return to Citizen Politics* (New York: Free Press, 1989), 82-83.

5. Samuel G. Freedman, *Upon This Rock: The Miracles of a Black Church* (New York: Harper Collins, 1993), 332; Boyte, *Commonwealth*, 83.

6. Boyte, *Commonwealth*, 83; Studs Terkel, *Hope Dies Last: Keeping the Faith in Difficult Times* (New York: New Press, 2003), 233-42.

7. Boyte, *Commonwealth*, 83.

8. Freedman, *Upon This Rock*, 307-44. In an article in the July 31, 1996, issue of the *New York Beacon*, published shortly after the death of I. D. Robbins and his cousin Lester, Bernice Powell Jackson wrote, "I. D. Robbins was a New York City builder whose vision of a single-family home for all Americans became a reality for some 2,800 poor families in Brooklyn and the South Bronx. The tragedy is that the political, financial and contracting worlds kept that dream from becoming a reality for many thousands of poor Americans across the nation. The Robbins cousins were successful builders who were convinced that simple row houses were the key to the vitality of the cities and to the nurturing of families. I. D. Robbins figured that a family earning $20,000 a year could own a $40,000 home. . . . When the Industrial Areas Foundation learned of Mr. Robbins' dream, they brought together 36 congregations in one of Brooklyn's poorest neighborhoods, East New York. These churches put up $8 million for a revolving fund for construction and without federal assistance began to build homes in Brownsville ... these three bedroom, brick houses sold for $39,000. They were built on large tracts of cleared, city-owned land, with foundations for whole blocks being poured at one time. They were 18 feet wide and 32 feet deep, with front and back yards and full basements. Mr. Robbins believed these were the answers to many of the city's problems which he blamed on high density, high-rise government-subsidized housing projects" (8).

9. Freedman, *Upon This Rock*, 339.

10. Jean-Pierre Ruiz, "Of Walls and Words: Twenty-First Century Empire and New Testament Studies," *Union Seminary Quarterly Review* 59 (2005): 122-30.

11. Samuel P. Huntington, "The Hispanic Challenge," *Foreign Policy* 141 (2004): 30-45.

12. Samuel P. Huntington, *Who Are We? The Challenges to America's National Identity* (New York: Simon & Schuster, 2004), 31.

13. Huntington, "The Hispanic Challenge," 44-45; Lionel Sosa, *The Americano Dream: How Latinos Can Achieve Success in Business and in Life* (New York: Penguin, 1999).

14. Freedman, *Upon This Rock*, 332.

15. Curiously, the New Revised Standard Version translation of this verse suggests that fear of the inhabitants of the land was the reason for which Jeshua and Zerubbabel set up the altar as they did: "They set up the altar on its foundation, because they were in dread of the neighboring peoples, and they offered burnt offerings upon it to the LORD, morning and evening" (On the text of Ezra 3:3, see H. G. M. Williamson, *Ezra, Nehemiah*, Word Biblical Commentary 16 [Waco, TX: Word, 1985], 41).

16. Ibid., 159.

17. Ibid., xxiii.

18. Joseph Blenkinsopp, *Ezra-Nehemiah: A Commentary*, Old Testament Library (Philadelphia: Westminster, 1988), 179.

19. Blenkinsopp, *Ezra-Nehemiah*, 351.

20. On the identity and background of Sanballat the Horonite and Tobiah the Ammonite," see Blenkinsopp, *Ezra-Nehemiah*, 216-19. Blenkinsopp suggests that "Tobiah belonged to a distinguished Jerusalemite family with close ties to the high priesthood and the aristocracy, and at the time of Nehemiah's mission he was the Persian-appointed governor of the Ammonite region" (Blenkinsopp, *Ezra-Nehemiah*, 219; Daniel Smith-Christopher, "The Mixed Marriage Crisis in Ezra 9-10 and Nehemiah 13: A Study of the Sociology of the Post-Exilic Judaean Community," in *Second Temple Studies 2: Temple Community in the Persian Period*, ed. Tamara C. Eskenazi and Kent H. Richards; Journal for the Study of the Old Testament Supplements 175 [Sheffield, UK: Sheffield Academic Press, 1994], 258-59).

21. Blenkinsopp, *Ezra-Nehemiah*, 226-27; Williamson, *Ezra, Nehemiah*, 192-93.

22. See Cheryl B. Anderson, "Reflections in an Interethnic/racial Era on Interethnic/racial Marriage in Ezra," in *They Were All Together in One Place? Toward Minority Biblical Criticism*, ed. Randall C. Bailey, Tat-siong Benny Liew, and Fernando Segovia; Semeia Studies 57 (Atlanta, GA: Society of Biblical Literature, 2009), 47-64; Jon L. Berquist, *Judaism in Persia's Shadow: A Social and Historical Approach* (Minneapolis: Fortress Press, 1995), 117-19; Mary Douglas, "Responding to Ezra: The Priests and the Foreign Wives, *Biblical Interpretation* 10 (2002) 1-21; Tamara Eskenazi, and Eleanore P. Judd, "Marriage to a Stranger in Ezra 9-10," in *Second Temple Studies 2: Temple Community in the Persian Period*, ed. Tamara C. Eskenazi and Kent H. Richards; Journal for the Study of the Old Testament Supplements 175 (Sheffield, UK: Sheffield Academic Press, 1994), 265-85; Philip F. Esler, "Ezra-Nehemiah as a Narrative of (Re-Invented) Israelite Identity," *Biblical Interpretation* 11 (2003): 413-26; Christine E. Hayes, *Gentile Impurities and Jewish Identities: Intermarriage and Conversion from the Bible to the Talmud* (New York: Oxford University Press, 2002), 27-34; Jonathan Klawans, "Idolatry, Incest, and Impurity: Moral Defilement in Ancient Judaism," *Journal for the Study of Judaism* 4(1998): 391-415; Smith-Christopher, "The Mixed Marriage Crisis in Ezra 9-10 and Nehemiah 13," 243-65; idem, "Between Ezra and Isaiah: Exclusion, Transformation, and Inclusion of the 'Foreigner' in Post-Exilic Biblical Theology," in *Ethnicity and the Bible*, ed. Mark G. Brett (Leiden: Brill, 1996), 122-27; Saul Olyan, "Purity Ideology in Ezra-Nehemiah as a Tool to Reconstitute the Community," *Journal for the Study of Judaism* 35 (2004): 1-16; Harold Washington, "The Strange Woman (אשה זרה / נכריה) of Proverbs 1-9 and Post-Exilic Judaean Society," in *Second Temple Studies 2: Temple Community in the Persian Period*, ed. Tamara C. Eskenazi and

Kent H. Richards; Journal for the Study of the Old Testament Supplements 175 (Sheffield, UK: Sheffield Academic Press, 1994), 217-42; idem, "Israel's Holy Seed and the Foreign Women of Ezra-Nehemiah: A Kristevan Reading," *Biblical Interpretation* 11 (2003): 427-37; Gale A. Yee, *Poor Banished Children of Eve* (Minneapolis: Fortress Press, 2003), 143-46. On the text of Nehemiah 13:23-24, see Williamson, *Ezra, Nehemiah*, 393.

23. Blenkinsopp, *Ezra-Nehemiah*, 363.

24. Ibid., 363; Williamson, *Ezra, Nehemiah*, 398; E. Ullendorf, "C'est de l'hébreu pour moi," *Journal of Semitic Studies* 13 (1968): 125-35.

25. Blenkinsopp, *Ezra-Nehemiah*, 363.

26. Smith-Christopher, "Between Ezra and Isaiah," 122.

27. Williamson, *Ezra, Nehemiah*, 397.

28. Ibid., 398.

29. Blenkinsopp, *Ezra-Nehemiah*, 363.

30. Ibid., 363.

31. John Hutchinson and Anthony D. Smith, eds., *Ethnicity* (Oxford: Oxford University Press, 1996), 6-7; Esler, "Ezra-Nehemiah as a Narrative of (Re-Invented) Israelite Identity," 414.

32. Yee, *Poor Banished Children of Eve*, 144-45.

33. Ibid., 143.

34. Ibid., 144; Mary Douglas, "Responding to Ezra," 1-21.

35. Yee, *Poor Banished Children of Eve*, 144.

36. Ibid., 146.

37. Jon L. Berquist, *Judaism in Persia's Shadow: A Social and Historical Approach* (Minneapolis: Fortress Press, 1995), 117-18.

38. Ibid., 118.

39. Ibid.

40. Alejandro Portes and Rubén G. Rumbaut, *Legacies: The Story of the Immigrant Second Generation* (Berkeley: University of California Press; New York: Russell Sage Foundation, 2001), 144.

41. Portes and Rumbaut, *Legacies*, 144.

42. See Carmen Nanko-Fernández, "Language, Community, and Identity," in *Handbook of Latina/o Theologies*, ed. Edwin David Aponte and Miguel A. De La Torre (St. Louis: Chalice, 2006), 267-69; idem, *Theologizing en Espanglish: Context, Community, and Ministry* (Maryknoll, NY: Orbis Books, 2010).

43. Huntington, "The Hispanic Challenge," 45.

44. Portes and Rumbaut, *Legacies*, 113.

45. Pedro A. Cabán, *Constructing a Colonial People: Puerto Rico and the United States, 1898-1932* (Boulder, CO: Westview, 1999), 131.

46. Portes and Rumbaut, *Legacies*, 113.

47. Ibid., 114.

48. Paula A. Arriagada, "Family Context and Spanish-Language Use: A Study of Latino Children in the United States," *Social Science Quarterly* 86, no. 3 (2005): 599-619; Richard Alba, John Logan, Amy Lutz, and Brian Stults, "Only English by the Third Generation? Loss and Preservation of the Mother Tongue among the Grandchildren of Contemporary Immigrants," *Demography* 39, no. 3 (2002): 467-84.

49. Alba, Logan, Lutz, and Stults, "Only English by the Third Generation?" 471, 478-79.

50. Gillian Stevens, "Nativity, Intermarriage, and Mother-Tongue Shift," *American Sociological Review* 50 (1985): 81.

51. Stevens, "Nativity, Intermarriage, and Mother-Tongue Shift," 81.

52. Frances Negrón-Muntaner, "English Only Jamás but Spanish Only Cuidado: Language and Nationalism in Contemporary Puerto Rico," in *Puerto Rican Jam: Essays on Culture and Politics*, ed. Frances Negrón-Muntaner and Ramón Grosfoguel (Minneapolis: University of Minnesota Press, 1997), 259.

53. As cited in Cabán, *Constructing a Colonial People*, 131.

54. Kal Wagenheim and Olga Jiménez de Wagenheim, eds., *The Puerto Ricans: A Documentary History* (Princeton, NJ: Markus Wiener, 1994), 111.

55. As cited in Cabán, *Constructing a Colonial People*, 133.

56. Negrón-Muntaner, "English Only Jamás but Spanish Only," 263.

57. Ibid., 281.

58. Ibid.

59. Ibid., 280.

60. Ibid., 281.

61. Ilan Stavans, *Spanglish: The Making of a New Language* (New York: Harper Collins, 2003), 1-54; Alberto Sandoval Sánchez, "Puerto Rican Identity Up in the Air: Air Migration, Its Cultural Representations, and Me 'Cruzando el Charco,'" in *Puerto Rican Jam: Essays on Culture and Politics*, ed. Frances Negrón-Muntaner and Ramón Grosfoguel (Minneapolis: University of Minnesota Press, 1997), 189-208; Agustin Lao, "Islands at the Crossroads: Puerto Ricanness Traveling between the Translocal Nation and the Global City," in *Puerto Rican Jam: Essays on Culture and Politics*, ed. Frances Negrón-Muntaner and Ramón Grosfoguel (Minneapolis: University of Minnesota Press, 1997), 169-88.

62. Tato Laviera, *La Carreta Made a U-Turn* (Houston, TX: Arte Público Press, 1979), as cited in Stephanie Álvarez Martínez, "¡¿Qué, qué?!—Transculturación and Tato Laviera's Spanglish Poetics," *Centro Journal* 37 (2006): 25-46.

63. Álvarez Martínez, "¡¿Qué, qué?!" 34-35.

64. Tato Laviera, *AmeRícan,* 2nd ed. (Houston, TX: Arte Público Press, 2003).

8. THE VIEW FROM NORTHERN BOULEVARD

1. Daniel J. Harrington, *The Gospel of Matthew*, Sacra Pagina 1 (Collegeville, MN: Liturgical Press, 1991), 283.

2. Bernard Brandon Scott, *Hear Then the Parable: A Commentary on the Parables of Jesus* (Minneapolis: Fortress Press, 1989), 282. See Michael L. Barré, "The Workers in the Vineyard," *The Bible Today* 24 (1986): 173-74.

3. Barbara E. Reid, *The Gospel according to Matthew*, New Collegeville Bible Commentary 1 (Collegeville, MN: Liturgical Press, 2005), 100.

4. Scott, *Hear Then the Parable*, 282.

5. Joachim Jeremias, *The Parables of Jesus*, 3rd rev. ed. (London: SCM Press, 1972), 37.

6. Harrington, *The Gospel of Matthew*, 284.

7. Ibid.

8. Bruce J. Malina and Richard L. Rohrbaugh, *Social Science Commentary on the Synoptic Gospels* (Minneapolis: Fortress Press, 1992), 124.

9. Ibid., 125.

10. John H. Elliott, "Matthew 20:1-15: A Parable of Invidious Comparison and Evil Eye Accusation," *Biblical Theology Bulletin* 22, no. 2 (1992): 61.

11. José David Rodríguez, "The Parable of the Affirmative Action Employer," *Apuntes* 15, no. 5 (1988): 423.

12. Ibid., 424.

13. Ibid.

14. William R. Herzog II, *Parables as Subversive Speech: Jesus as Pedagogue of the Oppressed* (Louisville, KY: Westminster John Knox Press, 2004), 11.

15. Ibid., 7.

16. Ibid., 84.

17. Ibid., 85.

18. Ibid., 86.

19. Ibid., 87.

20. Jeremias, *The Parables of Jesus*, 37.

21. Arlene Martinez, "The Region: Risks Are Part of a Day's Work; Amid a Laborer's Abuse Allegations, Others Seeking Temporary Jobs Tell Their Own Stories of Being Victimized," *Los Angeles Times*, May 18, 2004, section B.

22. Abel Valenzuela, Jr., Nik Theodore, Edwin Meléndez, and Ana Luz González, "On the Corner: Day Labor in the United States," Center for the Study of Urban Poverty Working Papers (January 23, 2006), www.sscnet.ucla.edu/issr/csup/uploaded_files/Natl_DayLabor-On_the_Corner1.pdf.

23. Ibid., iii.

24. Ibid.

25. Federation for American Immigration Reform, "How Day Laborer Hiring Sites Promote Illegal Immigration," www.fairus.org/site/News2?page=NewsArticle&id=16767&security=1601&news_iv_ctrl=1007.

26. Ibid.

27. Herzog, *Parables as Subversive Speech*, 92.

28. Ibid., 93.

9. THE BIBLE AND THE EXEGESIS OF EMPIRE

1. Jean-Pierre Ruiz, "Taking a Stand on the Sand of the Seashore: A Postcolonial Exploration of Revelation 13," in *Reading the Book of Revelation: A Resource for Students*, ed. David L. Barr; Resources for Biblical Study 44 (Atlanta, GA: Society of Biblical Literature, 2004), 122-23.

2. See David A. Sánchez, *From Patmos to the Barrio: Subverting Imperial Myths* (Minneapolis: Fortress Press, 2008). Also see Jean-Pierre Ruiz, "The Bible and U.S. Hispanic Theological Discourse: Lessons from a Non-Innocent History," in *From the Heart of Our People: Latino/a Explorations in Catholic Systematic Theology*, ed. Orlando O. Espín and Miguel H. Díaz (Maryknoll, NY: Orbis Books, 1999), 100-20.

3. Pope Leo XIII, encyclical letter *Quarto abeunte saeculo* on the Columbus Quadricentennial (July 16, 1892), available at www.vatican.va/holy_father/leo_xiii/encyclicals/documents/hf_l-xiii_enc_16071892_quarto-abeunte-saeculo_en.html.

4. National Council of the Churches of Christ in the U.S.A., "A Faithful Response to the 500th Anniversary of the Arrival of Christopher Columbus" (May 17, 1990), www.indians.org/welker/faithful.htm. Pope John Paul II, Leo XIII's successor, expressed similar sentiments in 1992: "The Church has always been at the side of the indigenous people through her religious priests and bishops; in this Fifth Centenary how could she possibly forget the enormous suffering inflicted on the peoples of this Continent during the age of conquest and colonization! In truth there must be a recognition of the abuses committed due to a lack of love on the part of some individuals who did not see their indigenous brothers and sisters as children of God their Father" (John Paul II, "Message to Indigenous People," in Fourth General Conference of Latin American Bishops, *Santo Domingo Conclusions* [Washington, DC: National Conference of Catholic Bishops, 1993], 185).

5. On this, see, for example, Allan Figueroa Deck, "The Trashing of the Fifth Centenary," *America* 167 (1992), 499-501.

6. See Elisabeth Schüssler Fiorenza, *Rhetoric and Ethic: The Politics of Biblical Studies* (Minneapolis : Fortress Press, 1999).

7. "Incipit liber sive manipulus de auctoritatibus, dictis ac sententiis et prophetiis circa materiam recuperande sancta civitatis et montis Dei Syon ac inventionis et conversionis insularum Indye et omnium gentium atque nationum, ad Ferdinandum et Helysabeth reges nostros hyspanos" (Roberto Rusconi, ed., *The Book of Prophecies Edited by Christopher Columbus*, trans. Blair Sullivan; Repertorium Columbianum 3 [Berkeley: University of California Press, 1997], §003). All English translations of material from the *Book of Prophecies* are taken from this edition. Another critical edition and translation into English of the *Book of Prophecies* is Delno C. West and August Kling, *The Libro de las profecías of Christopher Columbus* (Gainesville: University of Florida Press, 1991).

8. This is a reference to the work of Nicholas of Lyra (c. 1270-1349).

9. "Reverendo y muy devoto padre: Quando vine [aquí] començé a sacar las autoridades que me parescía que haçían al caso de [Jerusalem en un] libro para después tornarlas a rrever e las poner en rrima en su lugar en los [sea] al caso. Después sucedió en my otras ocup[aciones, por donde no ovo lugar de proseg]uir my obra, ni lo hay. E ansý os lo [enbío] que le vedieses. [Podrá ser que el anima os] incitará a proseguir en él e que nuestro [Señor vos alunbrará auctoridades muy a] unténticas. En la Biblia es de continua[r, e en muchos lugares la Glosa a]provecha e alumbra, e es de haçer d'ella muncha [memoria, al tiempo se oviese se s]acar en lympio."

10. Rusconi, "Introduction," in *The Book of Prophecies*, 6.

11. See the outline of the *Book of Prophecies* in West and Kling, *The Libro de las profecías of Christopher Columbus*, 98-99.

12. The third voyage concluded with the arrest of Columbus and his return to Spain in chains.

13. "Començé a sacar las autoridades que me parescía que haçían al caso de [Jerusalem en un] libro para después tornarlas a rrever e las poner en rrima en su lugar en los [sea] al caso."

14. Hector Avalos follows mainstream Columbus scholarship in suggesting that "Columbus intended to integrate the prophecies into a poem" and adds, "This poem, however, was to be nothing less than an epic with Columbus as the hero" ("Columbus as Biblical Exegete: A Study of the *Libro de las profecías*," in *Religion in the Age of Exploration: The Case of Spain and New Spain. Proceedings of the Fifth Annual Symposium of the Philip M. and Ethel Klutznick Chair in Jewish Civilization*, ed. Bryan F. Le Beau and Menachem Mor; Studies in Jewish Civilization 5 [Omaha, NE: Creighton University Press, 1996], 72). Also see West and Kling, *The Libro de las profecías of Christopher Columbus*, 35. Rusconi disagrees (Rusconi, "Introduction," in *The Book of Prophecies*, 6 n. 25).

15. On the history of the manuscript, see Rusconi, "Introduction," in *The Book of*, 8-11.

16. Henri Harisse, *Notes on Columbus* (New York, 1866), as cited in Delno C. West, "Wallowing in a Theological Stupor or a Steadfast and Consuming Faith: Scholarly Encounters with Columbus' Libro de las Profecías," in *Columbus and His World: Proceedings, First San Salvador Conference*, ed. Donald T. Gerace (Ft. Lauderdale, FL: College Center of the Finger Lakes, 1987), 50.

17. This was the edition of Cesare de Lollis, *Autografi di Cristoforo Colombo con prefazione e trascrizione diplomatica*, Raccolta di documenti e studi pubblicati della R. Commissione Colombiana per il quarto centenario della scoperta dell'America (Rome: Ministero della Pubblica Istruzione, 1892-94).

18. Filson Young, *Christopher Columbus and the New World of His Discoveries* (Philadelphia: J. B. Lippincott, 1906), 146, as cited in West, "Wallowing in a Theological Stupor," 50.

19. Gianni Granzotto, *Christopher Columbus*, trans. Stephen Sartarelli (Garden City, NY: Doubleday, 1985), 246.

20. So, for instance, Pauline Moffatt Watts, "Prophecy and Discovery: On the Spiritual Origins of Christopher Columbus' 'Enterprise of the Indies,'" *American Historical Review* 90, no. 1 (1985): 73-102; Leonard I. Sweet, "Christopher Columbus and the Millennial Vision of the New World," *Catholic Historical Review* 72, no. 3 (July 1986): 369-82; Djelal Kadir, *Columbus and the Ends of the Earth: Europe's Prophetic Rhetoric as Conquering Ideology* (Berkeley: University of California Press, 1992).

21. See Francisco Álvarez, "Cristóbal Colón y el estudio de la Sagrada Escritura," *Archivo hispánico* 17 (1952): 129-40; John V. Fleming, "Christopher Columbus as a Scriptural Exegete," *Lutheran Quarterly* 5, no. 2 (1991): 187-98.

22. Hector Avalos, "Columbus as Biblical Exegete: A Study of the *Libro de las profecías*," 59-80. Also see Hector Avalos, "The Biblical Sources of Columbus's '*Libro de las Profecías*,'" *Traditio* 49 (1994): 331-35.

23. Fernando F. Segovia, *Decolonizing Biblical Studies: A View from the Margins* (Maryknoll, NY: Orbis Books, 2000), 22.

24. R. S. Sugirtharajah, "Biblical Studies after the Empire: From a Colonial to a Postcolonial Mode of Interpretation," in *The Postcolonial Bible*, ed. R. S. Sugirtharajah; The Bible and Postcolonialism 1 (Sheffield, UK: Sheffield Academic Press, 1998), 16.

25. Sanjay Seth, Leela Gandhi, and Michael Dutton, "Postcolonial Studies: A Beginning," *Postcolonial Studies: Culture, Politics, Economy* 1, no. 1 (1998): 8, as

cited in R. S. Sugirtharajah, *The Bible and the Third World: Precolonial, Colonial and Postcolonial Encounters* (Cambridge: Cambridge University Press, 2001), 246. See *The Post-Colonial Studies Reader*, ed. Bill Ashcroft, Gareth Griffiths, and Helen Tiffin (New York: Routledge, 1995). Helpful introductions to postcolonial theory are available in Leela Gandhi, *Postcolonial Theory: A Critical Introduction* (New York: Columbia University Press, 1998); as well as Ania Loomba, *Colonialism/Postcolonialism* (London: Routledge, 1998). Many of the "foundational" texts of postcolonial theory are excerpted in *Colonial Discourse and Post-Colonial Theory: A Reader*, ed. Patrick Williams and Laura Chrisman (New York: Columbia University Press, 1994). I am especially interested in the postcolonial theory arising from the context of Latin American reflection on imperialism and neocolonialism. See J. Jorge Klor de Alva, "The Postcolonization of the (Latin) American Experience: A Recosideration of 'Colonialism,' 'Postcolonialism,' and 'Mestizaje,'" in *After Colonialism: Imperial Histories and Postcolonial Displacements*, ed. Gyan Prakash (Princeton, NJ: Princeton University Press, 1995), 241-75; Walter D. Mignolo, *Local Histories/Global Designs: Coloniality, Subaltern Knowledges, and Border Thinking* (Princeton, NJ: Princeton University Press, 2000).

26. Sugirtharajah, *The Bible and the Third World*, 255.

27. Among the books known to have been owned by Columbus are Pierre d'Ailly, *Imago Mundi* (published between 1480 and 1483), with 898 marginal notes in Columbus's own hand; Aeneas Silvius Piccolomini, *Historia rerum ubique gestarum* (Venice, 1477), with 861 marginal notes in Columbus's own hand; Marco Polo, *Consuetudinibus et conditionibus orientalium regionium* (Antwerp, 1485), with 366 marginal notes in Columbus's own hand; Pliny, *Historia naturalis* in the Italian translation of Cristoforo Landino (Venice, 1489), with 24 marginal notes in Columbus's own hand; an anonymous fifteenth-century concordance of the Bible, *Concordantiae Biblicae Cardinalis S.P.*, with markings in the margins that highlight texts Columbus found important; Saint Antoninus of Florence, *Sumula confessionis* (1476); a fifteenth-century palimpsest containing Seneca's *Tragedies*; Abraham Azcuto, *Almanach perpetuum, cuius radix est annun, 1473*, including folio copies by Columbus (see West and Kling, *The Libro de las profecías of Christopher Columbus*, 24).

28. See Avalos, "The Biblical Sources of Columbus's '*Libro de las Profecías*,'" 331-35. On the various editions of Nicholas of Lyra, see Edward A. Gosselin, "A Listing of the Printed Editions of Nicolaus of Lyra," *Traditio* 26 (1970): 399-426.

29. "He yo visto e puesto estudio en ver de todas escrituras: cosmografía, ystorias, corónicas e fylosofia e de otras artes, a que me abrió nuestro Señor el entendimiento con mano palpable a que era hasedero navegar de aquí a las Yndias, e me abrió la voluntad para la hesecución d'ello. E con este fuego vine a vuestras altezas."

30. "Todos aquellos que supieron de mi ynpresa con rixa le negaban burlando."

31. "Todas las çiençias de que dise arriba non me aprovecharon ni las abtoridades d'ellas. En solo vuestras altezas quedó la fee e constançia. ¿Quién dubda que esta lunbre non fuese del Espíritu santo, asý como de mí? El qual con rrayos de claridad maravillosos consoló con su santa e sacra Escritura a vos muy alta e clara con quarenta e quarto libros del Viejo Testamento, e quarto hevangelios con veynte e tres hepístolas de aquellos bienaventurados apóstoles, abinbándome que yo prosiguiese e de contino sin çesar un momento me abíban con gran priesa." On the number

of books in Columbus's canon, see John V. Fleming, "Christopher Columbus as a Scriptural Exegete," *Lutheran Quarterly* 5 (1991): 189-93. For a list of the biblical books and other materials cited in the *Book of Prophecies*, see West and Kling, *The Libro de las profecías of Christopher Columbus*, 23.

32. "Digo que yo deso todo mi navegar desde hedad nueva e la pláticas que yo aya tenido con tanta gente en tantas tierras e de tantas setas, e dexo las tantas artes e escrituras de que yo dyxe ariba; solamente me tengo a la santa e sacra Escritura, e a algunas abtoridades proféticas de algunas personas santas, que por revelación divina han dicho algo d'esto."

33. "Pudiera ser que vuestras altezas, e todos los otros que me conosçen, e a quien esta escritura fuere amostrada, que en secreto o públicamente me reprehenderán de la reprehension de diversas maneras: de non doto en letras, de lego marinero, de honbre mundanal, et cetera."

34. "¡O, Señor, que quisistes tener secreto tantas cosas a los sabios e rebelástalas a los ynoçentes!"

35. "Yendo nuestro Señor en Iherusalem cantaban los mochachos: '¡Osana fijo de David!' Los scribas por lo tentar le preguntaron sy oyá lo que desían, e él les respondió que sí disiendo: '¿No sabéys vos que de la boca de los niños e ynocéntes se pronunsçia la verdad?'"

36. "La sacra Escritura testifica en el Testamento viejo, por boca de los profetas, e en el nuebo por nuestro redentor Ihesu Christo, qu'este mundo a de aver fin: las señales de quando esto aya de ser diso Mateo e Marco e Lucas; los profetas abondosamente tanbién lo avian predicado."

37. "Segun esta cuenta no falta salvo çiento e çincuenta e çinco años para conplimiento de siete mill, en los quales dise arriba por las abtoridades dichas que avrá de feneçer el mundo. Nuestro Redentor diso que antes de la consumaçion d'este mundo se abrá de conplir todo lo qu'estava escrito por los profetas."

38. "Los profetas escriviendo fablavan de diversas maneras el de por venir pasado e el pasado por venir, e asymismo del presente, e disieron munchas cosas por semejança, otras propincas a la verdad e otras por entero a la letra, e uno más que otro, e uno por major manera, e otro no tanto."

39. The *Book of Prophecies* cites Isaiah 2:2-3; 5:26; 6:11-13; 8:9; 11:10-12; 11:11; 12:4-6; 14:32; 18:1-7; 19:19-20; 22:20-25; 23:1-2, 12; 24:14-16; 25:6a, 7, 9a, 9c-10a; 26:1-3; 27:13; 28:22; 30:18b-19a, 27a; 33:7, 13-14a, 20; 35:1a, 2b, 9b-10a; 40:1, 5, 9a, 17; 41:1-5; 41:1a, 5a; 42:1-4, 6-16; 42:3-4; 43:1-7a; 44:1-3, 23, 25b-28; 45:1-6a; 46:10b-13; 49:1-4a, 5b-6; 49:1a; 51:1-13a, 16-18, 22b-23a; 52:1-3, 7-15; 55:1a, 3-5, 13b; 57:13b; 59:18b-20a; 60:1-22; 60:9a; 62:1-12; 63:1a; 66:18-24; 66:19a.

40. "Ysaýas es aquel que más alaba san Gerónymo e san Agostín e los otros dotores, a todos apruevan e tienen en grande reverençia: de Ysaýa disen que es no solamente propheta, más hevangelista; este puso toda su diligençia a escrevir lo venidero e llamar toda la gente a nuestra santa fee católica."

41. "Yo vine con amor tan intrañable a servir a estos Principes, y e servido de servicio de que jamás se oyó ni vido. Del nuevo cielo y tierra que dezía Nuestro Señor por San Juan en el Apocalipsi, después de dicho por boca de Isaías, me hizo mensajero y amostro aquella parte. En todos ovo incredulidad, y a la Reina, mi Señora, dio d'ello el espiritu de intelligençia y esfuerzo grande y lo hizo de todo heredero" (from *Cristóbal Colón: Textos y documentos completos*, ed. Consuelo

Varela [Madrid: Alianza Editorial, 1982], 243); translation from Djelal Kadir, *Columbus and the Ends of the Earth: Europe's Prophetic Rhetoric as Conquering Ideology* (Berkeley: University of California Press, 1992), 153.

42. See note 38 above.

43. Kadir, *Columbus and the Ends of the Earth*, 146.

44. Angelus de Clavasio, *Summa angelica de casibus conscientiae* (Venice: Paganinus de Paganinis, 1499).

45. Jean Gerson, *De sensu litterali Sacrae Scripturae*, in *Oeuvres completes*, volume 3: *La oeuvre magistrale*, ed. Palémon Glorieux (Paris: Desclée, 1962), 333-40. On medieval exegesis, see the magisterial work of Henri de Lubac, *Medieval Exegesis*, volume 1 trans. Marc Sebanc; volume 2 trans. E. M. Macierowski (Grand Rapids, MI: Eerdmans, 1998, 2000).

46. "Quadruplex sensus Sacrae Scripture aperte insinuatur in hac dictione Ierusalem. Hystorice enim significant, civitatem illam terrestrem ad quam peregrini petunt. Allegorice, significant Ecclesiam militantem. Tropologice, significant quamlibet fidelem animam. Anagogice, significant celestem Ierusalem, sive patriam, ve regnum celorum" (translation from West and Kling, *The Libro de las profecías of Christopher Columbus*).

47. Avalos, "Columbus as Biblical Exegete," 61.

48. "Notandum quod in sacra Scriptura aliquando ponitur tempus pro tempore, sicut preteritum pro futuro et cetera."

49. Avalos, "Columbus as Biblical Exegete," 61.

50. Biblical citations inserted.

51. See Delno C. West, "Christopher Columbus, Lost Biblical Sites, and the Last Crusade," *Catholic Historical Review* 78, no. 4 (October 1992): 519-41. On Columbus as visionary, see Kadir, *Columbus and the Ends of the Earth*, 157-60. Also see Claude Kappler, "La vocation messianique de Cristophe Colomb," in *Voyage, quête, pèlerinage dans la littérature de la civilization médiévale: Sénefiance*, Cahiers du CUERMA 2 (Université de Provence, 1976), 255-71; Alain Milhou, *Colón y su mentalidad mesianica en el ambiente franciscanista español*, Cuadernos Colombinos 11 (Valladolid: Museo de Coloón y Seminario Americanista de la Universidad de Valladolid, 1983).

52. John Leddy Phelan, *The Millennial Kingdom of the Franciscans in the New World*, 2nd ed. rev. (Berkeley: University of California Press, 1970), 22.

53. Leonard I. Sweet, "Christopher Columbus and the Millennial," 371.

54. Paul Leicester Ford, ed., *Writings of Christopher Columbus Descriptive of the Discovery and Occupation of the New World* (New York, 1892), 28-29, as cited in Sweet, "Christopher Columbus and the Millennial Vision," 372. On the expulsion of the Jews from Spain, see Lewis A. Tambs, "Expulsion of the Jewish Community from the Spains, 1492," in *Religion in the Age of Exploration: The Case of Spain and New Spain. Proceedings of the Fifth Annual Symposium of the Philip M. and Ethel Klutznick Chair in Jewish Civilization*, ed. Bryan F. Le Beau and Menachem Mor; Studies in Jewish Civilization 5 (Omaha, NE: Creighton University Press, 1996), 39-57; Norman Roth, *Conversos, Inquisition, and the Expulsion of the Jews from Spain* (Madison: University of Wisconsin Press, 1995).

55. In his important book, Henry Kamen offers the following telling observation: "While Castilians enjoyed almost unlimited political horizons, they contracted their

cultural perspectives by defining in a wholly exclusive sense what it meant to be a 'Spaniard.' Unlike the Roman Empire before them and the British Empire after them, they attempted to exclude from their midst all alternative cultures, beginning with two of the great historic cultures of the peninsula. From the year 1492, which marked the capitulation of Granada and the expulsion of the Jews, both Islam and Judaism were effectively excluded from the Spanish concept of the universe" (Henry Kamen, *Empire: How Spain Became a World Power 1492-1763* [New York: Harper Collins, 2003], 342).

56. Kadir, *Columbus and the Ends of the Earth*, 71. A few pages earlier, Kadir observes that "So compelling are the linkages between ideological conviction and its worldly realization that in the case of Columbus certain historians of eminence have been persuaded that the Genoese mariner "discovered" the New World in 1492 for the second time, having already *realized* the undertaking he so relentlessly and, in the end, persuasively peddled to European royalty" (66). Among such historians Kadir ranks Juan Manzano Manzano, *Colón y su secreto: el predescubrimiento* (Madrid: Ediciones Cultura Hispánica, 1982).

57. The classic work on the influence of Joachim of Fiore is Marjorie Reeves, *The Influence of Prophecy in the Later Middle Ages: A Study in Joachimism* (Oxford: Clarendon Press, 1969). Also see Bernard McGinn, *The Calabrian Abbot: Joachim of Fiore in the History of Western Thought* (New York: Macmillan, 1985).

58. Kadir, *Columbus and the Ends of the Earth*, 30.

59. See Milhou, *Colón y su mentalidad mesianica en el ambiente franciscanista español*.

60. Michel de Certeau, *The Writing of History* (New York: Columbia University Press, 1988). As Kadir suggests, "Christianity and its providential rendering of human time and worldly events purvey the *ideological givens* that make *imperial taking* a natural right needing no further justification. In other words, prophetic history and its apocalyptic rhetoric serve as ideological shield for intricate and mixed motives for Europe's project in the New World" (*Columbus and the Ends of the Earth*, 30).

61. See West, "Christopher Columbus, Lost Biblical Sites, and the Last Crusade."

62. Terry Eagleton, "Poscolonialism and 'Postcolonialism,'" *Interventions* 1, no. 1 (1998): 24.

63. See Gandhi, *Postcolonial Theory*, 3.

64. Eagleton, "Poscolonialism and 'Postcolonialism,'" 26.

65. Arif Dirlik, *The Postcolonial Aura: Third World Criticism in the Age of Global Capitalism* (Boulder, CO: Westview Press, 1997), 5.

66. See Kadir, *Columbus and the Ends of the Earth*; Sugirtharajah, *The Bible and the Third World*.

67. Seth, Gandhi, and Dutton, "Postcolonial Studies: A Beginning," *Postcolonial Studies: Culture, Politics, Economy* 1, no. 1 (1998): 8, as cited in Sugirtharajah, *The Bible and the Third* World, 246.

68. See Jean-Pierre Ruiz, "Cardinal Francisco Ximénes de Cisneros and Bartolomé de las Casas, the 'Procurator and Universal Protector of all the Indians in the Indies," *Journal of Hispanic/Latino Theology* 9, no. 9 (February 2002): 60-77; Walter Mignolo, *The Darker Side of the Renaissance: Literacy, Territoriality, and Colonization* (Ann Arbor: University of Michigan Press, 1995).

EPILOGUE: READING THE NEW NORMAL

1. International Organization for Migration, *World Migration Report 2010: The Future of Migration: Building Capacities for Change*, *Executive Summary* (Geneva: International Organization for Migration, 2010), 1, www.iom.int/jahia/webdav/shared/shared/mainsite/published_docs/wmr-2010/WMR-Executive-Summary.pdf.

2. International Organization for Migration, *World Migration Report 2010 Executive Summary*, 1.

3. U.S. Census Bureau, *International Data Base*, Population Clock (March 8, 2011), www.census.gov/ipc/www/idb/worldpopinfo.php.

4. International Organization for Migration, *World Migration Report 2010 Executive Summary*, 1.

5. See, for example, Fabio Baggio and Agnes M. Brazal, eds., *Faith on the Move: Toward a Theology of Migration in Asia* (Manila: Ateneo de Manile University Press, 2008); Jehu J. Hanciles, *Beyond Christendom: Globalization, African Migration, and the Transformation of the West* (Maryknoll, NY: Orbis Books, 2008); Kristin E. Heyer, "Social Sin and Immigration: Good Fences Make Bad Neighbors," *Theological Studies* 71 (2010): 410-36.

6. From this imperative to intercontextual (and not only interdisciplinary) conversation, it follows that the theological consideration of migration among Christian scholars, pastoral agents, and activists will call for efforts to engage in increased interreligious understanding. While that task lies beyond the scope of this book, it must be on the agenda. James H. Kroeger writes, "Today's reality of migration results in persons of diverse religions and cultures living together—whether they are prepared or not for their new reality" (James H. Kroeger, "Living Faith in a Strange Land: Migration and Interreligious Dialogue," in *Faith on the Move: Toward a Theology of Migration in Asia* (Manila: Ateneo de Manile University Press, 2008), 224).

7. See the well-framed critique by Gemma Tulud Cruz of Carlos Abesamis's use of the Exodus "as a paradigm in the struggle of Filipinos for justice and freedom," in Gemma Tulud Cruz, *An Intercultural Theology of Migration: Pilgrims in the Wilderness* (Leiden: Brill, 2010), 310-18, at 310. She cites Carlos Abesamis, *Exploring Biblical Faith* (Quezon City: Claretian Publications, 1991), as well as Carlos Abesamis, *Exploring the Core of Biblical Faith: A Catechetical Primer* (Quezon City: Claretian Publications, 1988).

8. M. Daniel Carroll R., *Christians at the Border: Immigration, the Church, and the Bible* (Grand Rapids, MI: Baker Academic, 2008), 19.

9. See Jean-Pierre Ruiz, "Taking the Local: Toward a Contemporary Theology of Migration," in Jean-Pierre Ruiz and Nicholas DiMarzio, *From Strangers to Neighbors: Reflections on the Pastoral Theology of Human Migration* (New York: St. John's University Vincentian Center for Church and Society, 2004), 2-18.

10. See Carmen M. Nanko-Fernández, "Beyond Hospitality: Implications of (Im)migration for Teología y Pastoral de Conjunto," in her *Theologizing en Espanglish: Context, Continuity, and Ministry* (Maryknoll, NY: Orbis Books, 2010), 110-19: Nanko-Fernández notes, "Even the posture of hospitality contains a hidden power differential revealed in the sentiment of a parishioner from . . . [a] Tulsa, Oklahoma parish: 'The English-speaking parishioners have tried to be

welcoming to the Hispanics. But many feel the newcomers have not reciprocated and that the Anglos' contributions are not valued.' The power resides on the side of the one who has the ability to welcome or to turn away. The problem with hospitality as the predominant paradigm is that current usage of the language of 'stranger' fails to appreciate that the stranger is not only the newcomer to the land, but also the inhabitant encountered by the sojourner" (119).

Index